PEOPLE-CENTERED PROFIT STRATEGIES

101 COMPETITIVE ADVANTAGES

PAUL PEYTON

Edited by Camille Akin

The Oasis Press® / PSI Research
Central Point, Oregon

Editor: Camille Akin
Book Designer: Constance C. Dickinson
Compositor: Jan Olsson
Cover and Illustration Designer: Steven Burns

Please direct any comments, questions, or suggestions regarding this book to The Oasis Press®/PSI Research:

Editorial Department
P.O. Box 3727
Central Point, OR 97502
(541) 479-9464
info@psi-research.com *email*

The Oasis Press® is a Registered Trademark of Publishing Services, Inc., an Oregon corporation doing business as PSI Research.

ISBN: 1-55571-517-6

Printed in the United States of America
First Edition 10 9 8 7 6 5 4 3 2 1

 Printed on recycled paper when available.

TABLE
OF
CONTENTS

PREFACE

Twenty-eight percent of American corporations are experiencing declining sales volumes. An additional seven percent are experiencing an incredible increase in sales accompanied by declining profits. Nearly one million businesses go bankrupt every year. The American trade imbalance has grown progressively more negative since 1982. Currently, Americans are shipping their standard of living overseas at the rate of $165 billion a year. The good news is that this troubling and persistent trend can be reversed — one business at a time.

So! Another management book? Not exactly. Although thousands of great management books abound, they only tell you the details of hundreds of theories of organization, teamwork, and conflict resolution. What they don't tell you is which of those theories works. You don't need to know the names of a hundred theories or the definitions of a thousand acronyms; you need to know what solid action you can take to add profits to the bottom line. I wrote this book because of the thousands of business managers who ask what they can do to increase profits. Business schools focus on big business with heavy financial and legal issues. Many professional societies are becoming internalized and irrelevant. Small business development centers (SBDCs) are underfunded. Until now, there was no step-by-step set of directions telling you how to increase profits. Until now, managers were faced with the frustration of a series of try-this-and-see-if-it-works theories.

This book will counter the rising tide of aggressive teaching of mismanagement. I recently attended a seminar in which the instructor denounced profits as an "irrelevant traditional measure of business success."

The seminar was focused on managing the business in a manner that disregarded profitability in favor of issues like politics, society, and personal preferences. The teachings of this seminar are common to the flood of mismanagement theories of today. They may sound good, but they cannot survive the tests that they will encounter in the real world.

My experience in manufacturing exceeds a quarter of a century. I have tested my share of unworkable theories. I have found — repeatedly — that the basic elements of leadership, planning, motivation, and cost control will reliably produce spectacular results. Prepare yourself: the spectacular results will not come as a starburst. The results accumulate in microamounts, one-tenth of a percent at a time. The spectacular results will become apparent only with a backwards glance. In other words, only in the future will you be able to compare your new results to the conditions of past. Based on this experience, you are given a step-by-step method that will produce profit growth that others call a turnaround.

This book is focused on the reality and the necessity of profit. Profit will drive higher wages, motivate investment, and fill the public coffers. Profit increases your standard of living and will enable a clean environment. Profit will reverse the trade imbalance and guarantee freedom. This book provides you with a clear definition of what to do to increase profit — and to sustain the increase indefinitely.

PAUL PEYTON
July, 1999

INTRODUCTION

Do you want your business to become more profitable? Do you want to increase your profits with a minimum of capital outlay? Are you open to learning simple techniques that will multiply your profits permanently? If you answered yes to the above questions, you have realistic expectations. You can manage your business in such a way that you will drive costs down and drive revenues up. The reliable result is higher profits; profits that are permanent and can be achieved with little or no capital outlay.

This book will take you from the foundational concept of leadership psychology all the way to the final action steps to initiate and measure a turnaround of profits. Along the way, you will learn how to:

- ► Develop a team of pro-profit employees, customers, and suppliers.
- ► Build a business plan that drives priorities, decisions, and organization.
- ► Control costs.
- ► Build high morale.
- ► Use an early warning system.
- ► Develop unique competitive advantages.
- ► Predict and control secondary events that ultimately determine your business' fate.

The profit pointers outlined in this book apply to most businesses. The terminology and examples used are from manufacturing businesses for two reasons.

1. Manufacturing is the most complex business to master. The acts of management have the most leveraged effect in manufacturing. It follows that if you can manage a turnaround in a manufacturing business, you have the skills to turn around many other types of business. Further, manufacturing terminology relates easily to other businesses. A bill of materials in the manufacturing field is the same as a recipe in the restaurant business. In fact, if the restaurant business begins packaging meals to ship to remote customers, it becomes a manufacturing business.

2. Manufacturing is the sector of the American economy that has seen the greatest declines and neglect. Prosperity in manufacturing is required for any society to prosper: manufacturing drives the service, retail, and financial sectors. The ripple effects of one manufacturing turnaround will drive the turnarounds of numerous other businesses.

When you apply the principles and concepts of this book to your business, you will develop a complete system — that is, the interaction of all business functions to produce a predictable and desirable result — that will work efficiently. Your business' complete system will exhibit Just-in-Time (JIT) techniques. Tomorrow, the JIT fad will be gone and the name will be different. By whatever name, your complete, efficient system will lead to higher profitability. When you reach that plane of efficiency and high profits, you won't care what name tag the experts hang on your accomplishment.

You have most of the resources that are required to turn your business into one that is efficient and highly profitable. All you have to do is establish a means of properly organizing and directing those resources.

PART I

ATTITUDE MATTERS

Little things control big things. Consider the ease of steering a battleship if one knows how to use the rudder.

As a smart business owner, you understand that developing a well-managed company is critical to surviving and prospering in today's marketplace. Most business owners have the tools that are required to become measurably more profitable, well-organized, predictable, and easy to run. These essential tools — equipment, products, markets, employees, and expertise — constitute 99 percent of business operations, even in companies that appear to be poorly managed. However, what many business owners and managers fail to understand is that the 99 percent is controlled by the last one percent. The last one percent is like the rudder that steers a battleship.

The last one percent of your business' operations controls the fate of your business. Many managers misunderstand and overlook that last one percent. That last one percent is controlled by the human mind — much like the hand of the captain that controls the rudder of the battleship. Your attitude has a tremendous impact on the key players within your business world. Your attitude will make the difference between keeping your business afloat or watching it sink.

In Part I, you will learn how to use your own attitude to enhance the profit-influencing acts of the four critical groups that affect your business: leaders, employees, customers, and suppliers. A destructive attitude in any one group alone can send your business marching into bankruptcy court. The constructive attitude — cooperative and mutually supportive — in all four groups is the most important single element in business success. If your business possesses cooperative and mutually supportive attitudes in its leaders, employees, customers, and suppliers, your business will be able to succeed in spite of problems with technology, materials, or quality. Conversely, if your business has a combative attitude in even one of the four areas, you can do nothing to compensate. High technology will not win alienated customers. Trendy materials management techniques will not override irate suppliers. A demoralized workforce will build and ship defective products in a shop that has achieved the ultimate quality verification — the International Standards Organization (ISO) 9000 Certification. The cooperation and mutual support among leaders, employees, customers, and suppliers generates a power that is unlimited in its ability to push profits upward.

CHAPTER 1

UNDERSTAND LEADERSHIP PSYCHOLOGY

Good followers are a serious problem for poor leaders. They keep doing exactly what they are told.

Engineering the turnaround of a business is a task that requires you to undertake dozens of activities simultaneously. The magnitude and cross-functional nature of a turnaround project require the work of a team of people that possesses diverse aptitudes, priorities, and abilities. The challenge to your ability is to lead this diverse group to work in a manner that is mutually supportive and strives to achieve a common goal.

Successfully leading such a diverse team is the fundamental requirement of the person who is in charge of correcting a distressed business. Fortunately, there is a simple, basic, leadership psychology that will enable you to lead people in any situation. It has universal application — it applies to your business now and it will apply ten years from now.

This simple psychology is changeless and is summarized in three people-centered rules.

1. People always achieve what they want to achieve.
2. People always possess greater ability than they use.
3. People always respond to stimulus.

Combine these three universal rules into a single principle to guide you in a successful business and it is this: stimulate people to achieve and they will respond with great ability.

As a businessperson who may be focusing on the bottom line, it is easy to pass over that single principle of profits. Businesspeople are constantly bombarded with seminars, books, and consultants that purport similar ideas. Stimulation of people, however, is a fundamental key to an exceptional understanding of leadership psychology.

Look at your own business situation. Is it an every day furor of activity? Is it a mass of individual deeds that accumulate to burp up an occasional saleable product? You bet it is.

The way to improve profitability is to improve the quality and efficiency of the thousands of individual deeds. You can't do that with a giant stride of technology. You can't make one decision or incorporate one trendy management fad that will make the big difference. You will have to stimulate the people around you to achieve. They will — with great ability.

Stimulate Your People

Envision two manufacturing firms who are direct competitors. One grows to significant success while the other struggles on the perpetual brink of bankruptcy. Why is there such a difference? Two retail stores struggling with diminishing profits. One stages a dramatic and permanent turnaround while the other declares bankruptcy. Why the difference?

The difference between success and failure is in the cumulative efforts of the people who work for the companies. Leadership psychology correctly applied will make a big difference in your business success.

- ► Effort is driven by desire.
- ► Desire is driven by influences.
- ► Influences are driven by leadership.

The complex interaction of desire, effort, influence, and leadership is psychology. The leaders of great accomplishments know psychology, whether or not they have formally studied the subject. One of the foundational tasks of leadership psychology is to stimulate desire.

How to Stimulate Your People

Stimulating ordinary people to achieve great things is a rare ability. When great things need to be achieved in business, a common error is to hire a superstar in a specific field to "lead" people of lesser ability to turn in higher

PROFIT POINTER

◄► 1 ◄►

levels of performance. The superstar affinity is a short cut that will result in dismal results in the long term. Imagine the following two contrasting examples of stimulating people set by Short Cut Enterprises and Diligence, Inc.

Short Cut has mastered the concept of stimulating employees to achieve at higher levels of ability. Short Cut is a business in which every employee is motivated and rewarded and is achieving high levels of success. However, Short Cut has motivated people by placing them in competition with one another. Rewards and recognition go to the person who can set individual goals and achieve them. You can predict the result. Competition among individuals will be intense. That competition will exhibit symptoms of undermining plans of others, backstabbing, and duplication and opposition of efforts. Infighting and office politics will prevail. By stimulating individual performance, Short Cut believes that it will benefit from the accumulation of the effects of multiple superstar performances. It believes that the rewards for the superstars will coax higher performance out of an average employee.

Diligence, Inc. has instituted a contrasting approach. Diligence owners have studied the low-tech management model called "horse and wagon." If the load is too heavy for one horse to pull effectively, horse and wagon management responds by adding one more horse."

Diligence has studied beyond the obvious. It knows about the last one percent. Diligence owners know that there is more to the technique than just adding one more horse. No matter how strong, well-trained, beautiful, or well-groomed the second horse may be, it is of absolute, vital importance that the second horse pull in the same direction as the first horse! You probably recognize the idea as logical, elementary, and obvious.

Short Cut's approach is wrong. Unfortunately, Short Cut is typical of too many American businesses. If a hot demand allows Short Cut to live long enough to be as large as IBM or General Motors, it will be 500 percent overstaffed at the corporate level. It will be inefficient, slow-moving, and bureaucratic. Its products will be overpriced to compensate for its overstaffing and inefficiency. Every minor downturn in business will cause the owners to panic and think of downsizing. Short Cut has planted the seeds of its own demise by rewarding and enhancing individual performance. The superstars will work in competition with one another throughout the life of the company. The cost is incalculable.

Unfortunately, employees who pull in the same direction are not common. The common practice among American businesses is to hire a superbly qualified individual and then motivate that individual to straighten out a mess. Such companies trek from one mess to another, one superstar to another. Every mess straightened out in one department is at the cost of a mess in other departments that were properly structured and efficient. Every high-profile superstar rises over the disgruntled remains of one, or many, low-profile, hard-working team players.

The prognosis is that Diligence will never perceive a need for superstars. The business will operate smoothly from day to day, month to month, and year to year on the organized efforts of a modest number of average employees. Diligence will display characteristics that are universally recognized as successful and the results will prove:

- ► Predictable and stable profitability;
- ► Low employee turnover rates;
- ► Minuscule error rates;
- ► Insignificant infighting;
- ► High morale;
- ► Industry standard quality;
- ► Enviable customer satisfaction; and
- ► The lowest product costs.

Diligence will never overstaff during the good times nor lay off large groups when a decline in business dictates that costs be controlled. Investors will consider Diligence as a safe, profitable, and prudent investment. Stock prices will increase steadily without the heart-rending roller-coaster ride that frightens investors.

Stimulating employees to higher levels of total performance is the goal of true leadership. Be aware that high-performing individuals working in conflict will lead to chaotic and costly final results. Average individuals working in unison toward a common goal will lead to predictable and cost-effective results.

Achieve Unity of Effort

Unity of effort means that all people in your business are striving in the same direction to achieve the same ends. It means that every task is performed only once, without duplication or conflict. Unity of effort eliminates wasted effort. You can achieve unity of effort by creating a competent plan, communicating it to your employees, providing tools and training, and eliminating roadblocks. Unity of effort is the product of effective leadership.

Profit Pointer

❧ 2 ❧

Expect High Performance

Effective leaders expect high performance and they get it. The expectation of high performance stimulates high performance. The phenomenon is called the Pygmalion Effect. The Pygmalion Effect can work wonders in your business.

First, believe that your employees have the genuine ability to rise to higher levels of performance. Your belief alone will stimulate new resourcefulness and energy. Employees will come to you asking for opportunities to prove their newfound abilities. Note, you cannot fake your expectation of high performance; employees will see through your facade to your real beliefs almost immediately. Second, believe in the goals that you have set. You must believe that they are attainable. For your employees to be willing to believe that the goal you have set is attainable, you must be able to help them understand the path of progress from the present conditions to the reaching of a future goal. This means that you must do some analysis and planning before you present high-sounding goals to your employees. If you know how to reach the goals, you can help your employees believe that the goals are, indeed, attainable.

Your belief in your employees and in the goals you expect them to achieve result in a total positive expectation. You will never have to speak about your expectations: you communicate expectations in your nature of speech and in your everyday actions. Employees pick up your expectations and rise to the level of your beliefs.

Coach, Counsel, and Train

The mark of exceptional leaders is that they can influence others to achieve without using force or intimidation. Leaders who can stimulate a voluntary desire to achieve are rare; these types of leaders are best. Desire to achieve is one side of success; ability to achieve is the other. Once desire has been stimulated in a group of employees, the task of the leader is to enhance the ability to achieve. Ability is enhanced by coaching, counseling, and training. A top-notch leader spends a great percentage of time in the coach-counsel-train mode.

Unfortunately, many leaders still choose force and intimidation, which have heavy effects on the performance of their employees and, in turn, the profitability of their businesses. One example of such intimidation is the written warning. The written warning is issued for one reason only — to uphold a denial of unemployment benefits when an employee is dismissed. So, when you give a written warning, what are you really doing? You are saying to your employee, "I expect you to make this same mistake again. When you do, I will fire you and deny unemployment."

Predictably, the employee will goof again. You will dismiss the employee. You will hire and train again. You will absorb mistakes again, write warnings again, fire again, and hire again. If your business is engaged in this self-defeating routine, try this simple formula: counsel-coach-train. It works — if you give a little extra effort to help a marginal employee succeed, that employee will not forget your effort. You will be repaid with loyalty and heightened performance forever.

Devise Attainable Goals

Believing in a goal is essential, but there is more. A goal must be stated in terms that are meaningful in the mind and language of your employees. A goal must be tangible and measurable. A goal statement that reads, "To be better tomorrow than we are today," is not tangible or measurable. Your employees' definitions of better and your definition of better may be very different. They may be thinking that smiling more equates to better. You may be thinking that $100,000 in cost reductions means better.

The goal that this book refers to most often is the goal of a business turnaround. But the goal of turnaround is too big a goal for your employees. You first must determine subelements of the goal and write them down in measurable terms. If, for example, a landmark event, such as a foreclosure, will occur in 90 days unless profits are increased, use 90 days out as a deadline. If the business is averaging $100,000 in the red, then $150,000 in reduced costs in 90 days is an excellent goal statement.

To make the goal meaningful, make it visual. All people comprehend tangible things better; things that they can see and feel. While $100,000 in losses might seem very real to a top manager or to an owner, it is abstract and theoretical to the people who are buried in the challenges of the day-to-day operations. A simple way to make the abstract goal meaningful is to chart it. Place the chart where everyone can see it and post it daily. It should be attractive and neat. The target should be very prominent.

There is an interesting principle associated with charting. Anything that is charted gets better. You may have difficulty accepting that concept, because it does not bear a logical connection. The connection goes back into rather deep psychology. It is easiest to explain by remembering the Pygmalion Effect. Charting implies that you are expecting the condition being charted to get better. Employees will rise to your expectation and the condition will get better. For an excellent example of a charted goal statement, refer to Chapter 7.

PROFIT POINTER

❖ 3 ❖

To get even better results, break the goal down into bite-size pieces. Instead of stating that the goal is to reduce costs by $150,000 in 90 days, break it down into smaller pieces — $50,000 every 30 days for 3 months, for example. Then, break each $50,000 chunk into manageable elements. Ask your key department managers to help break down the goal, such as:

- ► Can the purchasing department trim one percent per month out of parts and materials?
- ► Can the sales department save $5,000 in operating costs?
- ► Can the production department save one percent in labor?

Then, instruct each department to divide and reassign even smaller pieces of the project. The object is to get the overwhelming, larger, overall goal divided into pieces of individual responsibility and commitment. Individuals can handle small, well-defined pieces of a greater plan with innovation and ability. You will be surprised and delighted at how well your employees respond to this sort of assignment of responsibility. You will rarely find a case in which a person will refuse to shoulder part of the load.

This approach will provide you with a side benefit that is always a source of surprisingly significant improvements. As you make cost-reduction assignments, you will be deluged with employee suggestions. For every one idea you have for reducing costs, your employees will offer a dozen.

PROFIT POINTER

❖ 4 ❖

Reward High Performance

Another condition of effectively stimulating an employee to higher levels of performance is reward. Reward is not motivation. Motivation arises within an individual when a reward is expected.

Both negative and positive rewards exist. You have probably heard a lot to discourage the use of negative rewards. There is no question that positive rewards produce great results. But there are cases when the negative side of things must be faced with maturity, such as the case of a business with declining profits.

Your employees are intelligent, perceptive adults. Mature adults respond poorly to exaggerations and hoopla. If your business' profits are declining, tell your employees the truth. Tell them that if profits keep declining, the business will fail and they will lose their jobs. If your employees are going to be a part of the solution, then they must know the full nature of the problem.

They must know in total, truthful detail — including numbers, dates, trends, costs, and profits. Let them know that a large part of their reward is that things will stay the same — they will keep their jobs. Do not threaten, intimidate, or blame your employees for the condition of your business. Don't even hint of casting blame. You owe your employees honesty — after all, you expect honesty. A fearful or resentful employee will do you no good. Employees who understand the condition of the business and believe that they can make a difference will do a lot of good!

Recognition and Fulfillment

You will have to offer positive rewards if you want innovative, creative change. Financial rewards are nice and traditional. However, if your business is distressed, a financial reward for your employees is likely not your wisest choice. Financial rewards do not provide the motivation that most managers and owners think. There is, however, a reward system that costs nearly nothing. It is a reward system that provides more incentive than financial rewards. All people respond to it. It can be described in two words: recognition and fulfillment.

Recognition can be as simple as mentioning an employee in your company newsletter. The traditional compliment is recognition. The whole idea is for you to let employees know that they are important to you and to the business. Recognition imparts a feeling of security. The feeling of security frees an employee to operate at higher levels of resourcefulness and energy.

Fulfillment is the warm feeling that results when a person has achieved something special. Why is it important to your business for your employees to feel fulfilled? First, fulfillment results from having done something creative or resourceful; you want your employees to be creative and resourceful to carry your business to higher levels of success.

Fulfillment is essential for a second reason. All people have a basic human need for fulfillment. They will seek out situations in which the need for fulfillment will be satisfied. If your employees find fulfillment in the workplace, they will not seek it elsewhere. Remember, they may seek employment from your competitor to find fulfillment.

There is no substitute for the involvement of the people that do the work in a business. Dozens of names and formal programs dedicated to involvement of the general workforce exist, including empowerment, participative management, self-directed work teams, and quality circles. All are formalized methods of recognizing employees and of supplying some degree of fulfillment.

An employee-of-the-month program is a vehicle of recognition used by many companies which can do more harm than good. An employee-of-the-month program can turn into a competition among employees. It is a competition in which a small group of employees will normally dominate. The group that dominates depends on your own rules of the competition. Employees outside the dominant group quit trying and the result is low morale.

To prevent an employee-of-the-month recognition from turning into a competition, make it part of a much larger plan of employee recognition. Have several methods in which employees can achieve recognition. Try to keep them noncompetitive. Most people do not appreciate requirements to compete with their fellow employees in order to fulfill a basic need.

You do not need a formal program with a recognized name to enjoy the magnificent benefits of a workforce that is genuinely involved in the welfare of your business. To involve your employees, first become involved with their welfare. You are the leader. Act first and your employees will follow. It is one of the basic truths of leadership psychology. To learn more about building employee morale, see Profit Pointer 10 in Chapter 2.

PROFIT POINTER

◈ 5 ◈

Remove Disabling Conditions

As you lead your employees on the path to high performance, you will discover that they will complain of roadblocks. Many leaders dismiss their complaints as excuses. In reality, employees that are motivated and involved make few excuses. They are anxious to get on with the job. Your job is to listen to their complaints and act. You will soon find that employees are asking you to do two things:

1. Remove disabling conditions.
2. Provide enabling conditions.

Removing disabling conditions and providing enabling conditions are essential tasks of leadership. For example, if an employee needs a special tool to complete an assigned task, and that tool is being repaired, then the lack of that tool is a disabling condition. When you provide the tool for the employee, you have removed the disabling condition. The employee can then complete the task.

Eliminating roadblocks is often called "putting out fires." Putting out fires is an ineffective form of management. In fact, it is not management at all. It is nothing more than problem solving — problems that should have been anticipated and prevented.

Even in the case of excellent management, there will always be a few unanticipated disablers that crop up in day-to-day operations. When a disabler occurs, good leaders will:

- ► Quickly eliminate the condition; and
- ► Learn from the condition and take steps to prevent its reoccurrence.

Preventing the reoccurrence of disablers is called proactive management by trendy theorists and academicians. To stay grounded in reality, understand that the only true form of management is proactive. The opposite form of management is reactive. Reactive means that the leader simply responds to stimulus from chaos in the operation. Responding means following. Following and responding are not parts of effective management.

A proactive manager plans, leads, organizes, and controls. There is little that is reactive in good management. Your goal as a leader should be to predict and prevent disabling conditions.

Provide Enabling Conditions

The difference between providing enabling conditions and removing disabling conditions is subtle. Removal of a disabler allows progress to resume after it has stalled. Providing an enabling condition allows progress to continue smoothly without stalling.

Most leaders understand the importance of removing roadblocks. What they often overlook is the importance of removing roadblocks at the right time. Think about it: what is the best time to remove a roadblock — before or after it becomes a hindrance to progress?

As an effective leader, your priority is to remove roadblocks before they are a recognized hindrance. Many managers, however, do not see far enough into the future to predict a roadblock and remove it before it becomes a hindrance. A mark of superb managers is the ability to foresee roadblocks and remove them before the workforce stumbles and stalls. Such leadership ability is rare and valuable. Excellent business leaders develop systems to predict roadblocks in time to develop corrective measures or alternative plans.

Planning is the key. When you operate your business according to a plan you can predict roadblocks, usually in plenty of time for management to clear the path. However, planning alone will not eliminate roadblocks. Planning must be complemented with communication with employees, resourcefulness, and a closeness to the action.

PROFIT POINTER

◄► 6 ◄►

Successful removal of roadblocks before they are encountered can reduce operational costs substantially. To get an idea of the effectiveness of removing roadblocks before they hinder progress, think of the cost-reduction potential in terms of ten percent cost-reduction minimums and unlimited cost-reduction maximums.

As you begin to provide enabling conditions, think in terms of materials, product design, tools, morale, documentation, and employee training. You will commonly find a need to develop enabling systems in the following areas:

- ► Parts and materials that are always available;
- ► Designs that prevent errors and induce efficiency;
- ► Tools that are in good condition, accurate, and readily available;
- ► Morale that fosters resourcefulness, energy, and communication;
- ► Bills of materials, routings, and drawings that are accurate and instructive; and
- ► Functional training for employees.

When you systematically master these six areas, you will realize superb performance from a workforce comprised of ordinary people.

PROFIT POINTER

◈ 7 ◈

Provide Leadership

Leadership has been defined and redefined thousands of times. It has been misused millions of times. To properly lead your employees in noteworthy success, you must master the principles of leadership. Four simple principles of leadership exist.

1. People follow plans — give them a plan.
2. People follow because they choose to follow — give them a reason.
3. People follow the easiest path — remove the disablers.
4. People follow if they are able — provide the enablers.

What do these leadership principles mean to you in the daily grind of trying to get employees to do what you want? If you attempt force, you will expend enormous amounts of energy maintaining the force to extract mediocre performance. However, if people are following willingly, then you do not have to apply the force. You do not have to expend the energy, and the performance will be superb!

Directive versus Participative Management

Two styles of management exist. Simply compared, the directive style issues directives and enforces compliance. The participative style asks for suggestions and expects employees to volunteer for action. The directive style is best suited to emergency situations or war. The participative style is best suited for the more mundane task of making silk purses out of sows' ears on a daily basis.

Directive managers give orders. They rarely ask questions or listen to opposing views. They rarely change a mindset or revise a plan. They dominate conversations. They press on against all odds. They go down with the ship. But the 100 percent directive manager will rarely benefit from the ideas or the creativity of others. In fact, directive managers are often undermined by their subordinates.

The directive style is not leadership — it is driving from behind. If it is used in the conduct of day-to-day business, it will be resented and resisted. Directive managers will breed emergency situations to get results. They will fabricate conditions that cause employees to come asking for directions. The directive style cannot promote, share credit, train, or ask an employee, "How would you like this done?"

Participative managers lead others to achieve. Participative managers will devise plans that are achievable by the people who must do the work. Participative managers will ask questions, then listen more than they talk. They give credit for all accomplishments to the group who did the work. Indeed, they never accomplish much; their people do. They devise rewards. They never run a department; the department runs itself. They never stand in the spotlight; they direct the spotlight. They do not direct people; they manage resources, information, and situations. They create plans, share responsibility, and delegate authority. They coach, counsel, and train. They won't go down with the ship; they will create a plan to keep the ship from sinking. The participative style encourages high performance from a group. The downside of the 100 percent participative style is that it is likely to muddle decision making when a crisis demands quick action.

Excellent managers will have the flexibility to adopt the style of management that is best suited to the reality the situation at hand. Lee Iacocca best expressed the proper mixture of leadership styles when he said, "I listen to what everybody has to say, then I make a decision." His management style is a blend of participative and directive. Great leaders are capable of both styles of management, combined to fill the needs of the situation at hand. They have the ability to recognize the needs and abilities of human nature. Great leaders know leadership psychology.

Participative Works Better

An inflexible, directive style of management dominates the American business world, as indicated by a 1994 U.S. Department of Labor workplace study. One of the disturbing facts was that only five percent of all workplaces has effective participative management. The study revealed that 50 million American employees would like to participate in workplace decisions, but are prohibited from doing so. The study emphasized that those 50 million employees express anger, frustration, resentment, and hostility toward the managers of the companies who employ them. These are the attitudes that lead to business failure.

Directive management is normally less effective than participative management. A company that is riding high on a wave of hot demand may thrive with a directive management style. It is not the directive style that causes the success; the success is caused by hot markets. Hot markets compensate for the costs of chaos and internal conflict caused by directive management. When the hot markets cool and contract, when costs must be controlled, when innovation and creativity are required for survival, participative management will pull the rabbit out of the hat.

If you are attempting to lead a business in a turnaround effort, there is an interesting condition that can be quite a challenge to you if you are not prepared. Employees in a business who have been abused by an overly directive management will appreciate a participative style. They will respond with enthusiasm. You will receive energetic cooperation. Your turnaround project can be quite easy. The opposite is true for employees in a business who have been nurtured into softness by over-participation. They will resent your directive initiatives. They are accustomed to second-guessing and revising plans forever. Your directives will be received with anger. The business that has gone too far into the participative realm is more difficult to bring around than is the over-directed business.

You will be faced with the probability that you will have to fire some key people to shock others out of their complacency. Firing key people is a two-edged sword. On one hand, they are leading the resistance to your directive efforts. On the other hand, they probably possess genuine expertise about the business. There is not an always-right answer to this one; it is your experience and judgment that will make the difference. Remember, firing people speaks more about your own inabilities than it does about their inabilities.

Identify Your Style

If you find that people under your influence must be driven hard to achieve mediocre results, then you should closely examine your management style to determine if you are heavily directive. You probably are. In fact, the U.S. Department of Labor study cited earlier indicates a 95 percent chance that you are part of a company with an unacceptable degree of directive management. To determine your management style, complete the Mindset Evaluation located at the end of this chapter.

If you find that you are too heavily directive or too heavily participative, then you have one of three alternatives:

1. Change nothing. This is the easiest and most common choice of the three alternatives. It doesn't work, but it is easy.

2. Coach and motivate yourself. This is the most difficult choice. There is an adage that pointedly states the mind that created a problem cannot solve the problem. Self-correction requires a level of maturity and self-discipline that is rare.

3. Bring in an outsider. This is the most risky choice. Too many trendy consultants advocate unproven theories of their own concoction. If you can find a competent, ethical person to assist you, this is a good choice.

Alternative number two is the plan that will provide the best long-term results. If you want to develop the expertise to operate a high-performance business, you must be willing to make personal change.

Get Close to the Action

PROFIT POINTER

❦ 8 ❦

Distancing is a condition in which the leadership of a business loses contact with the business' day-to-day operations — also called the front lines. On the front lines, employees interface with customers and create products and services. Thousands of decisions are made daily on the front lines. Unanticipated disablers crop up and are resolved. Products and schedules are changed and employees come and go. Every change is a deviation from what the business was yesterday. A savvy businessperson will determine if the business is changing in the direction of higher quality and lower cost or in the opposite direction toward bankruptcy.

Distanced leaders never think they are distanced. For that reason, you need to recognize the symptoms of distancing in your business. If you see the symptoms, then you are distanced and need to get back on the front lines. Some examples of the symptoms of distancing are:

► Quiet employees;

► Departmentalization;

► Lengthy, detailed job descriptions;

- ▸ Rigid policies;
- ▸ Formalized communication;
- ▸ Quiet customers;
- ▸ Irate suppliers;
- ▸ Superstars; and
- ▸ The Big Fix Syndrome.

Quiet Employees

Quiet employees are a prime indicator of distanced leadership. The people at the top do not converse with the common employees. Guess which of those two groups really knows what is happening in the workplace? Guess who know about the problems with quality, excess scrap, downtime, overtime, and skyrocketing costs? Guess which group never gets told? Leaders should spend some time every day listening to the employees who are doing the front lines work.

Departmentalization

Departmentalization means that employees have bonded into tightly-knit groups with common functions. People departmentalize themselves as a defensive measure when leadership becomes distant. Communication to distant leadership often results in unworkable directives. It follows that people discuss problems with one another rather than seeking leadership advice. Problems run around in circles within a department. It becomes convenient to dismiss problems as, "not the responsibility of this department."

Lengthy Job Descriptions

The lengthy and detailed job description is another manifestation of distancing. Like departmentalization, lengthy job descriptions are a defensive measure. People use the job description as a substitute leader. A job description should be brief and flexible; one page is plenty. It should be prepared by the leader responsible for the function, not by the employee in the job. If a leader cannot write the job description for a subordinate, then that leader is distanced.

Rigid Policies

"There's no reason for it, it's just our policy." You have probably seen such a sign over a retail counter somewhere. Policy making is prevalent when leadership is distant. It is another protective measure that employees take who are frightened by a lack of close contact with the leaders of the business.

Formalized Communication

In the company that has distanced leadership, formalized communication is a method to avoid directly talking or listening to each other. Face-to-face communication is strained and is often hostile in the distanced business. The stand-up, spontaneous, hallway meeting is replaced by prepared and scheduled presentations. Have a great idea? Write up a proposal and schedule it for the next staff meeting with an opening on the agenda. Distancing filters communication until leadership hears only what it has indicated that it wants to hear — the good stuff — nothing negative and no early warnings. The source of the early warnings — employees who are dealing with reality — is silenced, resulting in fewer innovation, stagnation, and animosity.

Quiet Customers

A symptom of distancing is that top leadership no longer hears customer complaints. When customers seem silent, it is because your company has indicated that it does not want to hear customer complaints. Your business can only develop improved products and services if you hear the responses of your customers. Remember that customers truly wish to let you know how you are doing — make it easy for them. Refer to Chapter 3 to learn how you can use customer complaints to your benefit.

Irate Suppliers

Supply is vital to every business. Distancing of suppliers breeds ill will and eventually erodes profits. No materials management technique or system will compensate for the wrath of an irate supplier. Chapter 4 will help you develop suppliers who will support the success of your business.

Superstars

Distanced leadership will predictably hire high-performance individuals. The hope is that a few superstars will correct problems in a business. When the leaders of a business begin to look for superstars, it means that they have no intent to go where the action is and remedy their own problems. The superstar affinity is the result of leadership that has been distant for a long time.

The Big Fix Syndrome

An expensive symptom of distancing is called the Big Fix Syndrome. The Big Fix occurs when distant leadership discovers that the business is losing profits. By the time distanced leadership discovers a problem in the business, the problem is normally deep-rooted and quite complex. It is the kind of problem that will require extensive analysis and involvement by leadership to implement a cure. Distant leadership, however, cannot and will not perform the analysis and work required to solve difficult business problems. A distant leader will opt for the Big Fix.

The Big Fix will be a major project, such as buyout or a merger. It might be a massive consulting project or a trendy management technique with a sophisticated name. Often, the fix is a dose of high-technology; it could be bigger or smaller buildings. Sometimes the fix calls for downsizing, upsizing, or reengineering. Too often, the Big Fix involves closing American plants and moving production to a foreign country.

The Big Fix is sometimes effective, but for the wrong reasons. The Big Fix is always much more costly than accurately diagnosing and correcting the causes of business distress. The reason that the Big Fixes are sometimes effective is that they are such complex and difficult projects that most of midmanagement and the workforce become involved in making them work. They meet and talk to one another. They listen and ask questions. They discover some of the real causes of business distress and correct them.

Big Fixes are unpredictable. They are complex, difficult, and normally divide company efforts. Complexity is the opposite of what you want to implant into your business to improve its performance. Simplicity is the hallmark of the perpetually successful business.

Get close to the action. Even a half-hour a day in the shop (or wherever the action is in your business) will keep you informed of the little things that eventually amass into big things. Remember that the last one percent of your resources and energies determines the fate of your business. You control that last one percent. Be willing to receive constant input to know which way to steer your business and employees.

Chapter Recap

You will find that using the right leadership psychology makes managing a business fun and easy. Remember a few pointers to keep you on the right track.

- ▶ Stimulate people to achieve and they will respond with great ability.
- ▶ You will get what you expect.
- ▶ Subdivide goals into manageable, attainable pieces.
- ▶ Remove disabling conditions.

- ► Provide enabling conditions.
- ► Develop a mostly participative style of leadership.
- ► Get close to the front line action.

Leadership psychology is the basis for creating a pro-success business environment. That psychology affects your attitude and the attitude of those under your influence. Your attitude drives action. The next three chapters are dedicated to helping you understand how the attitudes and actions of employees, customers, and suppliers will affect the future of your business.

Mindset Evaluation

This evaluation will help you develop a winning psychology of leadership. The column on the left lists attitudes that facilitate business success. The column on the right lists attitudes that contribute to business failure. Between the columns is a row of numbers, five to one. Honestly estimate your own attitude, then circle the number that is closest to your position. Use the mindset evaluation rating scale on the next page to determine what your score means.

85 percent of everything that goes wrong is a management responsibility.	5 4 3 2 1	85 percent of everything that goes wrong is because of employee errors.
We have specific plans that lead to becoming the high-quality, low-price leader.	5 4 3 2 1	We plan to become the sales leader.
We make efforts to assure that our suppliers are healthy and profitable.	5 4 3 2 1	We buy from the lowest bidder.
We seek out customer complaints.	5 4 3 2 1	We never receive customer complaints.
A competent receptionist takes all calls.	5 4 3 2 1	A voice processing system takes calls.
A carefully-designed business plan guides the day-to-day decisions of managers.	5 4 3 2 1	We take advantage of every opportunity. Our employees must respond quickly.
Our training budget ensures that all key people will receive business training this year.	5 4 3 2 1	We sometimes allow training if the employee can convince us that it is worthwhile.
Managers often go into the shop to listen to employees to stay close to day-to-day operations.	5 4 3 2 1	Employees can come into managers' offices to speak up.
Our organization and plans help to assure that all employees are striving in the same direction in a unified effort.	5 4 3 2 1	We like to see the best people achieve dominance. "The cream rises to the top."
Success depends upon a good plan, tools, training, performance measures, and a good system of rewards.	5 4 3 2 1	A great factor in business success is hiring highly talented people.
People will perform according to the expectations of the leader.	5 4 3 2 1	People will shirk work any chance that they get.
Long-term success is the result of doing thousands of little things right, everyday.	5 4 3 2 1	The big things — contracts, projects, and technologies — are what count.
Good leaders discover the strengths of people, then devise plans to use those strengths.	5 4 3 2 1	Good leaders give commands, then make sure that they are carried out.
We strive to eliminate fear from the work environment. Fear disables competence.	5 4 3 2 1	Fear is the only thing that keeps employees in line. Fear is the greatest motivator.
Respect for customers depends upon top managers treating employees with respect.	5 4 3 2 1	Employees are paid to treat customers respectfully. Employees here get the respect that they earn.

Mindset Evaluation Rating Scale

Now, check your results. Total the numbers you circled. Locate your score total below to learn your current business mindset.

———————————

60–75 You have a pro-profit attitude that is contagious.

30–59 Your attitude is adversely affecting profits. Work on your lowest scores first.

 0–29 Your attitude is a constant antagonist toward the people who govern your profits. Work fast to move your attitude qualities into the left column.

CHAPTER 2

FOSTER PRO-PROFIT EMPLOYEES

People do what they want. Great leaders know what people want. Great leaders devise plans that fit with the aspirations of the common person.

Employees do the bulk of what gets done every day in your business. They make thousands of choices and perform thousands of individual deeds. Those thousands of deeds and choices may ultimately encourage profits, discourage profits, or have a neutral effect on profits. Whether those deeds and choices are pro-profit depends on the effects of your leadership. Consider the following example of this manufacturer.

The president of a western U.S. manufacturer was arguing with the manufacturing manager. The manager had implemented a scrap reporting policy as part of a system to identify and reduce costly errors in production. Employees responsible for errors were required to sign scrap tags. Predictably, the key offenders did not like the policy. They convinced the president that the policy was demoralizing. The president demanded that the policy be revoked.

The manager argued that if the policy was revoked, then scrap rates would increase. The accountability brought on by signing scrap tags was, he argued, the factor that had brought scrap down from five percent to the acceptable level of one-half of one percent. The president roared, "Nonsense. People don't like the idea. They will create scrap just because they are mad at you."

The president revoked the scrap policy and fired the manufacturing manager. A year later, scrap was up from one-half of one percent to one percent. A troublesome trend, but not a sure indicator that the manufacturing manager was right. Three years later, the scrap rate was a whopping 17 percent!

The cost, time, and enforcement of the assignment of responsibility of scrap was so minuscule compared to all the other costs of the business that it would not make a pencil-line width of difference in charting profits. But remember from Chapter 1 that it is a tiny part of that last one percent that determines the fate of a business. And, in the above example, the resulting 17 percent increase in costs was enough to neutralize the profits of the company.

If you are engineering a turnaround of profits, consider the scrap scenario in reverse. In other words, if your company is experiencing a 17 percent scrap rate, start asking questions. Find out what is being rewarded. Don't quit looking until you find the condition that is rewarding scrap.

The cause of the problem will be subtle, tiny, and hard to find. It can be easily disguised as some reward or requirement for doing something else properly. Or, as in the above example, it might pose as an idea for improving workplace relations.

Develop Pro-Profit Pressures

PROFIT POINTER

❖ 9 ❖

In the previous example, rewarding scrap encouraged its increase; penalizing scrap encouraged its decrease. Whether the scrap tag is signed or unsigned, the immediate measurable difference in scrap rate will be buried in the normal fluctuations of scrap from month to month. Such minuscule decisions and actions are called pressures — because they exert a continuous force that will drive a measurable element of a business either up or down. When enough pressures accumulate on a measurable element of a business — such as the scrap rate — it will reliably and predictably move in the direction of the accumulated pressures.

Make sure you understand the concept of business pressures. Pressures are such seemingly insignificant acts that they are overlooked by most owners and managers. But, pressures are ultimately the factors that make the big differences. Your competitors have tools, equipment, products, people, and buildings. You have little advantage over the competition in those areas, since you have similar tools, equipment, products, people, and buildings. Any advantage that you might have is probably a small advantage and is costly. Pressures, on the other hand, involve the control over the use of your tools, equipment, products, people, and buildings. Control over pressures is free or nearly free. Concentrate on things like:

- ▶ Quality of decisions;
- ▶ Recognition;
- ▶ Communication; and
- ▶ A thousand little things, like signing scrap tags.

Unrelenting upward pressure on revenue; unrelenting downward pressure on costs — these actions drive the idea of controlling the last one percent of your business' operations. Controlled exertion of those pressures is a unique competitive advantage. Do enough of the little things correctly to exert pressures that are pro-profit and you can expect a significant change in the profitability of your business.

PROFIT POINTER

❧ 10 ❧

Recognize the Profit Potential of Employee Morale

The profitability of your business is determined by thousands of decisions made daily by your employees. Whether those decisions are pro-profit or couldn't-care-less in nature depends on your level of morale. Research indicates that low morale pervades nearly all U.S. companies — it follows that you likely have low-morale employees whether or not you recognize the condition. Unless you have taken identifiable action to create high morale, then you should assume morale is low.

The first step in correcting low morale is to recognize that top leadership is the source of conditions that affects morale. The second step is for those leaders to become motivated to raise morale. If only a few employees are antagonistic toward your company, they can cause it to fail in spite of superb management efforts. On the other hand, if they want the company to succeed, their contributions will override less-than-perfect techniques.

High morale is a vital foundational element of profit. Employee morale drives thousands of decisions every day. These are the lowest level decisions that drive profit pressures in microamounts. Whether those pressures are driven up or driven down depends on the condition of your employees' morale. To determine your employees' morale, complete the Morale Evaluation at the end of this chapter. Low morale will cost you in the following ways.

High turnover

Demoralized employees will seek a situation that is upbeat and encouraging. Turnover costs in more ways than just rehiring — you pay for lost production, training of new people, and errors. The most subtle cost of high turnover is in the lack of contributions by senior employees — contributions that are never made because you never develop senior employees.

Sabotage

Not all sabotage is deliberate destruction. For every act of notable sabotage, there are a hundred acts of negative progress. Negative progress is a failure to do something constructive, such as not reporting an error; not volunteering for a critical project; not reporting a great cost-saving idea; not helping a fellow employee; or not reporting to work on a beautiful day.

Inefficiency

You can find inefficiency in the thousands of microdecisions every day, such as how fast to walk to the bathroom; how much paint to apply per pass; how close to the operation to place the material; how quickly to pull the trigger on the screw gun. Inefficiency mounts up in the tiniest increments, like grains of sand. Employees can double their output just because of improved morale.

Quality

Quality is dependent on morale. No amount of money can buy a great quality program if morale is in the gutter. Demoralized employees are a contributor to poor quality. They simply allow errors to happen.

Creating high morale is like planting a fruit tree. You must do many right things before you harvest the fruit. Once the fruit begins to come in, however, minor maintenance is all that is required to assure a continuously bountiful crop. Keep your sights set on the goal. Remember that a high morale workforce makes a company self-perpetuating. Ultra-performing management is not required. A high-morale workforce carries the load — with competence, a light heart, and self-motivation. A company with high morale is efficient, regularly profitable, and easy to manage. You can expect to see continuous improvement in the following areas.

Costs

High-morale employees are caring and efficient. They devise better methods. They bring cost-incurring conditions to the attention of the proper persons. They exhibit higher levels of energy. They come to work regularly and stay longer. They work without supervision, take care of tools and machines, turn off lights, spend less time in the bathroom — and they walk faster. All of these things contributes to total control of costs, one grain of sand at a time.

Quality

High-morale employees watch for errors and suggest improvements. They help other employees; they train newcomers; they keep tooling in good condition. High morale employees do not conceal errors.

Customer service

High-morale employees want to fill orders completely. They meet production schedules and volunteer for overtime. They communicate with the sales department and help other departments to catch up on late work. They keep accurate inventories. They fill backorders quickly. All of these actions contributes to higher levels of customer service.

The essential intangible elements of high morale are comfort, excitement, and value. You are responsible for providing these elements.

Create Emotional Comfort

Emotional comfort is the overlooked issue. A no-patience-for-foolishness supervisor once asked, "Am I supposed to babysit these employees?" The answer to that question is closer to yes than it is to no. Building a successful company means building competent individuals. To achieve that, you will have to delve into emotional and psychological issues. Emotional comfort is a prerequisite to high morale — which is an enabling condition. You can create emotional comfort by establishing two key conditions.

Security

Employees must know that they will not be fired or disciplined without just cause. Just cause is defined by your employees. You set the precedents. If one employee can come in late ten times without being subject to discipline, then all other employees expect the same treatment. Employees should be treated like you would treat your friends — or like you would prefer to be treated if you were an employee. Courtesy and respect are necessary to increased feelings of security. Intimidating tactics are harmful to morale. Employees should not be subjected to temper tantrums, abusive language, yelling, or any other demeaning behavior.

Acceptance

Acceptance — defined as a feeling of belonging — is recognized as a basic human need that must be filled before a person can achieve at higher levels. Let your employees know they are doing well. Offer encouragement. Job definitions and performance evaluations help employees feel like they belong. Performance evaluations should be frequent — every 90 days. Informal evaluations should happen much more often — the occasional smile or kind word, the pat on the back, remembering names, asking about family, and asking for opinions. Public recognition conveys acceptance. Acceptance and security allow employees to rise to higher levels of performance.

Generate Excitement

Enthusiasm is a type of excitement; so is anticipation. Excitement stimulates energy and thought processes. The drab routine of repetitive manufacturing is depressing. You can imagine the difference in performance between employees who are stimulated and employees who are depressed. Your job is to keep an ebb and flow of excitement in the workplace. Keep employees involved in something new. Stimulate controlled change. Be aware of the degree of change that employees will accept. The change must fall within their abilities to perform. Change that is too dramatic simply breeds resistance. The way to know what your employees will accept is to maintain close communication with them. Get to know what projects your employees will dive into and what projects they will resist.

Eliminate the fear of consequences

Fear is what breeds resistance to new projects. The fear is not, as often believed, a fear of failure; it is fear of the consequences of failure. You can improve employee acceptance to new projects by eliminating the consequences of failure and the adverse consequences of success.

What do your employees expect to happen if they fail at some new project? If they expect termination, a cut in pay, a cutoff from further opportunities, embarrassment, or an angry tirade, they will not allow themselves to be placed in a position in which they might fail. There will be the well-known resistance to change. Replace the fear with incentive. Offer a chance for recognition or promotion if the project succeeds.

Managers get one chance to implement an efficiency measure. If it results in an immediate layoff, employees will resist success in future efficiency projects. If a project is successful and eliminates the need for some employees, try to incorporate them into other departments or let them lead other efficiency projects. Also, you can train them for advanced positions, or let them help in other departments until a vacancy opens up, or even give them a vacation with pay. Anything is better than punishing your employees for success.

Certain types of changes promote employee excitement and involvement. Employees are naturally drawn to anything new or different. Nothing excites employees more than changes like new products, plant expansions, new markets, department re-arrangement, quality programs, cost-reduction programs, or new equipment installations. Any new direction arouses curiosity and stimulates thought and involvement.

Make sure you set up situations in which employees have a near certain chance of success. Success is good for both you and your employees.

Train and educate

Properly trained and educated employees are less likely to fail. Thus, they will harbor less fear of failure. Public education does not teach anything to help people succeed in the real world of business. Employers that train and educate find that their employees are more enthusiastic about new projects.

People want to succeed. They understand that training and education offered by their employer is a material contribution to their personal success. Training and education stimulate new ideas and involvement in company affairs and enable higher levels of competence. Employees cannot wait to apply newly learned skills in the reality of the workplace — that is excitement.

Training and education should include priorities. Knowing priorities enables employees to make competent decisions without consulting a top manager. To enable employees is to empower them. A common example of established priorities is simply informing employees whether you prefer to ship a defective product (for the revenue) or to hold and repair it (for customer satisfaction).

In addition, you should communicate your business' overall plans to your employees. Let them know things like shipping goals, profit goals, safety goals, and cost-reduction goals. Treating your employees like competent business partners will cause them to become competent business partners. Think about the Pygmalion Effect from Chapter 1. People know you are serious if you provide sufficient resources to achieve the objectives. If you do not make resources available to facilitate achieving a cost-reduction goal, then your employees will soon quit trying.

Further, your goal is to train your employees about methods to achieve goals like how to go about contributing to product design simplification and who to approach with a cost-reduction idea. Provide simple and basic explanations of how to get things done and you will get an employee's imagination stirring. Before long, you will experience innovative contributions that are beyond anything you had dreamed.

Encourage involvement in professional organizations

Most professional organizations offer superb educational offerings at a very low cost. Each organization offers a certification program. One organization that offers two certifications is the American Production and Inventory Control Society (APICS).

- Certified in Production and Inventory Management (CPIM) focuses on the technical specifics of materials and shop floor management.
- Certified in Integrated Resource Management (CIRM) focuses on the big picture — effective management of manufacturing.

Companies with long-term oriented management are recognizing the value of these certification programs. Some offer a significant pay increase to employees who achieve certification. They also pay membership dues, class fees, and testing fees. For more information, contact:

The American Production and Inventory Control Society (APICS)
500 West Annandale Road
Falls Church, VA 22046-4274
(800) 444-2742

The American Society for Quality Control (ASQC)
P.O. Box 3005
Milwaukee, WI 53201-3005
(800) 248-1946

The Society of Manufacturing Engineers (SME)
P.O. Box 930
Dearborn, MI 48121-0930
(313) 271-1500

The National Association of Purchasing Management (NAPM)
P.O. Box 22160
Tempe, AZ 85285
(602) 752-6276

Help employees career plan

In-house career planning represents your commitment to the success of your employees. If you want loyalty, low turnover, and long-term employees who know every aspect of your business, try career planning. Career planning is simple to implement. Develop a simple plan for (and with) all employees. The plan should document what employees would like to be doing and earning each year for the next ten years.

Counsel your employees and develop plans to achieve those goals. Show that you care by helping employees achieve their goals. A very simple career planning effort lets your employees know that they have a future with your company that agrees with their personal desires. A half-hour of counseling and planning every six months will encourage enthusiasm and loyalty.

Give promotions

A promotion represents a pat on the back; it is recognition and security. A promotion is your way of rewarding employees for doing a good job. Frequent promotions within the workforce stimulate a higher level of productivity as employees compete for the honor. Promotions do not have to be accompanied by large pay increases to be an incentive. Your employees strive for recognition much more than for money.

Be fair when promoting. Treat all persons equally. Personal friends, members of the same church, and attractive people should be treated equally to those that are not so well-placed or blessed. Remember to discern between talkers and doers. Your employees know the difference. Promote a talker and you discourage the doers.

Also, promote on the basis of performance that is objectively measured. Performance-based promotions create incentives for all employees to perform better. Give an opportunity to all employees who may be qualified via job posting. Just picking someone to fill an opening may be expedient, but it is a practice that is discouraging to the rank and file.

Many companies adopt a wage scale that will allow employees to graduate to a higher scale. When they have learned a certain number of tasks, they are cross trained. Graduating from scale to scale is an acceptable substitute for conventional promotions. It agrees with the ideas of training and education and it supports career planning.

Make Your Employees Feel Valued

Feeling valued is an absolute human need that must be fulfilled. Human beings seek out situations in which they will feel valued and needed. Low feelings of value are a cause of high turnover and other undesirable employee behavior. The need to feel valued causes people to seek out situations in which they are needed. People will change jobs or move across the country. They will accept lower rates of pay to find a situation that fulfills their need to feel valued.

Your employees require much more than a once-a-year pat on the back and a three percent raise to feel needed. They require regular reinforcement of the message. The day-to-day relationship between managers and their employees is what verifies the message. The following messages will tell your employees that you value them.

Approval

Let your employees know when they have done something right. A mixture of verbal and written approval is best. Approval builds employee competence in other ways — it guides performance without disciplinary action.

Courtesy

Treat people with dignity and respect. To be courteous, you will request rather than order and you will criticize in private and praise in public. Refrain from using abusive language, yelling, and angry outbursts. Extend courtesy to your employees and you will raise morale and win personal respect.

Pay

The rate of pay must be acceptable in the mind of the employee. A common misunderstanding is that high pay results in high morale. Employees themselves contribute to this error. The first demand of a demoralized workforce is more pay. They ask for more pay because they are uncomfortable asking for fulfillment of emotional needs and willing to accept high pay as compensation for demoralizing conditions.

A high rate of pay will not create high morale. You can pay employees enough so that they will smile in the face of abusive conditions; you can pay them enough to endure abusive conditions until they retire. You cannot pay them enough to buy their enthusiastic involvement in the success of your company. Only high morale can motivate enthusiastic involvement in the success of a company.

Caring

Acknowledge that your employees are human with everyday human problems. Work with employees to minimize the effects of personal trials: an illness in the family, marital problems, runaway children, deaths of loved ones, and civil or legal challenges. Personal difficulties are devastating for a moment in time. Your job is to minimize the effects of personal issues in the workplace without adding to the burden of your employee.

When the emotional trauma is over, the employee will return to acceptable levels of performance. If you have been a source of strength in times of trial, your employees will respect and appreciate you. If you added to the burden of a distressed employee through reprimands and disciplinary action, your employees will universally resent the act.

Inclusion

Include employees in all matters that will affect them. Ask for opinion and input. A meeting or formal hearing will net poor results; most of your employees will not speak freely in large groups. One-on-one communication is the method that will net the best results.

Communication

Most companies promote one-way communication — from the top down. You should promote two-way communication. To promote bottom-up communication you will need to put employees at ease. Ask them to voice their frustrations as well as their support. Inclusion allows employees to voice opinions about decisions before they become final. Announce the decision and invite responses, then modify the decision so that it will work in the real world. The employees must make the decision work. If they contribute to the final decision, they will contribute to making it work. If it is purely a management decision, made in isolation, the response of employees will be one of noninvolvement.

American manufacturers have a reputation for resisting bottom-up communication. The result is that top managers are very unaware of the real effects of management decisions. In management schools, we learn about the theoretical effects of decisions only. You need to be aware of whether your decisions create the desired effects. Your employees will tell you, but only if you encourage them. Unimpeded bottom-up communication will markedly improve the quality of your decisions.

Consistency

Consistency is fairness and justice. It means that you are treating all employees equally — equal discipline for equal offenses, equal praise for equal achievement, and equal pay for equal work. Your employees expect consistency of treatment. Consistent treatment will not improve morale. However, inconsistent treatment is demoralizing.

Inconsistency is viewed by employees as favoritism, injustice, or unfairness. It is called racism, sexism, or prejudice. In many cases it is illegal. Superficial efforts that bear the appearance of consistent treatment may fulfill the legal obligations of the company, but it does little good for morale. People quickly see through the facade. True consistent treatment enables morale to thrive.

High morale comes spontaneously from within an individual. Management cannot create high morale. Management can only enable morale by removing morale-disabling conditions. Use the Morale Disablers Checklist at the end of this chapter to help you correct and remove morale disabling conditions.

Remember that morale enhancements are a foundation for long-term profitability and growth. Do not expect to see quick results on your bottom line. In six months don't expect to see an additional $42,353 in profit as a return on morale enhancements. Instead, expect to see a multitude of tiny improvements that place a continuous upward pressure on revenues and a downward pressure on costs.

Manage by Opportunity

Management by Opportunity is a term used to describe the philosophy of taking advantage of opportunities to move in the right direction. Every business offers literally thousands of opportunities daily. Some are opportunities to press toward greater profit; some will press toward lower profit.

The prerequisite to making Management by Opportunity work is to discern which actions will genuinely aid and which will degrade profit in the long term. A common error among today's business owners is to move in a direction that will increase profit in the short term while creating secondary responses that will degrade profits in the long term. Secondary responses are discussed in Chapter 13.

Management by Opportunity may seem to be a disorganized approach when compared to more structured management techniques. It is not intended

PROFIT POINTER

⋘ 11 ⋙

to replace the structured discipline of planning and goal setting; it is a complementary technique that you should use to bolster morale and to use the unique contributions of individuals. Management by Opportunity does not have specific goals. Instead, it has directions — up for revenue, down for costs. Management by Opportunity grabs every fleeting chance to make a right move, no matter how small or seemingly insignificant.

Structured, goal-setting management techniques are valid but limited. Employee contributions that do not fit the structured pattern are excluded. Employees who are not formally included in a specific project are left out. Structured, goal-setting techniques are poorly flexible and are management-oriented. Management by Opportunity is flexible, responsive and employee-oriented. This type of management fosters enthusiasm and team spirit; it is spontaneous and doesn't require administration. To help you understand the great potential of Management by Opportunity, consider the following example (based on an actual case).

Smith is a tool grinder who has mastered the trade. During routine chores, Smith has time to think and one day asks his manager if it is okay to buy a backup diamond wheel for carbide.

Smith's manager recognizes a chance to apply Management by Opportunity. The manager asks Smith to explain why the company needs an extra wheel. Smith explains, "Sometimes they break. Takes six weeks to get another one. The people in purchasing won't buy an extra one because it costs $98. They don't understand that we are exposed to up to six weeks of downtime if I break a wheel at the wrong time. I think it's inexpensive insurance."

Smith's manager figures if $98 will save even one hour of downtime at any time in the future of the company, the investment will be paid back hundreds of times over. The manager clearly sees the opportunity to press costs down and revenues up in one simple decision and says, "Do it!"

A spike on the profit chart will never be seen from Smith's contribution. When the contribution makes a difference, it will be that it prevented a loss. Mega-managers will quickly pronounce such a tiny improvement as insignificant. With Management by Opportunity there is no such thing as an insignificant improvement. Even if Smith's idea never actually prevented a loss of profits, it is worth the $98 to encourage new ideas from other employees.

Promote Simplicity

Ideas that come from the shop floor are almost always ideas to simplify. A wise manager will welcome ideas for simplification and may hang a sign on the wall that reads "Complexity Costs — Simplicity Saves."

The ideas that come from the shop floor are often so simple that the full impact of them is hard to understand. The ideas are often so perfectly thought out that they can be implemented with little cost. They often can be expressed in one or two sentences.

- ► "Make the door swing the other way."
- ► "Move the bucket over there."
- ► "Put a pin in the fixture. That way, you can't do it wrong."
- ► "Why weld this? Make that part an eighth longer and it will stay in place."
- ► "A backup grinding wheel could save us six weeks of downtime."

Your response can be equally simple — do it! If you want to move light years ahead of your competition in cost and quality, try implementing one idea for simplification every week for a year.

Most American businesses need to simplify in a number of areas, including:

- ► Product models and options
- ► Shop floor layout
- ► Product design
- ► Administrative procedures
- ► Numbers of suppliers
- ► Numbers of customers
- ► Inventory flow and storage

However, instead of simplifying in these areas many American business owners move their operations to foreign countries in the hopes that lower labor costs will improve their profits. They are neglecting to consider the soft (hard to define) costs that result from the increased complexities of employing foreign labor to build products that are always specified in American terms.

Many business owners end up moving their operations back to the United States after they learn that the additional complexities are horribly costly. If you are considering a move to use foreign labor, make sure that you first predict the additional costs that result from more complex logistics, communication, quality management, and unwritten cultural codes of the area.

A second trend that will last well past the year 2000 is the pursuit of high-technology. The complexities of high-technology reach beyond the full understanding of even the people who develop and sell the stuff. If you are considering some high-tech solution, make sure that the added complexity is offset by substantially lower costs or higher quality.

PROFIT POINTER

◁⧓ 13 ⧓▷

Stimulate a Pro-Profit Attitude

The new manufacturing manager asked the owners and managers a pointed question: "Do you think your employees want the company to succeed?" The answer was a lengthy tirade explaining that the employees had darn well better want the company to succeed — after all, it was their livelihood. The manufacturing manager's question was spurred by remarks made by key shop employees about unacceptably high error rates. Employees had revealed an attitude of hostility toward the owners. The hostility bred an "I-don't-care" attitude regarding the health of the company. The owners and managers did not believe that employees could possibly hold any attitude other than one that is pro-company. They were wrong. They did not understand what drives employee attitudes. The attitude and conduct of the leadership of a company are the factors that drive employee attitudes.

- ▶ Loyalty begets loyalty.
- ▶ Respect begets respect.
- ▶ Generosity of pay begets generosity of performance.
- ▶ Trust begets trust.
- ▶ Quality begets quality.

If top managers work to help employees succeed, then employees will work to help top managers succeed. The reverse was true in the example above. Top management held the attitude that employees should be treated like errant children. As a result, the employees were intimidated and threatened daily. Terminations were carried out weekly. Only a handful of employees had managed to stay with the company for more than a year. Just some of the characteristics of the attitude and performance of the employees included:

- ▶ Hidden errors;
- ▶ Defective product shipped;
- ▶ Failed production plans;
- ▶ Infrequent and deceitful shop-to-management communication; and
- ▶ Slow-moving employees.

Do these characteristics sound familiar? If they do, look to the leadership at the top. Top leadership sets the style, tempo, and atmosphere of your business. Your top leaders have the ability to either stimulate success or failure. A pro-employee attitude on the part of your company's leadership stimulates a pro-company attitude on the part of your employees.

Foster Willing and Capable Employees

PROFIT POINTER

❧ 14 ❧

People love to achieve. While it is true that some individuals need a mundane routine with no change, most people love the excitement and fulfillment of achievement. How many of your employees are excited about the idea of achieving something that will benefit your company? If you can think of only one in a hundred, you have a problem. One in a hundred, or one percent, is not enough to qualify as a competitive advantage. You need to strive for 50 percent or more.

Think of the contribution to profits that would materialize if 50 of your employees came up with an improvement in costs of only one-tenth of one percent, one time each year. That will provide you with a total of five percent per year in lower costs to add to your business' bottom line. If your profits are now five percent, another five percent will double your profits. This kind of contribution is not only possible, but it is common in companies with willing and capable employees.

You may think that you already have employees that are willing. You often hear the agreeable phrase, "Tell me what to do and I'll do it." That is good, but it is not enough. Management cannot constantly give directions to employees throughout the day. There is a big difference between passive willingness and active willingness. Passive willingness waits for instructions. You want active willingness. The active willing employee seeks out opportunities to achieve something significant. The four-part enabling sequence that fosters willing and capable employees includes:

1. Responsive, cooperative, and supportive management enables passive willingness, which is a prerequisite to your goal of active willingness.
2. Passive willingness enables the employee to accept instruction.
3. Instruction enables capability. The employee understands more and can do more.
4. Capability enables active willingness.

Active willingness results in aggressive involvement in the success of a business. Aggressive involvement can happen only after you, as the leader, have built a foundation based on the above enabling sequence.

Develop Aggressive Involvement

Aggressively involved employees contribute to the profits of your business in ways that are diverse, unexpected, and often imaginative. Instruction is the tool that converts passively willing employees into aggressively involved employees. There are two distinct kinds of instruction that you can provide your employees to start them on the path to becoming aggressively involved — training and education. The difference between training and education is subtle but critical.

Training instructs employees in how to do something. Typically, training provides instruction in how to achieve some technical task, such as drilling holes, painting, printing invoices, or answering the telephone. Training removes the roadblock — the disabler — and gives the employee the ability to perform a task.

Education is a motivator. Education teaches employees the reasons why it is important to perform a task in a certain way. Understanding the reason behind technical instruction is the stimulus that results in aggressive involvement. Consider the benefits of education in this story.

———➤✦◄———

A perfect example of the value of education occurred in a rapidly growing steel fabricator in northeastern Washington. Evans was the fabrication supervisor who had the responsibility of driving costs down while bringing production up. Evans started by instructing Harris, the shear operator, on how to hold closer tolerances and how to check sheared blanks for squareness. Harris understood and was able to operate the shear competently.

Within days, the welding line had slowed to one-fourth the normal pace. Upon examination, Evans found that a fabricated U-shaped component was higher on one side than the other. Welders were grinding a tapering one-eighth inch off the top of one side of the component — which takes a lot of time. Costs went up while production went down. Evans told Harris again how to control tolerances and squareness. Quality and productivity improved for a couple of days, then the welding line slowed to a snail's pace again. The same component had the same problem again. Evans talked to Harris, again. Harris understood, again. But this time, Evans went a step further by inviting Harris to visit the welding line.

Harris watched and grimaced as the welder labored to grind off the one-eighth inch accumulated error. Evans showed Harris all the fabrication steps that depended on accuracy at the shear:

how a 0.030 inch shearing error could double and redouble until it accumulated to a full one-eighth inch. Harris was impressed. From that day on, Harris was motivated to make certain that there were no errors originating at the shear.

Reliable, error-free performance resulted when Evans educated Harris by showing why it was important to hold tolerances and squareness. Harris knew how to make the parts error-free all along, but was not motivated. Harris was motivated to a higher level of achievement by learning why exacting squareness and size were so important.

The postscript is that it was repeatedly heartwarming to see Harris visiting the welding line to inspect parts. As the company grew large enough to warrant a second shift shear operator, Harris took the new employee to the welding line to show why meticulous shearing was so important. Harris' competence rubbed off on the new employee.

Expect great things when you develop aggressively involved employees. If you train for technical competence and educate for aggressive involvement, then you can accomplish many objectives with one effort. You will help your employees develop a higher level of technical competence and establish common grounds for communication. Training and education stimulate the mind and spark new ideas. They break the mundane routine of endless repetition that is common to most production employees.

A great step toward a complete training and education program starts with "basic training" of new employees. See the checklist at the end of this chapter.

Chapter Recap

Unless you have experienced the contributions of enthusiastic pro-profit employees, you will be overwhelmed by the benefits that you will realize. Active, motivated, aggressively involved employees make a company easier to manage and automatically more profitable.

There is just no way to lead a company in the direction of higher profits unless you have a friendly relationship with the psychology that drives humans. What you have already learned in chapters 1 and 2 will give you a competitive advantage. What you will learn further in this book will provide you with specifics of what to do based on this foundation of business psychology. Then you will have a towering advantage over your competition.

You may know of a competitor who has achieved spectacular success in a hot market without knowing business psychology. But that competitor will not have the rock-solid core of goodwill that is required to endure.

American manufacturing is facing a test from very competent foreign competitors. The structure of U.S. manufacturing will be shaken — severely — in the next 20 years. A solid foundation is absolutely necessary for survival. A workforce that is aggressively involved today is the competitive advantage of tomorrow.

Morale Evaluation

The true condition of your employees' morale is difficult to assess by any method that you may commonly use. Objective evaluation of certain indicators is the most reliable method of diagnosing the morale of your workforce. The column on the left lists indicators of high morale. The column on the right lists signs of low morale. Circle the number — five through one — that is closer to the position of your company. Then, use the morale evaluation rating scale on the next page to see what your score means.

High Morale	Rating	Low Morale
Employee turnover is low. Most employees leave due to retirement.	5 4 3 2 1	Employees quit often, sometimes without notice.
Absenteeism is low. When employees are out, it is rare and justifiable.	5 4 3 2 1	Absenteeism is a problem. Employees find excuses to be late or gone.
There are few complaints about pay, even though the pay is average or less than average.	5 4 3 2 1	Everyone gripes about low pay, but pay is above average for the area.
Employees are impressively competent. Managers can be gone, yet work goes on.	5 4 3 2 1	A manager has to be on hand at all times or work will drag to a halt.
Employees voluntarily find core causes of costly problems and work out the corrections.	5 4 3 2 1	Employees make costly errors. Many errors are repeated.
Employees will call managers into their work area to ask for assistance or direction.	5 4 3 2 1	Managers are resented in the work area. Employees don't frequently speak to managers.
Employees detect errors early and bring them to the attention of management.	5 4 3 2 1	Errors are passed through to the customer.
Employees ask to be trained to enhance their careers with the company.	5 4 3 2 1	Employees express no interest in training.
Managers are expected to help employees through times of personal or family difficulty.	5 4 3 2 1	The employee is expected to deal with personal issues without them affecting work.
Conversations with employees are respectful and courteous.	5 4 3 2 1	Conversations include angry outbursts, threats, and profanity.
Managers offer continuous training and counsel to help employees improve performance.	5 4 3 2 1	Employees are expected to know their jobs and how to improve their performance.
Employee opinions are requested and respected in major decisions.	5 4 3 2 1	Employees are paid to do what they are told.
Employees receive quick, formal recognition for a job well done.	5 4 3 2 1	Recognition is given during the normal performance reviews.
Employees are reviewed and counseled every 90 days.	5 4 3 2 1	There is an annual pay review.
Managers speak to employees on a first-name basis.	5 4 3 2 1	Managers do not know the names of most employees.

Morale Evaluation Rating Scale

Now, check your results. Total the numbers you circled. Locate your score total below to learn the true condition of your employees' morale.

———————

60–75   You have a workforce with high morale. Your employees are willing to help your company succeed. Keep up an effort, however, to continuously improve.

30–59   Your workforce is complacent. Substantial performance gains will be realized by improving morale, especially if your score is 30–45.

0–29   You have high costs and inefficiency. Sabotage of your product is likely. Your employees do only what they have to do. You should implement morale enhancements as a top priority. Otherwise, important projects will fail.

Morale Disablers Checklist

The following is a list of conditions that will destroy morale even if you have many morale-enhancing conditions in place. In the blank provided in the far right column, write the date on which you have successfully eliminated the described morale disabler. Remember, you must remove all of these morale disablers to effectively enhance your employees' morale.

_____

Morale Disabler	Symptoms	Date Disabler Removed
Low pay	Pay that is too low to sustain an average lifestyle. Look for evidence in the type of cars your employees drive and the homes they own.	_____
Rude or abusive treatment	Yelling, temper tantrums, and profanity; any form of harassment; intimidation tactics.	_____
Fear	Silence or severely restrained talk in the presence of managers.	_____
Unpleasant workplace conditions	Cleanliness or temperature extremes; a noisy workplace; insufficient lighting.	_____
Injustice	Unequal discipline for equal offenses; unequal pay for equal work; unequal recognition; unequal promotions or other rewards. Establish reminders to help you assure equal treatment of all employees.	_____
Dishonesty	Employees are sensitive to lies. Always be truthful, insist that all managers speak and behave truthfully.	_____
Hazardous work conditions	Uncorrected hazards speak clearly that you do not care about the health or safety of your employees. They will respond with equal disregard for the health of your business.	_____

Basic Training Checklist

The training given to an employee on the first day at work is the most important single act of the employer regarding employee success. Businesses that adequately train employees experience higher productivity, higher quality, and higher morale. Use the following checklist to help you develop a checklist specific to your company.

Company Philosophy

- [ ] The attitude of your company toward the family/personal life of your employees.
- [ ] The attitude of your company toward your employees regarding career goals and work satisfaction.
- [ ] The attitude of your company toward the world, such as community, laws, and politics.
- [ ] Whether your company's management is directive or participative.
- [ ] The frequency and content of performance reviews and how they impact wages.
- [ ] The company definition of success and how it is measured.

Expectations of the Company

- [ ] Policies, rules, and conventions that employees are expected to obey.
- [ ] Work hours, break times, and lunch.
- [ ] The performance standards of the task of each employee.
- [ ] Whether your company values individual or team performance.
- [ ] Policies on overtime and voluntary work.

Priorities of the Company

- [ ] What your business values.
- [ ] Safety priorities.
- [ ] How performance characteristics are measured.

Specifics

- [ ] Meet immediate supervisor and work area.
- [ ] Acquaint employee with the product and explain how the employee's task relates to the product.
- [ ] Training by employee's supervisor, noting which tools are necessary to complete the task. Training should be done during a time when it will have the least impact on production.

CHAPTER 3

DEVELOP PRO-PROFIT CUSTOMERS

Attitude precedes action. Moreover, attitude initiates, governs, and drives action. Attitude wages war; it builds peace.

All of the profits that your business will ever realize are in the hands of your customers today. Those customers must be willing to allow you to make a profit. Envision the difference in the profits of your business if all your customers were pro-profit — they willingly gave you business and referred you to others. Now, envision the condition of your business if all your customers were anti-profit — they really wanted to see you go out of business.

You and your employees mold the attitudes of your customers. It is within your power to mold pro-profit customers.

—————

An initially courteous receptionist answered the telephone. With equal courtesy, the manufacturing engineer asked to speak to a salesperson. The receptionist told the engineer that all the salespeople were taking inventory and could not be bothered. The engineer told the receptionist that a major purchase was the reason for the phone call and the help of a salesperson was required. The receptionist became irate. The engineer pleaded to be allowed to buy from the company. The

*irate receptionist told the engineer to call the following day
and hung up. Instead, the engineer called a competing company, made a $55,000 purchase, and never bothered the irate
receptionist again.*

Examine Your Attitude toward Customers

PROFIT POINTER

⬥ 16 ⬥

What are your employees' attitudes toward your customers? Are your customers considered friends or do you treat them as competitors for your
profits? Are they equal in importance to your own time, priorities, and policies, or are they treated as second-rate nuisances? Are you honored when
customers call? Are you distressed when customers are disappointed in
your products or service?

You cannot hide nor camouflage your attitude toward your customers. Customers pick up on your attitude instantly and respond with the
same attitude toward you. There is a principle of human relations involved in the relationship between you and your customers.

Ninety-five percent of the people you meet do not have a precon-
ceived attitude toward you; they form their attitudes based on the attitude
that you display first, such as in the example below.

Your Attitude	*Customer Attitude*
Customers are a source of revenue.	I'll make sure they don't make money off me.
Customers deserve all the quality and service I can give.	These people deserve all the business I can give.
Customers bother my routine.	I won't bother their routine.
Customers are my honored friends.	These people are my friends. I want them to succeed.

A careless attitude toward your customers will have the same negative effects on your employees. You assume the position of leadership.
Assume the attitude that you want to see in your customers and they will
reflect it back to you.

The principles of managing a customer base are very simple.
Picture yourself looking in a mirror. If you look in the mirror and see a
dirty, unkempt image, what do you do? You spruce up your own face.
When you look in the mirror again, you will see a spiffy, attractive image
that you like. If you don't like what you see and hear when you deal with

your customers, look at your own business attitudes and practices. Clean up your own act and you will develop a customer base that reflects the desirable business traits that you reveal to them — honesty, integrity, loyalty, and helpfulness.

You can take a litmus test to find out how your employees are treating customers. If only one customer says, "I'll be delighted to see you go out of business," you should worry. You should worry because there might be a hundred silent customers with the same attitude. You should ask questions until you truly know the status of your customer relations.

If you find out that two or more customers hold the same negative opinion, you should investigate and take action to correct your company's attitudes and policies toward its customers. You should assume that you have a serious problem with customer relations. If you learn that three or more customers would be happy to see you go out of business, accept it as a final warning to take dramatic action.

Dramatic action means that you should personally contact key customers to find out what is going on. Terminate employees who are treating customers with rudeness or disrespect. Put all other projects on hold until you have repaired relations with your customer base and you are sure that your employees are on the right track.

Remember to look in the mirror first. Rudeness toward customers is very possibly rooted in attitudes that you display and, in turn, your employees copy. If your customers are so irate that they want to see your business fail, it will fail. If your customers are pleased and want to see your business succeed — it probably will succeed. Some businesses do fail in spite of a happy customer base. However, happy customers are an enabler of success. An enabling condition will allow success, but it doesn't cause success nor guarantee success.

PROFIT POINTER

◄ 17 ►

Be Proactive about Customer Attitude

Monitoring your customer attitudes will help you be proactive. Customer attitude can become sour long before the effect of disgruntled customers shows up on your financial statement. If you wait until you see a decline in sales volume, you will have waited long past the time when you should have taken corrective action. You should take action as soon as you pick up the smallest indicators of customer unhappiness.

Leading indicators will give you clues of what your customer attitudes might be. The first indicator is the attitude displayed by your own employees toward customers. A foul attitude toward customers first reveals itself in semi-caustic remarks that may come up in casual internal conversations. Something as simple as, "This is a difficult customer" scrawled on a warranty claim can indicate a deep pit of anti-customer sentiment. Take early remedial — instructive and exemplary — action to improve the attitude of your employees toward your customers.

If you witness open indications of a rude, surly disposition toward customers, like the example of the irate receptionist at the beginning of this chapter, you should be certain that you have a customer attitude problem that is larger than you might imagine.

Employees will always display a more model attitude in your presence than in your absence. If what you see is bad, what you don't see is worse. Remember, the attitude of your employees drives the attitude of your customers. Take a proactive approach and correct the problem on your side of the customer relationship before it develops into lost sales.

Demonstrate that You Are Pro-Customer

PROFIT POINTER

⋘ 18 ⋙

The best way to be proactive in guarding customer attitudes is to put yourself in the place of a customer — then you can predict what the response of a customer will be when you make changes in your business. Remember that when you are predicting customer responses, you need to be most concerned with the long-term responses. Consider the short-sighted actions in the following true story.

One of the few small aircraft manufacturers that still exists in the United States guessed that it was pricing its replacement parts too low. In response, it doubled prices on most parts. As a result, the customers complained. What do you think was the secondary effect? The replacement parts sales volume fell to nearly zero. Maybe the profit was too low in the first place, but after customers quit buying, the profit was still lower. Lack of profits on parts sales was the good news. The same customers who quit buying replacement parts were dealers who also sold new aircraft. They started selling something else. New aircraft sales fell to near-zero also.

It was a shortsighted, get-every-dollar-you-can attitude that doubled parts prices in the first place. Raising prices for the purpose of increasing profits is often an error. (See Chapter 10 for pricing strategies and errors.) Raising prices to get every dollar possible tells your customers that they are only a source of revenue. Excellent managers will imagine themselves in the customer's shoes. They will make sure that any changes in their business will benefit the customer.

In the aircraft example above, the first indicator that predicted customer hostility was the intent to dramatically raise parts prices. Astute management would have recognized the intent to double prices as an unacceptable attitude toward the customer base and would have acted to prevent the customer uprising that followed. The mark of good management is in how many serious problems never occur!

"But, if profits were low," you might ask, "wasn't management in a lose-lose position? If they didn't raise prices, wouldn't they lose money anyway?" The answer is no. The correct choice is to reduce the cost of manufacturing. Most manufacturers do not control costs adequately. Reducing costs is always possible. Reducing costs increases profits without exerting a downward pressure on sales revenue.

Remember, a prime goal in engineering an increase in profitability is to make decisions that will exert an upward pressure on revenue and a downward pressure on costs. Higher pricing exerts the opposite pressure on revenue. If anything, higher pricing relaxes the need to press costs downward. In the aircraft example, management made two errors.

▶ A negative attitude toward the customer was allowed to bear fruit in the form of customer vengeance.

▶ Management elected for an action that led to reduced revenues while relaxing cost control.

The most common error in managing a business is the failure to predict secondary responses. If you want to stay ahead of your competition, make decisions that have a high regard for secondary responses. That way, in the long term, the secondary responses of decisions you made months earlier will carry your business through the lean times. See Chapter 13 for a detailed discussion of the power of secondary effects.

PROFIT POINTER

◈ 19 ◈

Nix Voice Processing

No matter what words the computer answering device might use, the message that the customer hears is, "We don't want to talk to you." You know that the attitude your company displays first will cause customers to respond with a similar attitude.

What do you predict will be the customer response to a business that starts the sales relationship by saying, "We don't want to talk to you?"

You will probably correctly predict that the customer will respond with the attitude of, "I don't want to talk to you either!"

The terms that come up when companies are considering adopting a voice processing system are the same terms that are red flags preceding adversarial customer relations:

► "Talking to these people takes so much time."
► "It's a pain in the neck."
► "It costs less than a receptionist."
► "It's a full-time job just taking and routing calls."

These should not be the attitudes that you want to transfer to your customers. Voice processing — in whatever configuration and by whatever name — is not conducive to good relations with customers. There is nothing that promotes a good feeling in the customer more than having a call answered by a competent, courteous person who knows the business and who personally knows whether the sales manager is in or out. A smart business move is to have a competent person in charge of incoming calls. Pay this person well. You do not want high turnover in this key position.

There is one other misconception regarding voice processing systems that you need to understand. Often, a small company will configure a complex call routing and forwarding system thinking it will make them appear to be a big company. In reality, voice processing makes a business look like a small, poorly-managed company that cannot afford a full-time person to answer and direct calls. If you truly want to impress your callers, have a live person answer incoming calls with professionalism, courtesy, and competence.

Keep Repeat Customers with Quality and Service

Profit Pointer
◆ 20 ◆

Your company depends upon repeat business. Your cost of winning a new customer is four to six times greater than the cost of retaining a repeat customer. One step above and beyond satisfaction is required to keep customers coming back, year after year. Delighting your customers is the step beyond that you want to attain. To delight your customers, you must understand the difference between satisfied and delighted. Mere satisfaction keeps customers as long as no competitor offers a better deal. Satisfaction is treading the high wire; one slip and your customers become dissatisfied and actively seek to do business with your competition. Satisfied customers will placidly wait for your competitors to win them away from you. Customers that are satisfied, but not delighted, are easily won by a competitor.

Quality and service are your tools to create a delighted customer base. Quality means that the product does what the customer expects it to do. Your customer learns what to expect from your products by three methods.

1. Logic and precedent. People normally expect universal levels of performance from certain types of products. For example, people expect the tires of a new car to hold air indefinitely.

2. Your competitors. The performance of the products of your competitors, or their advertising claims, tell people what to expect from your product. For example, if your competition claims 24-hour relief from one dose of cold remedy, then your customers will expect the same from your cold remedy.

3. Your advertising and sales information. You possess the power to create expectations of product performance in your customer. Claim a level of performance, then deliver more. If your product delivers more than your advertising claims, your customers will be generally delighted.

Giving customers one step above and beyond what they expect in quality is the first element of keeping repeat customers. Giving them a step above and beyond in service is the second element. Service is equal to quality in developing repeat customers. After-the-sale service offers the opportunity to meet with the customer face to face. Service representatives spend more time in personal contact with customers than do salespeople. The attitude of the customer is permanently formed by the attitude of service personnel and by the quality of after-the-sale service. Note the permanent negative attitude formed by the family in the following scenario.

———

A family of moderate income and conservative taste was test driving a used car. The control lever for the air conditioner was broken. The father asked the salesperson if it would be repaired if they bought the car. The salesperson replied, "Sure — no problem."

The family negotiated a price and agreed to buy the car. While the papers were being finalized, the car was sent to the service department for pre-delivery service. When the customers got into the car to leave, they noticed the air conditioner lever was not repaired. The service manager pointed out the as-is-no-warranty disclaimer on the rear window. The father tried to explain that the salesperson promised it would be repaired.

The service manager responded, "Salespeople can promise anything they want. The car is sold as-is. You have to pay for repairs." The customers left in an un-delighted frame of mind and vowed to never buy from that dealership again.

——————

Courteous service can do as much to retain customers as any other factor of a business. Several elements make service an asset.

Parts availability

The aircraft example cited earlier in the chapter hampered parts availability by doubling the price to a prohibitive level. A number of factors must be in place to assure excellent parts availability, including adequate factory stocks, logistics, pricing to encourage dealer stocking, and return policies.

Availability of competent service centers

Proper training and sufficient locations are key. Adequately trained technicians that can make proper repairs the first time, every time, are an asset. Local service outlets that can provide quick turnaround time are crucial.

Courtesy

Customers should be treated with high levels of courtesy and respect. For example, you and your employees can answer the phone on the first ring, smile, never argue, and assume a helpful attitude. Courtesy and respect are expected by most customers as a prerequisite to doing business.

Product design

Products should be designed to be easily serviceable. A manufacturer should know in advance which components are likely to need replacement. Troubleshooting and replacement instructions should be available when the product is introduced. Field service personnel should be trained regarding service and troubleshooting procedures before, not after, a new product is introduced.

Seek Out Complaints

No product is perfect; no service is perfect — customers will complain. How you receive and handle those complaints has a direct bearing on whether you will be in business five years from now. In today's business world, you should regard a customer complaint as a fabulous opportunity.

PROFIT POINTER

❧ 21 ❧

Competent response to complaints is becoming rare. Customers are experiencing discourtesy, red tape, runarounds, and incompetence on a large scale. A business that is able to gracefully accept customers complaints and handle them with competence has a distinct competitive advantage.

There are only two reasons for not hearing any customer complaints. Either you have created such fear in the workplace that employees quickly silence complaints before you hear them, or your customers have truly ceased to complain. If you have a fearful workplace, see Profit Pointer 10 in Chapter 2 and begin to upgrade employee morale. If you have customers that have truly stopped complaining, it is because they consider your company to be arrogant, incompetent, and callous.

The no-complaints symptom is akin to the condition of a terminally-ill patient who fades into a few moments of painless euphoria immediately prior to death. If your company has no complaints, then immediately break through all your self-imposed communication barriers with your customers so you can find out why they are no longer speaking. Encourage your customers to complain. Handle the complaints promptly, competently, and courteously. Your customers will appreciate your attitude and will reward your efforts with repeat business.

Chapter Recap

Your customers' attitudes drive their actions. When you offer a new product, will your customers accept it with enthusiasm? It depends on their attitude. When you increase prices, will your customers accept the increase or will they seek out a new supplier? It depends on their attitude. When you ask for your customers to assist you in developing a new product, will they give you valuable tips or will they manipulate you to their own advantage? It depends on their attitude.

Will your sales increase? Will your profits multiply? Will you attract new customers? Will existing customers buy more products? Will your customers help you find new markets? Will they help you refine your products and services? Do they resent your profits? Or, do your customers willingly play a vital role in the success of your business? It all depends on their attitudes toward your business — and their attitudes depend on the attitude that you display first.

CHAPTER 4

USE PRO-PROFIT SUPPLIERS

Today's battle winner is the loser on a grander scale. Those who avoid the cost of battle dominate in the end.

The most profitable long-term relationship with your suppliers is to strive continuously to increase the total profitability of both companies. Try to imagine the profit potential of complementing your own business expertise with the combined expertise of all your suppliers. This combination of pro-profit powers will often produce innovative and exciting cost-reducing events.

A great example of the benefits of a pro-profit supplier comes from a company that made commercial food preparation equipment.

The supplier provided welding gasses, filler wire, and expendables. The customer-supplier relationship had been stable for a number of years when the manufacturer began seeking more cost-efficient production techniques in the welding department. The supplier volunteered to send in its best welding engineer to advise.

When the engineer noticed that the company was using a very expensive mixed gas for welding cabinets, he commented that simple carbon dioxide would do the same job for less than

one-tenth the cost. The company implemented the suggestion
and saved $10,000 in the first year — a significant contribu-
tion to the profits of that year and to every year since.

———◆———

You should note that the $10,000 additional profits did not result
from hard-nosed purchasing negotiations. The supplier did not have to cut
into its own profits for the customer to realize a profit increase. In fact,
the supplier profit margin on the less costly carbon dioxide was greater
than the margin on the expensive mixed gas. Both the supplier and the
customer benefited from the change. Such a mutually profitable relationship is what you want to initiate with your suppliers.

Build a Mutually Beneficial Relationship

Suppliers to a difficult manufacturer were looking for any excuse to
"lose" the business. The purchasing department prided itself in its ability
to coerce and intimidate suppliers. Top leadership offered incentives to
"hammer" suppliers into providing shorter leadtimes, lower pricing, and
quicker responses to crisis schedule changes. What really happened was:

- ► Longer leadtimes;
- ► Slow responsiveness to schedule changes;
- ► Increased delay on credit for defects;
- ► Dramatic increases in shipment errors; and
- ► Higher prices.

Hoping for better results, the manufacturer changed suppliers frequently. Nobody wins in this kind of supplier relationship — the results
of this battle are losses on both sides. If you engage in a battle with a supplier, you will lose great contributions to your profits. Even if you are a
great intimidator and you succeed in putting a supplier completely out of
business, you win nothing. Your business needs a stable source of supply.
If you succeed in hard-nosed negotiations, you may be winning great
pricing by pushing other costs higher.

The I-Win-You-Lose (IWYL) style of supplier relations is very common in U.S. businesses. This practice works poorly in the short term and is
costly in the long term. IWYL relations require constant negotiations and
changing suppliers, which will cost your business dearly. You might think
that the IWYL style ultimately results in a lower per-unit cost, but it doesn't.
In the example of the welding supplies from the beginning of this chapter,
hard negotiations might have driven down the price of the expensive mixed

PROFIT POINTER

◆ 22 ◆

gas by a few dollars per year, but the whopping $10,000 price reduction would never have materialized except from the contribution of a friendly, involved supplier.

The goal is for you and your supplier to find a middle ground. That middle ground allows both parties to make a reasonable profit and to stay in business. The mutually beneficial relationship has important building blocks. You and your supplier will:

- ▶ Visit each other's facilities.
- ▶ Show concern for each other's schedules, costs, and quality.
- ▶ Offer mutual advice for improving quality and reducing costs.
- ▶ Commit to a long-term relationship.
- ▶ Communicate closely during product development.
- ▶ Be honest with each other.

When you achieve a mutually beneficial relationship with your suppliers, you will find that they will exhibit a pro-profit attitude. That attitude will drive pro-profit actions. Your business will enjoy a competitive advantage that is unavailable to your supplier-bashing counterparts. Imagine the benefits that will come to you — immediately and at little or no cost.

- ▶ Help in developing new products. Your suppliers have the inside scoop to help you determine the best ways to use their products or services.
- ▶ Help in reducing costs and improving quality. Your suppliers are experts in the use of their own products — they can recommend improvements in processes and products that will give you better performance at lower costs.
- ▶ Supplier financing of new product development. Suppliers will take on design tasks for components that they will provide — but only if they trust you to buy what they have designed. A side benefit is that they will design components that are easy for them to build, which will result in higher quality and lower costs.
- ▶ Assistance in hard times. Business downturns affect cash flow. Business expansions affect cash flow. A high-trust relationship that is mutually beneficial may motivate a supplier to assist you through cash shortages.
- ▶ Elimination of the cost of annual rewriting of specifications and seeking new bids. Every round of replacing suppliers

involves rewriting specifications and making new contacts. You may spend dozens of hours replacing one supplier.

► Elimination of the cost of introducing new supplier components or services into your business or product. New products may fit or perform differently from those of your last supplier. You may have to make extensive and unplanned revisions to your product.

► Elimination of the cost of maintaining relationships with numerous competing suppliers. In the case of a single, pro-profit supplier, your administrative tasks of expediting and coordinating are continuously reduced.

Sometimes your supplier is unwilling to meet you in a middle ground, win-win relationship. Sometimes your supplier is catering to a seller's market and unwilling to enter into any relationship that requires compromise that it perceives may minimize its profits.

In such a case, you should still take the initiative to build a relationship of mutual respect that supports the profitability of both the seller and the buyer. If that initiative is rebuked, then your only alternative is to negotiate the best terms you can for the short term and plan for the long term.

Be aware that suppliers that take advantage of a seller's market will often fail when the seller's market turns to a buyer's market. Poorly managed suppliers will proliferate during a seller's market. Seek out a supplier that shows evidence of good management and do as much business as possible with that supplier.

Remember, the supplier that offers the lowest price per unit is not always the best choice. Consider other important factors, such as order fill rate, product quality, return policies, and payment terms. Just a few percentage points difference in fill rate can be worth a substantial difference in unit price.

Seek the Lowest Total Cost

The supplier that provides the lowest total cost is your goal. To achieve the lowest total cost, both you and your supplier must understand the concept of lowest total cost. To begin, understand what costs are relevant to your business.

Lowest Total Cost versus Lowest Unit Cost

To fully understand the difference between lowest total cost and lowest unit cost, consider this example.

PROFIT POINTER

◄» 23 «►

Imagine that you are building a product that requires an electric motor. Two suppliers are in competition for your business. Cheap, Inc. offers you a price of $19 per motor. Service Providers offers a price of $23 per motor.

In a pure competitive bid situation, Cheap, Inc. would get the business by supplying the $19 motor. You would write a purchase order for a year's supply and start receiving motors on a scheduled basis. In this case, Cheap, Inc. is the supplier of the lowest unit cost.

Lowest total cost involves the related costs that are sometimes hard to define. Lowest total cost can be best understood by asking a series of questions.

Ask how much is added to the total "cheap" cost by:

► Minimum quantities. Do you have to buy more than you need to get the price?

► Schedule adherence. Will Cheap miss deliveries and cause overtime and inefficiency?

► Quality. Will Cheap motors fail in the field, requiring warranty claim service?

► Responsiveness. Can Cheap respond to your schedule changes?

► Stability. Will Cheap go out of business?

► Payment terms. Does Cheap want payment before delivery?

► Engineering assistance. Will Cheap help you solve applications problems?

► Customer receptiveness. Do Cheap motors drive away customers with noise?

► Defective products policy. Will Cheap provide quick credits for defective products?

► Completeness. Will you have to add paint, terminals, grease, or mounting brackets?

► Dishonesty. Will you have to pay extra to make the motors perform to specifications?

When you buy a Cheap motor, you may not pay the lowest total cost. You may get a motor that costs — in total — as much or more than the price quoted by Service Providers. Experience, maturity, and seeking wise business advice will help you understand that a higher unit cost may be evidence of a lower total cost.

Help Suppliers Keep Costs Down

You make it easy for suppliers to become pro-profit when you help them keep their own costs low. Often, U.S. manufacturers create situations that elevate the costs experienced by suppliers. Avoiding common mistakes will help your suppliers keep their costs down. Those lower costs will be eventually passed on to you. Lower costs will help you achieve a competitive advantage.

The following common errors that cause an increase in supplier costs exist.

Requiring supplier inventory

Inventory investment costs money. If you want Just-in-Time deliveries, make a schedule and keep it stable.

Schedule changes

When you require advanced or delayed deliveries or changed order quantities, excess costs for the supplier result. Make a schedule and stick to it.

Design changes

Even simple changes cause your supplier the cost of retooling and retraining. Test your design and stick to it.

Competitive bidding

Once your suppliers know that you will regularly price shop, they will all pad their pricing. The reason is that they must recoup start-up costs — the costs your suppliers experience when they must stock or produce an item that is new to them — quickly before you price shop again.

If they know that you will stick with them through the years, they will work to continuously improve pricing. Pick a supplier and stick with it.

Demanding short leadtimes

If suppliers are unable to provide genuinely short leadtimes, they will carry inventory to provide quick response. The cost is passed on to you. Work in partnership with suppliers to develop methods to shorten leadtimes. Dramatic reductions are possible through a team effort.

The final result: your suppliers will experience lower costs and they will help you experience lower costs. This will pave the way for both of you to experience higher profits.

Reduce the Number of Suppliers

You can increase profit by allowing your suppliers to do something that they already want to do. They want to sell more to you. From a supplier's perspective, the more similar products or services it can sell, the more cost effective it can become. All you have to do is to let your supplier sell more to you.

Your company receives double-barreled benefits by doing more business with fewer suppliers. First, supplier costs go down; these costs allow the supplier to be healthier and more stable and predictable. Some of the savings will ultimately be passed on to you, resulting in an even greater competitive advantage for your company. Second, your own costs go down.

As you reduce your supplier count, you reduce your business' workload in areas like purchasing, receiving, and accounts payable. You will experience reduced costs due to easier coordination of shipments plus the opportunity to combine shipments. Less total activity results in fewer opportunities for error. As you increase your level of purchasing with each of fewer suppliers, you will find that suppliers are more committed to you. Lower pricing and better service are the predictable results.

Chapter Recap

Long-term thinking is the key to developing pro-profit suppliers. Today's initiatives may require a year or two before the profit improvements begin to show on your bottom line. Even when you begin to see increased profits, you will find it is not easily traceable to suppliers. Often the cost savings are in the difficult to define (soft) areas, such as warranty claims, premium freight, overtime, and rework. When the savings arrive, you will have a profit-enhancing condition that many of your competitors cannot replicate.

PART II

CAUSES OF UNPROFITABILITY

The option of increasing revenues is fading. Those who learn to control costs will dominate.

Even if your business is profitable, you are more than likely still losing profits. Your first action is to determine why you are losing profits. You might be surprised at the competitive advantage that will result when you determine why you are losing profits. To move quickly, many of your competitors will skip the find-out-why step of the process and end up operating in chaos. You, on the other hand, will use the profit pointers in this book to identify the causes of lost profits. You will correct the causes and your profits will increase. The process really is that simple. You will be predictably successful when you seek out and remedy the conditions that cause lost profits. A triple-barreled blast of benefits is the result of seeking and remedying causes.

1. A root cause, once corrected, will always produce unpredicted side benefits. Those benefits are free; no analysis, corrective effort, or money is required.

2. Treating symptoms, the opposite of treating causes, is always costly — more staff, computers, technology, and buildings. Treating symptoms is a prime reason for high overhead and materials costs. Treating the cause not only eliminates the symptoms, but removes the need for all the costly palliatives.

3. Elimination of causes is normally at no cost to you (at least in monetary terms), and often will provide an identifiable payback. Often, you will find that a simple yes or no directive is all that is needed to remove a substantial cost-causing condition.

To be a successful leader of a profit-enhancement project, you will know the causes of lost profits. You may recognize many of the causal conditions in this section as conditions very common to your business and many other businesses. Remedying those conditions is conducive to improved business health, whether or not the business is actually losing profits. The causes of unprofitability include: misplaced priorities, declining sales, and a dysfunctional organization. Part II is devoted to identifying these causes and making significant changes in your business that will help you avoid unprofitable situations.

CHAPTER 5

PRIORITIZE FOR PROFITS

Doing the right thing with mediocre skill achieves far more than doing the wrong thing with the greatest of skill.

Misplaced priorities cause lost profits. If your priorities are not in order, you will expend resources doing things that yield unpredictable results — or results that cause further lost profits. If you understand how to avoid losing profits, then you have an advantage. Most of your competitors know, or think they know, the conditions that cause profits. They probably do not know, however, the conditions that cause profit loss. You should place a high priority on the skill of avoiding the conditions that cause lost profits. To gain this skill, know what actions will provide the greatest results. Many of your competitors are expending great resources to achieve something that will provide little or no payback — their priorities are wrong. You can rise above the competition by prioritizing the tasks that provide great returns.

Know the Profit Formula

Revenue minus cost equals profit. This is not rocket science. Most of the reading available to manufacturing practitioners today would make a new person in the field think that rocket science is simple when compared to manufacturing management. Most managers are inundated with concepts so complex that entire books are written about single topics, with buzz-words like:

- ► Time-based competition
- ► Supplier partnering
- ► Empowerment
- ► Demand flow
- ► Benchmarking
- ► Just-in-Time
- ► Materials Requirement Planning (MRP)

All of these concepts are valid parts of a well-rounded practice of managing manufacturing. But beware of spending an inordinate amount of time and money mastering the details of complex management techniques when you should be concentrating on basic practices. To effectively gain profit power, concentrate on the basics.

Never lose sight of the fundamental formula of profit: revenue minus cost equals profit. The quality of every decision you make and priority of every action you take should be based on a respect for that formula. Pay close attention to the relative differences in the significance of revenue and cost. Which deserves the most attention, revenue or costs? Of course, both are essential. But consider this example. If you have a choice of spending a $1,000 investment on either increasing sales by $10,000 or reducing costs by $5,000, which would you do? At a 10 percent profit margin, you will realize $1,000 of additional profit if you choose to increase sales. If you choose to reduce costs, you will increase profits by five times as much or $5,000. While the choice may seem obvious in this simple example, in the world of complex reality, many companies err by investing in more sales instead of implementing cost-control measures. Their priorities are wrong, and it costs them their competitive position.

The loss of competitive position means that many U.S. manufacturers are losing business to Japanese firms. This happens because Japanese manufacturers understand cost control as evidenced by their total emphasis on cost-controlled production. They entered markets with known potential and designed their entire companies to offer high-quality, low-cost products. High quality and low cost create a self-perpetuating cycle for a manufacturer — one that is at the top of the list of desirable outcomes. Consider the following scenario to help you understand how cost control can work for you.

Assume that you have chosen to invest your $1,000 in a cost-reduction project. You reduce costs by $5,000. The cost reduction not only improves your business' profitability, but it improves cash flow as well. You get the benefit before the product is sold. Plus, reduced costs enable a lower selling price. Lower selling prices tend to increase sales volume. Increased sales volume enables further cost reductions through economy of scale — lower prices equal more sales; more sales equal lower prices. Each complements the other throughout the life cycle of a product.

Now, imagine that you have the opportunity to invest your $1,000 in a project that will both increase sales and simultaneously reduce costs. If you chose such a project, you would add $6,000 to the bottom line. Actually, the increase in profits would be even greater, because the increased sales would be of a product that costs less. The perpetual cycle of improvement in this case will start sooner and each cycle will show greater improvements in sales and profitability.

Despite what you might hear, making a profit is not an obsolete and irrelevant measure of business success. You know better, but many of your competitors don't know better. The priority of keeping the profit formula in mind will guide your decisions, policies, and priorities.

Develop Internal Quality

One word describes a characteristic project that will simultaneously enhance sales and reduce costs. Japanese manufacturers have used it in manufacturing for decades. American manufacturers have fallen behind because they don't understand the pure power of one, single manufacturing concept: quality, specifically, internal quality.

Internal quality means that components fit. They work the first time. You don't have to foot the bill for repairs and rework. As a result, efficiency goes up, schedules are kept, backorders diminish, and premium freight decreases. If components work, your product will work, and that means warranty claims will diminish. With few warranty repairs, efficiency is increased. Dealers become more receptive to your product.

With profitable dealers and happy customers, your sales and production volume go up. High volume tooling, which generates products more rapidly at a lower per-unit cost, can be justified. Costs go down again, allowing reduced prices. Lower prices promote higher sales. The cycle repeats itself again and again — costs go down, sales go up, and profits soar. Key elements in achieving internal quality are:

▶ Product design that is easily within the capabilities of your people, machines, and processes;
▶ Accurate and easy-to-read drawings and process instructions;

- Tools that are more than adequate and in good working order;
- Machines that are capable of higher quality than the product requires;
- High-morale and highly trained employees;
- Materials that are of higher quality than the minimum required by the product;
- Dimensional tolerances of part-to-part fit that are tight enough to prevent errors of tolerance accumulation; and
- Subcontract services to a supplier that is easily capable of exceeding your requirements.

You may easily understand the profit potential of internal quality. However, many of your competitors expend great resources to promote inferior products, offer liberal warranties on defective products, move operations overseas, or implement the newest techno-wizardry. Your competitors may not understand the priority of internal quality. Develop internal quality and you will rise above the crowd.

Promote Simplicity

Simplicity is a major contributor to quality and cost control. Simplicity of design means fewer parts and easier assembly. Simplicity of design means the parts are easier to make. Fewer parts that are easier to make and easier to assemble mean fewer errors. Fewer errors equal lower costs, fewer product failures, and higher levels of customer satisfaction. Satisfied customers promote more sales, increasing production levels and reducing costs.

Your product line is the total range of product offerings — all models, variations, colors, options, and accessories. American companies have much to gain from product line simplification. Misplaced priorities cause a misdirected response when sales of a product begin a decline. The typical response is to offer more models and then offer two dozen options, thirty colors, and custom configurations. Sales increase and you may believe that you are successful. Don't fail to look into the shop to see the added complexity of scheduling, purchasing, and supervision. Be able to recognize the soft costs of:

- Ballooning inventories
- Unmanageable schedules
- Increased error rates
- Backorders
- Increased field failures

PROFIT POINTER
◆ 28 ◆

Whether you recognize it or not, complexity will make your costs go up and profits go down. To remedy the profit picture, you may increase prices. The result is that sales go down and costs go up again. You may buy a sophisticated software system and expensive employee training. You might even try flexible schedules. The more things that you "fix" to accommodate a complex product line, the more your costs go up.

The rule is to always strive to simplify your product and product line. Your profit potential will increase if you keep the following elements of simplicity in mind.

- Parts count. Eliminate parts — a 50 percent reduction from prototype is a good goal.
- Operations total. Combine or eliminate steps in the production process.
- Operations types. Strive for the same operations per part as much as possible.
- Operations sequence. Sequence your operations in the same order as the machines in the shop.
- Product type. Keep diversity minimal; use same skills, machines, and tools.
- Technology. Assure mastery before you attempt to implement.
- Stability. Seek to stabilize schedules, products, people, and systems.

Many of your competitors are rushing into more complex products, product lines, and technologies. As they achieve complex results, they also increase staffing levels, make higher demands on people, bloat their inventories, and multiply overhead costs. The irony is that complex products irritate consumers. Keep simplification high on your priority list and you will make more profits than your flamboyant competitors.

Control Materials and Overhead

The only industrial power that was not heavily damaged by World War II was the United States. The post-war world was a voracious and indiscriminate consumer of U.S. industrial production. American quality was sufficient because it was all there was in the world. The demand for product was so great that costs and quality were negligible issues. Meeting the demand was the challenge. Growth and marketing were the priorities of American business owners for the following 40 years. Promotions, new products, and new facilities were the disciplines that saw all the action. Creating revenue growth was easy. Of course, costs grew along with revenue. It became widely accepted that per-unit costs would normally increase as a business became larger and more diverse. Today, the bigger-company-equals-higher-cost belief has a large following.

The bigger-company-equals-higher-cost belief is incorrect. A large company with high production volumes has far greater innate opportunities to reduce costs than a small company. In reality, U.S. manufacturing has a serious problem with three cost culprits as companies become larger. Cost culprit number one is that overhead costs soar. Cost culprit number two is that materials costs soar. Cost culprit number three, labor efficiency, the most maligned of the three, is the smallest problem of U.S. manufacturing.

Many U.S. managers believe that the only controllable cost is labor. That belief is an error. Consider the figures in the following table to arrive at your own conclusion of where American manufacturing is losing cost control. The figures tell the story. The last column, relative efficiency, reflects how much better or worse we have become in each of the costs of manufacturing in 45 years.

Post-War and Current U.S. Manufacturing Cost Comparisons*

Costs	1945	1990	Relative Efficiency
Overhead	$10	$20	Down 50%
Materials	40	70	Down 43%
Direct Labor	50	10	Up 500%

* The cost figures are for an item with a total cost of $100 (in constant dollars).

As manufacturers grow, overhead functions become grossly inefficient and per-part costs inflate due to the increased overhead costs. Componentry is bought from "more efficient" outside suppliers. The result of buying parts from outside suppliers is that real overhead stays the same and the parts (materials) cost more.

In fact, due to the necessity of issuing purchase orders and handling more incoming material items, the real cost of overhead increases. Look at the figures another way to understand how poorly American manufacturers are performing. For the same amount of labor content (in constant dollars), a product that would have cost $100 in 1945 would cost $500 in 1990 — the entire $400 increase is due to overhead and materials. Overhead and materials are where U.S. manufacturing cost excesses reside. Ideally, overhead and materials are where you should apply your cost-control efforts.

Your priorities for controlling costs should include avoidance of common cost-increasing errors, including:

- ► Indiscriminate implementation of expensive high technology;
- ► Administration of complex products, product lines, and policies;
- ► Expensive marketing and sales of poor quality, complex products;
- ► Treating symptoms (the bandage approach) instead of causes;
- ► Conflict and duplication in organizational responsibilities;
- ► Inventory excesses, such as control costs, insurance, interest, handling, and storage;
- ► Purchasing componentry that should be made in house;
- ► Designs that result in materials waste;
- ► Frequent design changes — that translate into short product life;
- ► Inventory excesses that result in obsolescence and damage;
- ► Frequent jumping from supplier to supplier;
- ► Long logistics pipelines, especially to overseas suppliers;
- ► Frequent engineering changes, resulting in obsolete parts; and
- ► Poor internal quality, causing excess scrap.

The bottom line is that you will find the great profit improvements will come from a thorough analysis of the costs of overhead and materials. Much of your competition still believes that nothing can be done to reduce costs in these two areas of great waste. When you start chopping costs in areas that your competition believes is impossible, you will have another distinct competitive advantage. Keep materials and overhead cost reduction high on your priority list.

PROFIT POINTER

◄❧ 30 ❧►

Reward Cost Control

What effort receives the greatest reward in your company: cost control or sales increases? The greater priority is cost control — you must reward employees who develop cost-control techniques. You will get what you reward. Here's why.

Sales increases have been difficult to achieve during the 1990s. Companies that have achieved sales increases have done so at great expense: high marketing costs and an invasion of profit margin. The gains in sales that came easily in the 40 years after World War II will not come again in the foreseeable future. Whether in business or in government, the option of increasing revenues is fading. Control of costs is rapidly becoming the only avenue to increased profit.

Cost control has traditionally been the keystone of successful manufacturing. Cost control is the reason why mass production became the accepted method of the Industrial Revolution. When cost control is viewed from the obvious perspective of mass production, its position of dominance over manufacturing success is easily accepted. But in the reality of application, cost control as a regular discipline faces three obstacles.

1. Cost control is a new and unproven concept in the minds of modern U.S. business leaders who, through two generations, have seen amazing successes without having to study or apply the disciplines of cost control.

2. Cost control offers no glamour. It requires discipline, persistence, analysis, research, and unpopular decisions. Cost control makes microscopic, incremental gains — a tenth of a percent here, a tenth of a percent there.

3. Traditional American organizations do not reward cost control. The rewards are reserved for the dramatic sales increases. Cost-controlling employees are regarded as mundane administrators. Historically, they rise no higher than a midmanagement or staff position.

Development of a functional costing system — which is also called function-driven costing — is a priority of successful cost control. (Function-driven costing is discussed in detail in Chapter 10, Profit Pointer 54.)

Create Profit Pressures

Successful leaders of profit-enhanced businesses will increase revenues in microamounts. They will also reduce costs in microamounts. The turn-around results from the cumulative effect of dozens, even hundreds, of microcontributions in both directions. Those individual changes will be so small that they will not normally show up as an identifiable contributor on any financial analysis, chart, or graph. Microchanges and microcontributions, since they are immeasurably small, are referred to as profit pressures. The entire concept of a profit project is summed up as unrelenting upward pressure on revenues, unrelenting downward pressure on costs.

Unrelenting pressure means that a business will take advantage of every opportunity — no matter how seemingly insignificant — to press for more revenue or lower costs. Remember Management by Opportunity

PROFIT POINTER

◆ 31 ◆

from Profit Pointer 11? This is the application of Management by Opportunity: the measurable result of the accumulation of a tenth of a percent here, a tenth of a percent there. There is no such thing as an insignificant improvement.

Successful business leaders who regularly implement long-term successes are not tempted to seek out the one or two giant strides to success. When the giant strides are possible, they can be excellent contributors to the overall effort. But the giant strides have unpredictable results and are costly to implement. They should be attempted from a position of strength, not from a position of declining profits.

Chapter Recap

Getting your priorities in order saves you the cost and frustration of trying a tactic, failing, then trying again and again until something works. Your top priorities should include specific tasks to reduce the costs of materials and overhead. Devise a system of rewards that encourages employees to continuously improve control over costs.

Applying the right effort in the right direction not only saves you valuable resources, it also nets faster results. When your priorities are correct, you will have a significant competitive advantage.

CHAPTER 6

REVERSE SALES DECLINES

What goes up will come down. For anything to remain elevated, energy must be applied — in the right place, at the right time. Anything else is waste.

Declining sales will normally cause lost profits. The difference between you and your competitors is in how you respond to declining sales. Your competitors will predictably react to declining sales with promotions, special deals, and a candy store selection of colors, options, and accessories. What they will get in return is more sales — and escalating costs that ultimately erode profits. To have the advantage, custom tailor your response to declining sales. Your first task in custom tailoring a response is to discover the causes of declining sales. When you know the causes, you can focus your response without wasting resources.

Target the Root Causes

There is always a product that has reached its sales peak where you can see sales beginning to drop. As an astute leader, you should know:

► When the decline started, including sales of the product before and after the decline;

► The minimum sales volume that will generate a profit; and

► The cause of the cause, or root cause, of the decline.

A business that is committed to determining the root causes makes the difference between firms whose fates rise and fall with the tides of change and those firms who control their own destinies. How many managers do you know who discuss causes of causes?

To know your sales before and after a product's sales have peaked, you need to chart sales perpetually. Ideally, you will plot the units of sales, the total dollars of sales, and the real profits generated by the sales. Real profits are determined by function-driven costing; see Profit Pointer 54 in Chapter 10.

You might think this detailed charting and plotting is a lot of trouble. You are right; it is a lot of trouble. Remember, if you do the things that are considered as a lot of trouble when your competitors are not doing them, then that effort will prove to be a competitive advantage.

Charting sales is a plotting of a curve known as the product life cycle. Most manufacturers do not know where their products are on the product life cycle curve. It is vitally important to your business planning to know what the future holds for your products. Plotting the product life cycle helps you predict the future. Keeping the chart updated is a sales and marketing function.

Examine the following example of a product life cycle that has reached its maturity. Notice the normal fluctuations throughout the life of the product and the easily identified break-even point.

Product Life Cycle Chart Example

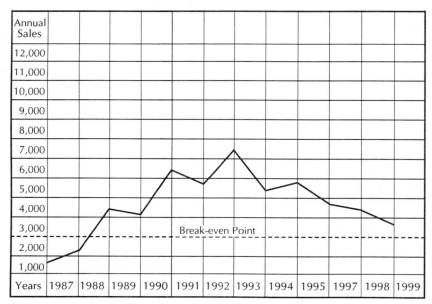

You can predict that sales will fall below the break-even point within a year. This product should be phased out soon. As an astute manager, you should have a replacement product prepared to take the place of the discontinued mature product. Product life cycle charts should be maintained and posted in full view for every product family. A blank product life cycle chart is located at the end of this chapter for your business' use.

To know the minimum sales volume that will generate a profit, mark that point on your product life cycle chart. As sales begin to approach the point of losses instead of profits, at least you will know you are entering a period of crisis before it appears on a financial statement. Knowing early enables you to respond with planned action rather than knee-jerk reaction.

To discover the cause of the cause (root cause) of a sales decline requires analysis and thoughtful investigation. Extensive sales histories and a product life cycle chart are the tools to help you discover the root causes and tailor your response. Quite often, the best response has nothing to do with the quality or intensity of your sales and marketing effort.

When you are planning your response to a given business condition, consider that your response will generate a primary effect — that is, what you hope to accomplish — and a secondary response to that primary effect. Regularly successful business leaders predict secondary responses. Business is dominated by a complex interaction of secondary responses. A secondary response is what happens long after the results you often expect (and measure) have come and gone. An obvious example is cutting wages. The primary effect is to reduce immediate costs and to increase profits. The secondary response is to demoralize the workforce. Demoralization causes a myriad of effects: increased turnover, increased training, more errors, more accidents, and more days missed due to illness. Profits may increase for 90 days, but the secondary responses of a wage cut hang on forever.

Your goal is to promote beneficial secondary responses (the effects that hang on forever). To get the beneficial secondary responses you want, you must delve into causes of causes. Secondary responses are mentioned throughout this book, especially in Chapter 13.

Prepare for Market Saturation

PROFIT POINTER

❧ 33 ☙

Sales may drop due to a natural product life end. There are several causes of the end of a product's life. Market saturation is one. Imagine that the product you manufacture and sell is a desktop stapler — the kind that most businesses use daily. Sooner or later, everyone who wants one of your staplers will have one. When they do, sales will fall to a low-level replenishment of staplers that wear out or break.

A sales decline due to market saturation is normal and predictable. When the market is saturated, the low-cost, high-quality producer will have the advantage. When total demand drops, all producers will begin to compete primarily on price. For your business to prosper in a declining market, you should be able to produce at a stable rate, very low cost, and a sustained high quality level. Plan for such a scenario early in a product's life cycle. Have your low-cost, high-quality product and production facility implemented and paid for long before the point of market saturation. Interestingly, as your competitors begin to lose profits and drop out of the race, you may gain enough sales to keep your production levels nearly as high as they were during the peak of demand.

As a product's life nears an end due to market saturation, you have two possible responses to prolong a product life cycle. One response is promotions and discounts. Promotions and discounts are properly used to initiate a new product. But they should rarely be used to increase sales of any product after introduction. Promotions and discounts erode profits and interfere with natural demand patterns. You need to have a history of natural demand to forecast effectively and plan responses near the end of a product life cycle. Manipulation of natural demand is a very common error — avoiding it is a competitive advantage.

The second response to extend a product's life is more effective — and more subtly dangerous if used unwisely. A product's life can be extended by adding options, colors, or new model variances. If you choose to use this technique, the danger is that it increases the total cost of the product line and that you are buying only a short respite before the product's life will end anyway. Utilize added options and variances as a strategy only to prolong a product life cycle in cases of emergency. A typical emergency is when a new product introduction is delayed, you can add options and variances to the old product to keep sales and production going until the new product is on-line.

Plan Responses to Superb Competition

A top-notch competitor can come up with a better product than your product that will serve the same function and the same market. That better product may even cost less. When you are surprised by such superb competition, you need to have a planned response that is in process beforehand. Planning for surprises is the hallmark of excellent leadership.

When a superb competitor blows your market away with a better product, you will be at an extreme disadvantage. Your reaction time may be entirely too long to allow financial survival. Your proactive response

PROFIT POINTER

◆ 34 ◆

should be to prevent the situation. Ten dollars of preventative management is worth a hundred dollars of what-do-we-do-now management.
Prevent the blindside competitive blow by staying close to your customers. Your customers have the ability to hear and see more than you.
They can keep you aware of your competitors' plans. Keep an excellent
relationship with your customers and they will keep you informed.

You may have competitors who do an excellent job of keeping new
product plans totally secret. If so, they are not including their customers
on new product development. Sooner or later, customer noninvolvement
will produce a market failure. Don't be afraid of the negative effects of
your competitors' moment of glory while waiting for them to have a market failure. You can do three things to properly respond to the superb
efforts of your competitors.

Plan an orderly flow of new products

Make sure the design is right before you go to market. Get a reputation for quality, delivery, and service. Make sure your designs
are conducive to quality and manufacturability: the keys to becoming the low-cost, high-quality provider. Long-term manufacturing
success depends on a steady flow of quality goods at a reasonable
price. Schedule new product introductions at regular intervals,
even if you do not know what the products are going to be!

Diversify, but not too much

Diversify to the extent that you are selling enough products so
that an unexpected sales decline in one area is not terminal. Three
diverse lines are normally sufficient to weather most conditions.
More is better up to the point of your own ability to manage the
diversity. Keep the basic processes similar. If you are in the market of manufacturing water heaters, you should stay with sheet
metal and welded products. You should not try to make upholstered furniture in the same factory.

Become the low-cost, high-quality producer

Place an unrelenting pressure to press costs down and to press
quality up even further. It may surprise you to know that most
manufacturers are functioning at the limits of their ability just to
make their products. Your competition likely does not have the
management prowess to consistently be the low-cost, high-quality producer. If you develop the ability to be the low-cost, high-
quality producer, then your competitor will never survive long
enough to affect you with a better product. An ounce of cost control and quality is worth a pound of reactive sales efforts.

If you know that a competitor is planning a new product introduction that will devastate your product offering, but you know it six months in advance, then you can prepare. You may be able to upgrade your own product. Or, you may elect to drop the price, empty your warehouses, and get out. You may have dozens more options depending upon your own product and market. The key is the advance warning system. With time, you can plan a successful counterattack or an honorable retreat without losses. To learn how to implement an early warning system, refer to Chapter 7.

Plan Responses to Regulated Obsolescence

PROFIT POINTER

❦ 35 ❦

A product that is successful today may be illegal tomorrow. Or, the process that you use to make your product may become illegal. A court liability decision could scare you out of producing more of your product. Such a surprise termination of your product life cycle can come as inconveniently as a surprise introduction of a new product by a competitor. You should take the same steps to prevent devastation as you would to protect yourself in the case of superb competition. You should strive to:

▶ Keep up the flow of new products;
▶ Diversify; and
▶ Become the low-cost, high-quality producer.

Read trade publications and other materials to keep you abreast of pending regulations so you will have as much forewarning of new regulations as possible. If you are politically motivated, try to influence your political leaders to show a greater concern for the welfare of the nation by supporting your business. Governmental regulation is creating rapid-fire product and process obsolescence. Letters to your leaders may defer or cancel a burdensome regulation.

Develop a Lonely Product Position

PROFIT POINTER

❦ 36 ❦

The most common reason why U.S. manufacturers are losing sales revenue is because of a crowded product position. Product position is a term that describes where your product is in relation to your competition. Selling price and quality determine where your product is located.

Strive to locate your product in a separate category that it is lonely. If you locate your product in a crowd of products of similar quality and price, then you are required to cut margins or to multiply your selling efforts to move your product. Look at the following product positioning map example and its quadrants' characteristics.

Product Positioning Map Example

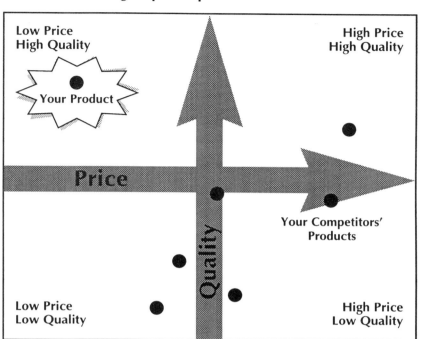

Notice that the products that fall in the upper left-hand quadrant of the map provide your business with a number of advantages. This quadrant's characteristics include:

- ► Low marketing costs
- ► Predictable sales volume
- ► Predictable profits
- ► High "natural" demand
- ► Cost control-oriented management
- ► Minimum competition
- ► High operations management expertise

Products in the lower right-hand quadrant make your business unpredictable and difficult to manage. This quadrant's characteristics include:

- ► High marketing costs
- ► Variable sales volume potential
- ► Requires emotional appeal to sell
- ► Heavy competition
- ► Sales-orientation

▶ Unpredictable profits
▶ Low requirement for management expertise

Somewhere in between you will find the high-price, high-quality quadrant, which is characteristic of:

▶ Medium marketing costs
▶ Low sales volume potential
▶ Repeat sales
▶ Limited competition
▶ Moderate management expertise

Additionally, you can see the low-price, low-quality quadrant, which is characteristic of:

▶ Moderate marketing costs
▶ High sales volume potential
▶ Off and on sales
▶ Heavy competition
▶ Sales-oriented management expertise
▶ Very short product life cycle

Most U.S. producers fall into the category of low price and low quality; it is a crowded position. The competitive advantage is to locate in the most lonely part of the product positioning map. You can be assured that the high-quality, low-price quadrant is the most lonely. A second advantage of being the high-quality, low-price producer is that you can move to any other part of the map very quickly if your location becomes crowded.

Notice that the characteristics of the low-price, high-quality producer include the trait of high operations management expertise. Higher levels of effort and competence in planning, analysis, organization, and general management are required to become the low-price, high-quality producer. That is why that part of the map is lonely; that is why it is the place that you should mark as your target. To map your product and your competitors' product positions, use the blank product positioning map at the end of this chapter.

The U.S. trade deficit, which occurs when we buy more foreign products than we can sell to foreign countries, has worsened every year since 1982. A typical low-quality, high-cost product position is the reason. Cost and quality are like the weather, everyone talks about them, but nobody does anything! If you want to prevent or remedy declining sales, do something about cost and quality. Part III thoroughly discusses what you can do to control costs and improve quality.

Adjust Your Marketing Strategy

If you are trying to sell iceboxes to Eskimos, then you need to adjust your marketing strategy. More than likely, your marketing strategy is off-the-mark in far less obvious ways.

If you believe you need marketing help, acquire the services of a marketing professional or find a good marketing book. Two such helpful guides, *Power Marketing for Small Business* by Jody Hornor and *Marketing Mastery: Your Seven Step Guide to Success* by Dorothy Otterson and Harriet Stephenson, are available from The Oasis Press. To learn more about the books that have helped thousands of small business owners with their marketing efforts, contact:

The Oasis Press
(800) 228-2275

For now, make a cursory examination to determine if your marketing strategy needs adjustment. If your marketing strategy is indeed in error, your sales decline will be accompanied by one or more of the following telltale indicators.

1. Your sales decline results in a loss of market share. A loss of market share means that the overall sales of your type of product are still strong, but sales of your brand are declining. Find out why. Look first at cost and quality. If you are competitive on those fronts, suspect an error in your marketing strategy.

2. Your sales decline immediately follows a significant change in people, policies, tactics, or territories. A major shift in the economy, politics, or laws can cause the need to revise your marketing strategy.

3. Your decline follows a change in buying preferences. Your competitors can alter the buying preferences of your market by heavily promoting some aspect of their product lines. If, for example, you have been successfully selling your vacuum cleaners based on low price, your competition may be able to sway the market to buy a vacuum cleaner with stylish good looks — and a higher price. In response, you will have to revise your tactic to sway the market back to some feature of your product — maybe service or parts availability.

Stimulation and manipulation of demand are marketing errors. Japanese manufacturers have invaded U.S. markets so successfully because they design products to align with a strong natural demand. They have done their market research and have given U.S. consumers exactly what they want. If you make a product to meet a strong natural demand, you have negated the need for strong efforts in selling, promotions, and advertising. U.S. analysts incorrectly teach that the Japanese advantage in market penetration is quality. In reality, the Japanese advantage is a precise alignment between product design and marketplace demand. You should strive to achieve a 100 percent alignment between what the market wants and what you provide. It follows that your marketing strategy may require adjustment in the design of your product.

Chapter Recap

Always view declining sales as a symptom. Since it is a symptom, you should resist the temptation to treat a sales decline by a direct attempt to increase immediate sales through traditional means, such as promotions, discounts, and special deals. If you want to be unique in the marketplace, find out the root causes of why sales are declining, then correct those root causes. Even if you are not certain of your root causes, you will always gain in sales if you master these three vital areas:

- ► Control over costs;
- ► Control over quality; and
- ► Precise alignment with a known demand.

Product Life Cycle Chart Instructions:

Use this chart to plot a product life cycle curve for each of your products. Simply plug in the annual sales dollars in the left-hand column and all applicable years of what you see as the product's life in the bottom row. You may want to use a ten-year span for instance. This chart will show you the product's normal fluctuations relative to sales and help you identify a break-even point. Additionally, you will be able to readily identify the point at which the product's life has matured.

This information will help you plan a proactive response to each product's peak points and low points and will guide your decision to end its life via phaseout.

Product Life Cycle Chart

Sales												
Years												

How to Use the Map:

Locate your competitors on the map. You do not need detailed price and quality information to locate their positions. A subjective appraisal is fine. Your goal is to position every company or product correctly relative to the others.

Now, position your own business. If you find that you are in a "crowd" of similar price and quality players, your goal is to move your business as far as possible away from the competition. This "distance" on the product positioning map is what makes your product offerings distinctly different from the customers' perspectives.

You will normally find that the low-price, high-quality quadrant is the least crowded. If that is the case, develop the necessary product designs management expertise to arrive in that quadrant.

Product Positioning Map

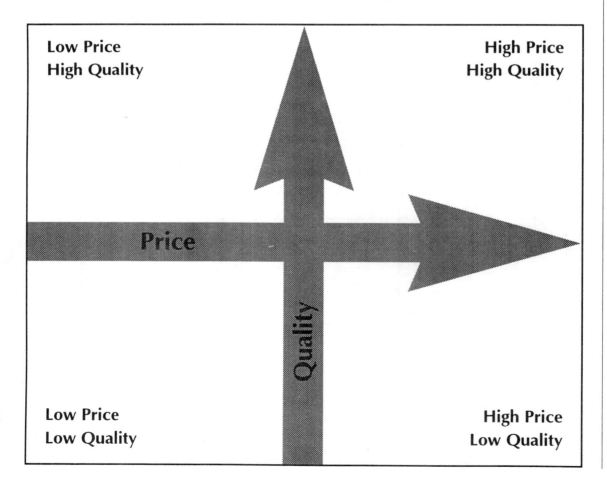

Low Price
High Quality

High Price
High Quality

Price

Quality

Low Price
Low Quality

High Price
Low Quality

CHAPTER 7

STREAMLINE YOUR ORGANIZATION

The purpose of an organization is efficiency: to do what needs doing once — no more, no less.

Your challenge, as a savvy business owner, is to set up an organization that will prevent errors, conflicts, and duplication. As a matter of simple routine, the effective organization will assure that every essential task is performed correctly and on time. It exhibits unity of effort.

Most managers try repeatedly to devise such an organization, but find that every new organizational concept has deficiencies that eventually cause errors, duplications, and conflicts. The organizational style that solves the short-term problems brings on deferred costs. The style that promises long-term benefits is rife with implementation conflicts and never matures to deliver the goods.

The reality is that your business, like most businesses, probably has a very ineffective (dysfunctional) organization. Dysfunctional organizations do many things twice, some things not at all, and expend great amounts of energy in conflict. A dysfunctional organization causes lost profits.

Consider how the following story illustrates the need to eliminate the dysfunctional nature of an organization to avoid profit losses.

---

*A manufacturer began buying welding gases from a new sup-
plier. The welding department supervisor negotiated the deal.
The purchasing department issued a purchase order and the
gases were delivered. The month-end invoice was sent to the
accounts payable department with a copy to the supervisor.
The supervisor initialed the invoice, indicating that the goods
were received, and forwarded the copy to the accounts payable department. The bill was paid twice. The bill was paid
twice because of organizational dysfunction.*

Before you begin to read the rest of this chapter, take a moment to
evaluate your business' organization. Use the Organizational Effectiveness
Evaluation located at the end of this chapter.

Recognize the Symptoms of Dysfunction

PROFIT POINTER

❧ 38 ❧

In the early life of a business, the leadership challenge is to get things
done. A new business is normally dealing with surging demand, growth-
related projects, rapid-fire hirings, capital projects, and a crushing cash
flow problem. In the rush to survive and adapt, there is no time to deal
with the trivialities. The legitimate priority is to just do whatever needs to
be done. The just-do-it style of management is not the wisest choice, even
for a start-up business. A startup is often dealing with hot markets that
absorb the high prices dictated by start-up inefficiencies. As the market
matures and cools and as more competition enters the market, then cost
control becomes a priority. The just-do-it style of management can generate enough extra cost through organizational inefficiency to significantly rob profits.

The second phase of the growth of a business thrives on an efficient, effective organization — one that is cool, controlled, and does
things right the first time. The fire and bubbling enthusiasm of the entre-
preneur must cool into a foundation of solid rock. The cool and controlled
style required of the management of an established company is often
adverse to the person who built a business from nothing. The entrepre-
neur has a fire in the spirit that cannot endure the calm order that is necessary in the cost-controlling stage of the company. The same fired up
spirit that founded a company will give birth to a chaotic, infighting, dysfunctional organization. You need to know the symptoms of dysfunction.
If you spot any of the following symptoms in your business, start building a functional organization immediately.

Frequent Reorganization

In his book, *Manufacturing Control: The Last Frontier for Profits*, George W. Plossl made a comment regarding the American propensity to reorganize. He said, "Reorganization is no substitute for a clear definition of primary functions and professional leadership with adequate systems tools to carry out these functions." In other words, the priority should be to develop regular, systematic methods to achieve your daily business functions. When you develop reports, charts, budgets, and responsibility assignments, you will enable people to get things done.

A multitude of theories exist regarding what might work in an organizational structure. The theories have many interesting, yet meaningless titles. Most of the theories do not work because they are devised in an effort to encourage interdepartmental communications. Poor internal communications have little to do with the structure of an organization. Organizational climate either promotes or discourages communication. If the structure of an organization is really poor, then it becomes a disabler of communication. When you develop an organizational structure, organize people in such a manner that encourages performing essential tasks only once.

An inept organizational structure promotes inefficiency and ineffectiveness. In other words, if you have organizational inefficiency and ineffectiveness, take a critical look at your organizational structure. There are specific symptoms that will tell you that you have problems with your organizational structure. The person who is experienced in profit-enhancement projects will quickly recognize problems with organizational structure, even without seeing the organizational chart.

Power Struggles

Organizational chaos breeds conflicts over territory and you end up with who's-responsible-for-what arguments. If you have this symptom, it is a cause of lost profits. The energy of talented people is drained trying to protect territory, justify actions, and define duties. Power struggles cost more than just the time spent in actual combat. There is the on-again-off-again nature of projects and plans that are stopped and started depending on who is perceived to be in power.

Low Management Morale

Low management morale is evidenced by high turnover and sour dispositions. Competent managers trapped in a chaotic organizational structure become quickly disenchanted. Interestingly, management disorganization attracts the politically-minded and repels the nose-to-the-grindstone crowd. The reason is that, with no clear responsibility assignments, the fast-talkers find it easy to claim responsibility for the "good" events and to pass the buck on the "bad" events. The hard-working, less-talkative true workers fail to get proper rewards for tasks done right, but get blamed for tasks done wrong.

Management Ineffectiveness

A dysfunctional organization causes inept management performance and poor quality decisions. Competent managers will perform if they know that recognition will follow achievement. In a chaotic organization it is often difficult for the top manager to know who is responsible for a given achievement. The same is true for failures. Incentives to perform do not exist. An interesting side issue is that those who would falsely claim credit for an achievement have no deterrent. In a poorly structured organization, top managers frequently cannot reliably identify their top performers. They do not know who is responsible for what.

Management versus Labor Hostility

The hostility between management and labor is normally expressed as a labor antagonism toward management. Infighting and waste in management circles breed a disrespect among ground floor employees. The results of management errors are usually corrected at the expense of the employees under them. An employee who makes $8.00 per hour will have much contempt for a $50,000-a-year manager who spends each day writing memos and fighting for territory. You can believe that the business with a hostile labor force also has poor morale. Poor morale leads to high error rates, high turnover, and inefficiency — all causes of lost profits.

Poor Communication

Poor communication is evidenced by many meetings, memos, and the always present I-didn't-know explanations. The organizational sin that inhibits communication is when two employees are responsible for the same function — a common occurrence in a dysfunctional organization. In such a case, a disagreement over methods turns into a competition. Competition breeds secrecy. Secrecy and competition result in chaotic conflicts of instructions to the people who are doing the work. Poor communication is a vicious cycle.

Computer Reliance

The dysfunctional organization will breed an incentive to computerize all sorts of management functions. Computers become a placebo that blocks the application of imagination and resourcefulness. In addition, computer projects offer a great opportunity to claim territory or to otherwise establish some degree of order. Such projects usually end up incomplete due to conflicts within the organization.

Nothing Gets Done

A dysfunctional organization blocks progress. The complaint of top management is that it is unreasonably difficult to push some project through the business. For example, a project is assigned during a regular staff meeting. At the following meeting, no one reports progress. Such a deficiency results because no one is certain of who is responsible for what business functions.

Overstaffing

Because of the nothing-gets-done syndrome, more employees are hired in a dysfunctional organization. More people in disorganization spur more chaos. More chaos invites more staff to solve the problems. Overstaffing is a prime result and cause of excess costs in a poor organization.

Reporting Tangles

Look at your organizational chart. Do you have multiple lines of reporting? Such lines imply that an individual is taking instructions from two bosses. Multiple bosses dilute the alignment of accountability and authority. This form of organizational structure makes meaningful performance evaluations impossible. Lines on a chart are to clarify divisions and subdivisions of functional responsibility. Unclear functional responsibility is a cause of conflict, infighting, duplication, and oversight — all of which are costly.

PROFIT POINTER

❧ 39 ❧

Cut the Costs of Dysfunction

The excess costs brought on by dysfunction fall into the category of soft costs. Soft costs are real costs that are difficult to define but can be divided into seven categories, including:

- ▶ Labor inefficiency
- ▶ Overstaffing costs
- ▶ Administrative waste due to errors and changes
- ▶ Management turnover
- ▶ Confusion in the non-salaried ranks
- ▶ Decision making errors
- ▶ Time spent trying new organizational techniques

If you tried, you could put a dollar estimate on these seven types of costs. Just to help you grasp the size of the problem, make a quick estimate of how much you think it costs yearly for any one of the seven costs in your own company. Pick one that you are most familiar with. Once you have your estimate, double it. You double it because for every dollar you know you are losing, there is a dollar you cannot see that you are losing. Now, take your doubled figure and multiply it by seven. (Remember, seven areas of soft costs exist.) The figure you have calculated is the amount you can add to your bottom line once you get your organizational structure in order. It will be worth your effort.

Additionally, there are intangible costs that are more deeply hidden than the costs you just estimated. You can call them the unknown losses of opportunity. For example, a dysfunctional organization loses great people. The people who stay are possibly as great, but they become quietly discouraged. The company loses in both cases. Other examples of unknown losses of opportunity are:

- ▶ New projects that are never proposed;
- ▶ Great ideas that are never voiced; and
- ▶ Bad ideas that are never criticized.

Organizational dysfunction smothers human resourcefulness, innovation, and creativity. People use their energies to protect territory and enlarge their importance. The profits lost because of losses of opportunity are impossible to calculate. Your safest bet is to assume you have an organizational structure problem and take steps to create a stable, functional organization.

Create a Functional Business Plan

PROFIT POINTER

❧ 40 ❧

The prerequisite to a turnaround of lost profits is the ability to turn a plan into action — action that is competent and efficient. A business that can act with competence is function driven. A function-driven business begins with a business plan that can be subdivided into functional units. It formulates plans that will perform the functions. It acts without conflict or guesswork. Building such an organization is the first act in a turnaround; it must always be done early in a business' life.

Your business' every decision and action should be a part of a larger plan. If you operate in this manner, you will experience less conflict, waste, and infighting that is symptomatic of a dysfunctional organization. Instead, individual acts will complement and support the acts of other individuals. The starting point for this kind of organizational efficiency is the larger plan. The larger plan is the overall business plan. The business plan is generic and is based on broad, sweeping objectives that indicate dates when a final goal is desired. Look at the following example of a proper business plan goal for a turnaround project.

Example of a well-stated business plan goal

Increase profits from an average monthly loss of $100,000 to an average monthly profit of $50,000; to achieve that goal 90 days from today. To gain profitability after that date to achieve a regular net profit of 10 percent.

Many successful businesses use the term profit plan to describe their business plans. Profit plan is a good name because it keeps everyone oriented toward the purpose of the plan. The top manager of the company is responsible for formulation of the initial generic statement of the plan. The profit plan will state what you need to achieve and when you need to achieve it, but will not state how you will achieve it.

How to achieve the goal will be defined by communication with the top managers of your business' four functional areas: manufacturing, product engineering, sales and marketing, and finance. These leaders, through communication with their employees, have the responsibility of defining the how-to portion of the business plan. How-to includes methods, objectives, and timetables. Look at the following example of goals by department that will help achieve the overall business plan.

Manufacturing department goal

Reduce scrap and rework from an average of five percent ($35,000) to three percent ($21,000). Increase production by ten percent. Reduce materials costs by two percent ($14,000). Reduce work-in-process (WIP) inventory by 25 percent. Prepare the production line for new product introduction in 90 days. Support prototyping of new product.

Product engineering department goal

Have new product ready for production in 90 days. Support scrap reduction via improved routings and drawings as required by the manufacturing department. Support production increase via design simplification of current products.

Sales and marketing department goal

Develop markets for sales of added ten percent production without discounting prices. Support production efficiency by stabilizing demand. Prepare distribution chain for new product to be able to ship in 105 days. Sell obsolete finished goods at discounts of up to 50 percent.

Finance department goal

Provide financing for inventories and facilities for new product line. Improve collections from 45 days to 29 days. Provide financing for new product development. Provide financial statement within first two working days of each month.

All departments are expected to cooperate with each other and support their coworkers' efforts. Individuals who must perform the daily work to achieve the goals of the department take instructions from the person who is held responsible for the performance of the department. They do not take direct instructions from anyone else. They are encouraged to honor requests for assistance from other departments. With this kind of planning, conflicting requests will be rare. When they do occur, they can normally be resolved at a lower level. Competent lower level decision making is a natural benefit of a good profit plan; everyone knows the plan so there is little opportunity for conflict of effort.

The functional subdivisions of your profit plan precisely drive the design of your organizational structure. In reality, there should be no differences between the functional responsibilities of the organizational structure and the functional requirements of the profit plan. If your business plan has four groups of functional requirements, then your organizational chart will have four groups of functional responsibilities. Each of the four groups is accountable for its functional performance.

For more tips on how to improve your profit plan, consider getting a copy of *Improving Staff Productivity* by Ben Harrison Carter. To learn more about this top-selling book, contact:

The Oasis Press
(800) 228-2275

Build a Function-Driven Organization

To structure your organization properly, you must begin to build a function-driven organization. A function-driven organization means two things. First, the term reminds you that the organizational structure really works — it is functional. Second, the term keeps you oriented to the concept that makes the structure work — it is driven by the need to function. When you draw a function-driven organization on paper, first draw a large rectangle at the top of the sheet. Label that largest rectangle profit plan. Then, draw four slightly smaller rectangles under the large rectangle and label them:

- ► Manufacturing plan
- ► Product engineering plan
- ► Financial plan
- ► Sales and marketing plan

Then, in a column under each of the smaller rectangles, list the corresponding functions. For example, the normal functions of the manufacturing plan are:

- ► Production
- ► Maintenance
- ► Manufacturing/industrial engineering
- ► Production control
- ► Purchasing
- ► Inventory control
- ► Warehousing

Look at the illustration of a function-driven organization below. The function-driven organization is defined by functions of your business plan, or profit plan. Note that the descriptions do not identify positions or employees' names. They are definitions of functions that must be carried out. All of those functions are necessary to the normal business plan. The goal at this stage of the organizational project is to recognize the relationship of functions to the achievement of the overall business objective. Names of people will ultimately be associated with each business function; thus, linking functional responsibility to specific individuals.

Also note the divisions of divisions of functional responsibility. For example, manufacturing is a division of the business plan. There will be a manufacturing plan that supports the overall business plan. Maintenance is a division of manufacturing. There will be a maintenance plan that supports the overall manufacturing plan. There may even be subdivisions within maintenance and numerous subplans that are part of the overall maintenance plan.

Keep in mind, the function-driven organization encourages teamwork and communication. It promotes acceptance of responsibility and enables proper accountability.

Now you can go back and assign names of people to each function. In a very small company, one person may take on many responsibilities. The person at the top — normally the president — may also take on the functional area of sales and marketing. Also, product engineering and manufacturing may be controlled by one individual.

The Function-Driven Organization

Profit Plan			
Manufacturing Plan	Product Engineering Plan	Financial Plan	Sales and Marketing Plan
Production	Design	Payables	Outside Sales
Maintenance	Research and Development	Receivables	Inside Sales
Manufacturing / Industrial Engineering	Prototypes	General Ledger	Advertising
Production Control	Bills of Materials	Cash Management	Forecasts
Purchasing	Drawings	Cost Accounting	Invoicing
Inventory Control	Document Control	Payroll	Pricing
Warehousing			

A very large company should never have more than one person in charge of a functional area. The responsibility for the manufacturing department, as an example, should never be shared by two people. No matter how logical and expedient it may seem to break up functional areas in the heat of some discussion or crisis, it will never work well. The reason is that such an act separates accountability and authority. If Chris and Jackie are sharing control of the functions of manufacturing, who is really accountable if the manufacturing gross profits begin to fall? Is it Chris who is in charge of inventory control and warehousing? Or, is it Jackie who heads up production? You can see how such an organizational error can lead to bouts of finger pointing.

Companies that endure the conflicts over responsibility know that it is time consuming and frustrating. It requires intervention by a higher authority who will never resolve the issue to the satisfaction of anyone. It makes otherwise competent and mature managers look like sparring kindergartners. You want an organization that is mature and responsible. Maturity and responsibility arise from situations that nurture those attributes. Build an organization that promotes maturity and responsibility. Then, you will enjoy the benefits of an organization that promotes high levels of responsibility and self-discipline. Once you have a documented function-driven organization, you will find that it looks like the hierarchical organizational structure that many of today's experts denounce. Don't worry about how it looks on paper. Pay attention to how well it works. The hierarchical organization appears again and again throughout history, from the organization of the Roman legions to the modern military to hospitals. The reason that it keeps reappearing is that it works so well. Failures of hierarchical organizations are not due to structure. Such failures are due to a lack of leadership, an uncertain business plan, and a conflict of goals communicated to lower levels of the organization.

Leadership, a business plan, and communicated goals are totally vital to success. They are so vital that, without them, even the best organizational structure cannot create success. Conversely, if they are in place, a poor organizational structure will probably get the job done — more than likely with some inefficiency and error.

Eliminate Functions that Don't Directly Impact Your Profit Plan

In a function-driven organization, only the top managers of the four functional areas report directly to the president of the company. So what about other functional tasks like personnel, data processing, and administration? When structuring your organization in a function-driven way, you must examine these types of tasks in light of your overall profit plan. For example, what function does an administration department perform that contributes to the success of your profit plan? Administration tasks can be handled by administrative secretaries or personal assistants. Be wary of an administrative department; such full-blown departments are usually costly bureaucracies that can grow into an unmanageable tangle. It is better to allow each functional area to be responsible for its own administrative tasks, such as:

- ► Personnel files
- ► Policy manuals
- ► Handling incoming calls and visitors
- ► System administration
- ► Travel arrangements
- ► Other routine office functions

Take a closer look at your personnel department. Depending on the size of your business, you may not need one. Direct supervisors should always conduct interviews and make hiring decisions for any people that work directly under them. Further, any regulatory compliance issues are the responsibility of whatever department is involved — usually the manufacturing department. Pay scales should be developed and maintained by the finance department with input from all supervisors. Personnel files can be easily maintained by someone in the payroll department, a division of the finance department. Consistent personnel policies are necessary to employee relations, but a full-time personnel manager is not required to formulate consistent policies. Company-wide policies should come from the president, with input from all departments.

Does your business have a separate data processing department? Full-blown data processing departments were questionable in the days of inept mainframes with no software. With today's personal computer based systems and software packages, there is no need for a data processing department. Instead, you can assign the system administrator responsibility, a part-time function, to a competent senior employee in any department, preferably the department with the greatest usage of the system.

Work Teams in the Function-Driven Organization

You may wonder if a function-driven organization will violate the concept of teamwork. It doesn't. A work team is a group of people working to achieve a common goal. They share their knowledge, information, and energies to support the efforts of one another. They should be in close proximity to facilitate regular communication. They should be aware of the efforts of one another so as to prevent duplication or conflict of effort. Those are the characteristics that enable teams to perform so effectively. The characteristics of work teams are the same as the characteristic of the function-driven organization. The function-driven organization is a design for a comprehensive set of work teams that complements and supports one another.

Use an Early Warning System

PROFIT POINTER

◆ 42 ◆

Managing manufacturing is like steering a battleship. If you want to maintain course, you must watch your instruments and charts and initiate course corrections before they are required. The charts of manufacturing are the profit plan and its functional subdivisions. The instruments of manufacturing are the charts and graphs called an early warning system. A wise captain will plot a course that avoids shallows and reefs. The captain will constantly monitor instrumentation to assure that the course is being followed. If the ship begins to drift toward a reef, the captain will make a course correction long before the reef is encountered. A foolish captain will wait until the ship has run aground before taking action. Once the ship is aground, all action is reactive:

- ▶ What happened?
- ▶ Why did it happen?
- ▶ Who is to blame?
- ▶ How do we recover?
- ▶ What is the damage?

Sounds just like a Monday morning staff meeting. Prevention of business disasters depends on a system of early warnings. The ideal early warning system consists of a number of regularly updated charts and graphs.

Reports of raw data are meaningless for most busy executives. Raw data must be mentally converted to meaningful trends. That requires keeping and rereading volumes of reports. Reading raw data is time consuming and distasteful for most executives. It is open to inconsistent interpretations. Charts and graphs offer instant visualization of important business trends. The data to chart depends on the business to some extent. Every operation has specific needs. Some data samples you may want to chart are listed below.

Data Samples to Chart in an Early Warning System

Direct Labor:
- Hours per unit.
- Labor dollars per unit.
- Employee turnover rate.

Materials:
- Purchased versus standard; expressed as a percentage of a predetermined standard cost (as in 110 percent of standard or 92 percent of standard). Even one percent is very significant on next month's bottom line.
- Freight variances.
- Raw and WIP per unit of production, expressed as a percentage of a standard.

Waste and Errors:
- Scrap and rework expressed as a percentage of completed work and compared to a standard (as in one percent acceptable, this month is running at four percent).
- The cost of warranty repairs expressed as dollars per unit sold (by product type).

Overhead Costs:
- General and administrative expressed in dollars per unit sold or shipped.
- The cost of selling (not cost of sales) expressed in dollars per unit sold or shipped.
- Manufacturing overhead expressed in dollars per unit produced, with a chart for each product line.

This type of detailed charting is a lot of work — a troublesome task that most of your competitors will never attempt. If you want a competitive advantage, stay ahead of costs. How many manufacturers do you know that can tell you how much it costs to get a given product sold? How many do you know who can quote to you the manufacturing overhead cost attributed to a given product? How many can tell you — based on fact and data — whether manufacturing overhead is going up or down for a given product? Having this kind of knowledge at your fingertips is vital to predicting and controlling profits. Do not be dissuaded by the fact that no one else in your business maintains this kind of information service. Doing what no one else does is a competitive advantage.

You may think computerized charts and graphs are your best bet. Actually, you should opt for the discipline of personally placing a dot and a line on a piece of paper. As you deal with the numbers, dots, and lines, you will be forced to awaken to reality. You will personally see when a trend begins. The updating of charts and graphs takes an hour or two. The task is routine. You will have time to think about the realities that forced the line to move up or down. The people in charge of your business' main functional areas should update their own charts for the same reasons.

You may be tempted to computerize this chore. Computers are capable of performing the task in less time and of doing it error-free — if the input is error-free. If you choose to generate the graphs via computer, you will inevitably end up ignoring the charts. They will be relegated to the same pile as the rest of the unread printouts. Management of a business is not a task that can be handled by a computer. It requires an occasional dose of human inspiration. It requires ideas, innovation, and changes of direction. The manual task of charting an early warning system will stimulate thought — thought causes ideas and ideas result in action. Look at the following early warning charts to learn how charting is vital to your business' operations.

Early Warning Chart – Positive Signs*

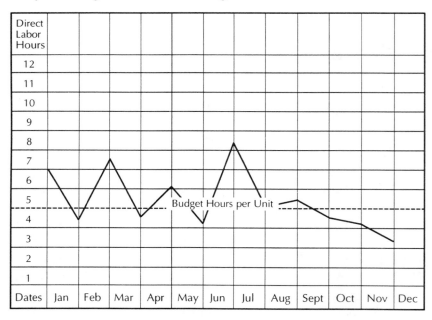

* Represents direct labor hours per unit of production for gas home heaters.

This early warning chart tells managers that the factors that influence direct labor on this product line are under control. The erratic nature of labor consumption ceased in August. Total labor per unit began a distinct downward trend at that same time. There are no red flags for the direct labor per unit of production.

Early Warning Chart – Negative Signs*

* Represents direct labor hours per unit of production for gas home heaters.

The chart above tells managers that the factors that influence direct labor on this product line are above budget and are trending higher. In August, labor consumption became higher than budget and became erratic. This chart indicates a red flag that tells managers some labor-influencing condition changed that began showing its effects in August. Use the blank early warning chart at the end of this chapter to help you locate any potential problems.

Your early warning charts should be arranged in plain view. You will be best served to keep them in your own office. That way you see them all the time. Putting them somewhere else is like placing the fuel gauge of your car in the trunk. You can bet that you will run out of gas if your gauge is out of sight.

Chapter Recap

A common cause of lost profits is the lost opportunities inherent in a dysfunctional organization. U.S. industries have, for the most part, lost sight of the purpose and proper structure of a functional organization. Today's trend is to embrace some really odd (unworkable) organizational theories. Organizing a business is straightforward and logical. You create a plan and make assignments: Tina does this, Joe does that — everyone reports when their tasks are complete — tell your superior if you encounter a problem.

A streamlined business organization will carry out the functional requirements to achieve its business objectives. It will do it with minimum effort and maximum competence.

Organizational Effectiveness Evaluation

This evaluation will help you determine the effectiveness of your organization. The column on the left lists indicators of an effective organization. The column on the right lists indicators of an ineffective organization. Circle the number that you believe is closest to the current condition of your business' organizational structure. Then, use the organizational effectiveness evaluation rating scale on the next page to help you understand your score.

All employees have clearly defined areas of responsibility. There are no conflicts over who is responsible for what.	5 4 3 2 1	Regular conflicts arise. People are unclear over who is responsible for which business function.
Management turnover is rare. Manager morale is high.	5 4 3 2 1	Managers quit or are fired often. Few managers have five years seniority.
Top managers are always aware of what people are doing which things. Achievement is always recognized.	5 4 3 2 1	Top managers are unaware of who completes daily tasks. Special projects are under- or over-managed.
There is no clear distinction between managers and the direct labor force. Employees respect the objectives of management.	5 4 3 2 1	Sharp boundaries exist. Employees will question the objectives and motives of management.
Management communications are mostly verbal. Meetings are regular, with agendas. Memos are for the dissemination of information.	5 4 3 2 1	Managers hold frequent, unscheduled, and long meetings with no agendas. Results are tentative and subject to change.
Computers are used as tools. Programs are designed for the business. Personal computing is rare. Important business functions are fully integrated.	5 4 3 2 1	A personal computer is located on every desk, with no network or custom programs. Our employees use spreadsheets and databases heavily.
Special projects and individual assignments are completed competently and on time.	5 4 3 2 1	There is always some roadblock to progress. "Nothing ever gets done."
Top management knows that there is no overstaffing; every person has a known set of functions.	5 4 3 2 1	We are uncertain of the right staffing level. Business downturns result in dramatic reorganizing and downsizing.

Organizational Effectiveness Evaluation Rating Scale

Now, total the circled numbers. Locate your score below to find out the status of your business' organizational effectiveness.

———————

32–40 Your organization is function-driven. You have the competitive advantage.

16–31 Your organizational structure is inefficient. Work on your lowest scoring areas first.

0–15 You have organizational dysfunction. Top managers do not recognize the chaos. Your costs are too high and you do not know why. Begin now to develop a function-driven organization.

Early Warning Chart Instructions

Use this early warning chart to instantly visualize important business trends. As discussed in the chapter, you can chart a number of different areas to learn whether problems are surfacing that will lead to disaster or will stabilize. Simply indicate the area you are studying in the left-hand column and indicate the timeframes — by month, by quarter, or by year, for example — for which the data applies. Then, plot your graph with simple dots and lines — this will help you and your team determine the reasons that make the line on the graph rise and drop. As you do this, you may see some red flags. The ability to see these red flags and respond appropriately is a competitive advantage.

Early Warning Chart

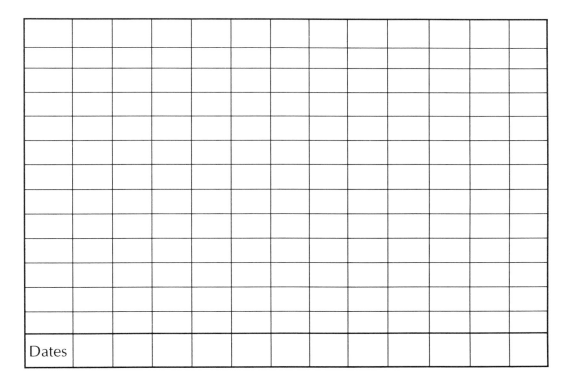

PART III

COST CONTROLS

The ultimate advantage in any endeavor is to master what others disdain.

If your business is showing decreasing profits with sales that are stable or increasing, then your costs are out of control. The logic for this conclusion is that stable or increasing sales indicate that your selling price is competitive with the rest of the players in the market. Your customers are accepting your product and pricing. If your profits are declining, then the only factor left is that your costs are out of control.

The era of easy price increases has offered little motivation for mastering the disciplines of cost control. If you are like other manufacturers, you have raised prices repeatedly to "cover costs." Today's businesses face a world that is filled with lean, hungry, cost-controlling competitors. This new breed of competitor works ten hours a day figuring ways to take a few more pennies out of the cost of products. Their parts counts are low. Their operations counts are low. Their quality is high. The prices of the products reflect their cost-controlling approach. If you want to compete with these producers, you have to out-manage them in cost control. You have two advantages. First, they have the cost of freight in order to sell in your turf. Second, they use methods that are native to this society — they were developed and perfected in this country.

Your business has three specific types of costs: labor, materials, and overhead. Part III will tell you what to do to reduce labor and materials costs. You will find that, as you gain more and more control over your business, overhead costs will automatically trend downward. For example, as you stabilize your production schedule, you will experience lower inventories and lower emergency freight costs.

Most of your competitors are becoming more focused on regaining lost sales in an era when more entities want a piece of the market pie. They are destined to spend lavishly on sales and marketing. The result will be little gain in sales and a decline in profits. When you focus on cost control, you can undercut your competitors' prices if needed and increase your profits — often dramatically — if you elect to keep your prices stable. You will gain the flexibility to respond to market conditions while your competition is locked into fighting for more sales at higher prices and costs.

CHAPTER 8

REDUCE LABOR COSTS

Out of sight, out of mind. The rule of the undisciplined. Nothing is more invisible than cost control.

The goal in reducing labor costs is to develop the means to work more efficiently. A common error is to reduce labor costs by buying products and services instead of producing them internally. While such a practice indeed reduces the dollars spent for labor, the total cost of purchasing — or outsourcing — is ultimately higher. The added costs are often in hidden areas, such as freight, administration, insurance, and inventory investment.

Although you learned in Chapter 5 that labor only constitutes ten percent of the cost of the average product, you should still dedicate resources to controlling the cost of labor.

There are two reasons for reducing labor costs. First, as you rectify conditions that are causing excess labor costs, you will find that those same remedies stimulate economies in other areas, such as administration, quality management, required floor space, inventory, and wasted material. Second, once the cost is reduced, you will find that you can make items in house more economically than you can buy them. When you reach that point of efficiency, you can capitalize on great savings on materials.

When you have successfully managed a labor-reduction project, you should find that the total labor content of your product has increased due to making items that you once bought. You should also find that your total cost of doing business is reduced much more than you can attribute to increased labor efficiency.

Rightsize Lot Sizes

Lot size is the amount of product that you make in one production run. Setting up equipment to make a run of a specific part or product involves a certain amount of time and cost. Due to the cost of setting up, wise cost-control practice dictates that you run a large enough lot size to minimize the setup cost per unit of production. However, lot sizes can be too large, resulting in costs of storage, repeated movement, damage, or spoilage. The dollar investment in a large run results in escalated inventory carrying costs. The right lot size is somewhere between the extremes of 1) so small that the setup costs consume all of the profit of the part, and 2) so large that inventory costs consume all of the profit of the part. To rightsize your lot sizes, you must know these financial figures:

► The share of profit for which the part is responsible;
► The cost of setting up to run the part; and
► The cost of carrying the part in inventory.

You can estimate the profit share of the part by calculating the percentage of the total cost of the product represented by the part. Then, you can use the same percentage to calculate the share of profit. For example, if the part represents one percent of the cost of the product, you can assume that it represents one percent of the profits of the product. Profit, in this case, is selling price minus materials and labor. Setup cost is calculated by multiplying the average (or estimated) setup time by the dollar-per-hour wage rate of the people performing the setup. If supplies are consumed in setup, then you can add the supply cost to the labor cost of setting up. Inventory carrying cost (per month) is usually calculated by your accounting department. If your accounting people cannot provide a carrying cost, use one percent per month as a starting point.

Use 10 percent of your per-part profit as a per-part budget for setups and inventory costs. This allows you to retain 90 percent of profit. You can then calculate a lowest profitable lot size by dividing your per-part setup cost by your per-part setup budget using this formula:

$ setup cost ÷ $ budget = lowest profitable lot size

You begin the calculation of a highest profitable lot size by first adding the materials and labor cost of the part to determine the inventory cost of the part. Then, multiply the inventory cost by inventory carrying cost; use your real cost or use one percent. Your answer is the per-part carrying cost in dollars. When calculating carrying cost, use only the material cost that is added. For example, if you already have the material on hand, it is creating a carrying cost already. In such a case, you would use a carrying cost only for added materials and added labor required to make the part that you will stock.

When you have a per-part carrying cost, you can calculate the highest profitable lot size by dividing the per-part budget by the per-part carrying cost using this formula:

$$\text{\$ budget} \div \text{\$ carrying cost} = \text{highest profitable lot size}$$

Your highest profitable lot size is stated in months of supply, since carrying costs are by the month. Because your consumption per month will likely vary, you must add your month-by-month projected consumption for the number of months of supply that your calculation has provided. Your total projected consumption of parts is your highest profitable lot size stated in number of parts.

The range between your highest and lowest lot sizes will vary from part to part. High-profit — profit compared to cost — parts will give you a wide range from highest to lowest. Low-profit parts will give you a narrow range from highest to lowest. This narrowing of choices reflects the true nature of managing a low-profit product versus managing a high-profit product. You will notice that, if your profit figure is zero, the calculation will recommend that you produce lot sizes of zero. This also reflects the true nature of how you should manage an unprofitable product.

You should use lot sizes close to your calculated lowest profitable lot size if your business has:

- ► Cramped inventory storage facilities;
- ► High inventory carrying costs, such as insurance and interest rates;
- ► Adequate or excess machine capacity; or
- ► Low or acceptable labor costs for setup.

You should use lot sizes close to your calculated highest profitable lot size if your business has:

- ► Adequate or surplus inventory storage facilities;
- ► Low or acceptable inventory carrying costs;

▶ Overloaded machine capacity; or

▶ High labor costs for setup.

If you have a blend of conditions, or if you are uncertain of your costs of labor and capacity utilization, then size your lots midway between the lowest and highest profitable lot sizes. You can reduce your total costs and increase your total production by scientifically rightsizing your lot sizes. As you perfect your lot sizes, your total labor efficiency will improve and labor costs will ease downward.

In addition, you can design your operations to accept any product mix without setup change or with minor setup change. In some cases, setup time reduction can be done with little or no cost. Sometimes, it can be done only at a great cost. Other times, it cannot be done. In any case, compare the costs to the cost savings to determine if the savings you experience through setup elimination will pay for the cost of the project. Your profit pressure should be in the direction of setup time reduction. As you reduce setup times, you can reduce lot sizes. Reduced setup times offer numerous benefits to a manufacturer, including:

▶ Smaller lot sizes, which equal lower inventory;

▶ Less labor dedicated to setups;

▶ Quick response to orders or to internal changes; and

▶ Flexibility to run large lot sizes when appropriate.

Setup reduction is treated as a complicated and mysterious issue. In reality, it is simple to achieve. An imaginative person with technical capability can work wonders in the realm of setup reduction. Reductions of hours down to minutes are common. To accomplish these types of reductions, you can:

▶ Do most of the setup work away from the machine.

▶ Keep tools, dies, and other instruments within a step or two.

▶ Standardize the setup components.

▶ Establish a repeatable step-by-step setup routine.

Setup time reduction offers direct and immediate benefit of labor reduction due to quicker setups. In the long term, quick setups improve total production capacity, reduce inventory, and improve total labor efficiency.

Manage Demand

Unanticipated fluctuations in demand result in unplanned changes in your master production schedule. Unplanned changes are referred to by a totally

PROFIT POINTER
◄ 44 ►

different term by the shop floor supervisors who implement them. The people who try to make the changes work call them disasters or emergencies.

Mass production thrives on planning. As a result, materials flow, employees are efficient, and errors become more rare. Properly executed plans allow time to create a more perfect plan for the next production cycle. Unplanned changes in a master production schedule can be likened to an atomic bomb detonation — shock is transmitted throughout the shop. Everyone goes into a reactionary mode. Old materials are moved out; new materials are moved in. Incomplete work in process goes to temporary storage. Purchase orders and work orders are revised, cancelled, or expedited. Something gets cancelled when it should have been expedited. Production errors occur. Production falls short of daily quotas. Overtime is scheduled. Morale sags. The secondary response is that inventory expands. All of the responses to schedule fluctuations are cost incurring.

To fully understand the cost impact on a shop by an unplanned change, spend a few weeks managing such changes. The damage to the order and efficiency of manufacturing cannot be overstated. To avoid this type of damage, stabilize your master production schedule. To stabilize the schedule, you must find the root cause of the fluctuations and correct the cause. The root cause is unmanaged demand.

Unmanaged demand is erratic. Highly successful manufacturing companies have achieved some degree of stabilized demand. Demand management is comprised of four techniques working together.

1. Simplification of the product line. Fewer total products mean that demand is confined to more manageable swings. Forecasting a simplified product line tends to be more accurate.
2. Commitment to the forecast. Selling to meet forecast quantities results in both a stable demand and in planning that is adequate to meet the demand. Monetary sales incentives to hit the forecast target are appropriate.
3. Forecasting, selling, and producing less than the maximum the market will bear. In short, you will be turning down sales to preserve stability and control in your production department.
4. Price adjustments. You begin by being the cost and quality producer. You then have the margin to allow discounts to increase volume up to the forecast levels.

You may come across theories that claim the better option is to develop a flexible factory so you can build what the customer wants, when the customer orders it, and in the quantity the customer orders — even one at a time. For traditional repetitive manufacturing, that concept is unworkable. The cost of developing that kind of flexibility is normally beyond any realistic payback. Work to manage your demand and stabilize your master production schedule — that is where the gold mine is located.

After you have mastered cost control, quality, setup reduction, and demand management, you might examine the concept of creating a flexible factory with great caution. One-at-a-time production will normally increase your per-unit costs and will divert your attention from the basics of making a profit.

Create Efficient Department Layouts

There is a story about a company that wanted to find out how much labor time was wasted through unnecessary material handling. The company president tracked the normal movement of one part. The idea was that if the one part indicated excess handling, then a larger study should be undertaken. The president found that the one part was moved a total of 26 miles — and in a plant that was only one-quarter mile long! If a company doesn't have any idea of whether there is excess material handling, what does that tell you?

- ► Have these people spent any time on the shop floor?
- ► Did the engineers who designed the sequence of operations know where the machines were located?
- ► Did anyone ever spend ten minutes in the shop lunchroom to overhear complaints?
- ► Did anyone ever wonder why there was so much work-in-process inventory?
- ► Did anyone ever look at costs and wonder what was wrong?

Excess material handling is a root cause of excess costs that drives bloated inventories. It should never be studied; it should be prevented at the time the product is conceived — when machines are installed and when buildings are built.

A business should not wait until someone suggests a study to find out if there is excess material handling. Material handling is a major unproductive cost in any manufacturing operation. Every operations planning decision should be made with an awareness of its impact on material handling.

Look at the following example of an inefficient plant layout. This layout is inefficient because travel distances from subassembly to assembly

PROFIT POINTER

◄► 45 ◄►

are too long. Forklift travel is restricted. Many items will be hand carried through cluttered passages. While the inefficiencies may seem small at first, the general chaos results in both lost time and a decline in morale.

An Inefficient Plant Layout

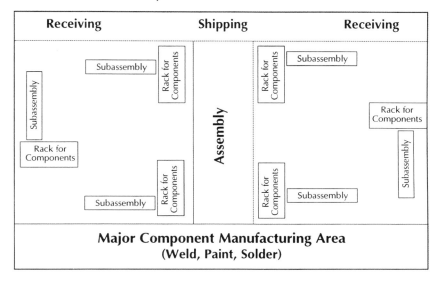

Now look at the following example of an efficient plant layout. This layout is efficient because travel distances are short. Subsequent operations are located in close proximity. Material storage areas are easily accessible by forklifts.

An Efficient Plant Layout

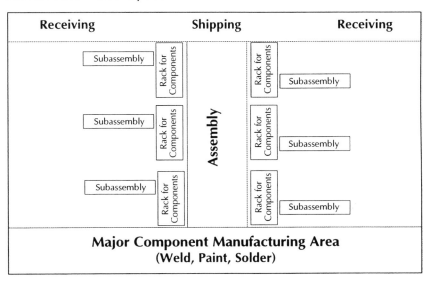

Departmental and plant layout can easily be costing you 50 percent in labor. An easy way to tell is to simply walk out into the shop and watch for three minutes. Count the number of people in your immediate field of vision who are doing direct work and count how many are walking somewhere. Do it ten times and average the number of people walking and the number of people working. Compare the two figures.

If you have 40 percent of your employees walking at any one time, then you can put all but five percent back to work by improving your department layout. If five percent of your employees are walking around, that is acceptable. Ask why employees must be walking instead of doing direct work. You will discover that those employees are trying to:

- ► Look for tools;
- ► Get materials;
- ► Find help to lift something;
- ► Locate someone to give them directions; or
- ► Tell someone about a problem.

Your job is to correct the causes of needless walking around. This task is usually simple and will cost you nothing. The trouble in American manufacturing is that most managers never take the time to correct the few simple, basic problems that lead to extravagant wasted motion. When you correct those simple problems, you will have a competitive advantage.

Control the Effects of Product Design

Eighty percent of your manufacturing costs are locked in. That means that 80 percent of your costs cannot be changed, no matter how carefully you manage inventories, labor, schedules, or quality. Product design accounts for 80 percent of the cost of a product over its lifetime. This cost is not just for materials. Materials costs are only a part of the total cost. Design determines the amount of labor required to build the product. Design determines the level of quality that is consistently attainable. To fully understand the profound difference that design makes in the cost of a product, consider the example of the designs of two competing products.

The first product is an old Western Electric touchtone telephone — a fine, reliable product. The second product is a Telko touchtone telephone with a pulse tone option and redial feature. The selling price of the Telko phone was about one-tenth the price of the Western Electric phone. If you disassemble and compare the two products, the comparison looks something like this:

PROFIT POINTER

◆ 46 ◆

Operations

Telko: Injection molding, soldering, assembly — a total of three operations stages.

Western Electric: Injection molding, soldering, assembly, screw machines, wire cutting/terminalization, zinc casting, rubber molding, sheet metal punching and forming, and riveting — a total of eleven operations stages.

Parts

Telko: A total of 85 parts.

Western Electric: A total of 79 parts, just in the keypad! In addition, this model has 19 parts in the metal base, 24 custom screws, 51 fabricated metal and composite parts, 34 wires and terminals, and 39 more miscellaneous parts — a total of 246 parts!

Just the parts count comparison implies that the Western Electric unit was three times as costly to build. But parts count alone is only part of the cost equation. The types of operations involved with the Western Electric units were nearly four times the number involved in building the Telko. When you think of the cost comparison, consider other cost factors, such as:

- ► Supervision
- ► Engineering problems
- ► Tooling maintenance
- ► Building size
- ► Work orders
- ► Stockroom shelving
- ► Opportunities for errors
- ► Material handling
- ► Physical inventories
- ► Skill levels required
- ► Inspections
- ► Drawings
- ► Engineering change orders

If you calculate a difficulty index to compare the two products, it would look something like this:

Difficulty Index Comparison

Telko: Operation types × number of parts (3 × 85) = 255

Western Electric: Operation types × number of parts (11 × 246) = 2,706

A ratio of difficulty comparing the two units indicates that the Western Electric unit should be 10.6 times as difficult (costly) as the Telko. The Western Electric unit costs almost exactly ten times the cost of the Telko unit.

Cost of production is directly related to the complexity of the design. A simple design equates to a design that costs less to build and requires much simpler efforts to produce reliably outstanding quality. Complex designs equal more cost, which equals greater selling price, which equals lost sales, which equal lost profits. If you have a complex design, begin a redesign for simplification now. In the competitive markets of today, you cannot afford the cost of a complex product. You can examine for excess design complexity in six areas.

1. Total numbers of products, models, accessories, or options;
2. Total numbers of parts required in the product. An initial design will typically contain 25 percent excess parts. There are cases in which the final parts count of the redesigned product was one-fourth of the original: 75 percent of the parts in the original design were excess;
3. Parts that overtax the capability of the available processes. Your process should be able to hold a dimensional (plus or minus) tolerance that is one-half (twice as tight) as your parts require;
4. Processes that overtax the skills of your workforce. Your process should be easily mastered by your normal employee under your normal training regimen. There will be exceptions, but keep them rare and under control;
5. Assembly. Some puzzling designs are difficult to assemble even when the parts are made correctly. Assembly should be straightforward. Expend your design efforts to make assembly procedures so obvious that little training is required; and
6. Stability. Engineering changes are costly. Make certain that your product is perfected before you release it to production.

Simplify and stabilize your product design. The cost benefits are probably beyond your imagination. Most of your competitors are not simplifying their designs. If you do, you will have one more competitive advantage in your favor.

Create Error-Proof Product Documentation

Employees are subject to human oversights and errors. The purpose of product documentation is to reduce the opportunities for oversight and

PROFIT POINTER

◆ 47 ◆

error. Consider the impact of improper documentation from the following example.

—————

Near the beginning of the second shift, a production employee asked the shift supervisor to approve a setup. The supervisor measured the length of the first part, a section of stainless steel tubing. The supervisor noted that the drawing for the part indicated a length dimension that ended in 5/8 of an inch. The supervisor noted that the routing form disagreed, showing a dimension that ended in 1/2 an inch. The supervisor was careful about errors and tried to determine the correct dimension.

One tube remained from a previous production run. The supervisor measured it — the dimension ended in 5/8 of an inch. That seemed to prove that the 5/8 of an inch dimension ending was correct. As a result, the supervisor approved the setup and the employee cut 300 tubes to length.

The tubes were cut one inch short which equaled $3,215 worth of scrap. There were additional costs, such as premium freight, overtime, delayed production, and general chaos. Technically, the supervisor was at fault — the setup was approved to cut the tubes at 27 5/8 inches when the correct dimension should have been 28 5/8 inches. The drawing was correct. But the supervisor's error was understandable. The routing and the drawing disagreed. The supervisor's attention was diverted from his primary responsibility — that of verifying that the machine was correctly set up — to an intense involvement in the investigation of the conflict between the drawing and the routing.

—————

This example is one of the best cases of the subtle manner in which product documentation can cause excess costs.

The engineering department made two errors. First, it included a dimension on the routing, which is a violation of standard practice. Routings tell how and where to make the part; drawings specify dimensions, materials, and tolerances. If a dimension is included on a routing, then the routing must be updated any time the drawing is updated. In the preceding example, the routing was never updated. The second error made by the engineering department is that it did not communicate the change via an engineering change order (ECO). One of the many purposes of the ECO is to call attention to the change. Without the ECO, harried production employees tend to make parts from memory even though the drawing has been updated.

A major complaint of engineering departments is that they are so pressed to make hurried product introductions that they never have time to design the product properly. That results in a flurry of changes after production starts. Their choices are to either flood the factory with trivial ECOs or refrain from issuing ECOs. To solve this problem, you can give the engineering department the time and resources to perfect designs to the point that they require few changes once production begins. Also, you must ensure that the engineering department knows how to properly document the product and communicate and control the documentation. Provide training if necessary.

There are several common documentation control errors that cause unnecessary cost.

Obsolete drawings in the shop

Obsolete drawings produce obsolete parts. Develop a system to assure that only current drawings are accessible.

Multiple configurations of the same part number

The source of this problem is an inadequate method of logging new part numbers. Part numbering is a science in itself. For more details on how to implement an effective part numbering system, refer to Profit Pointer 48.

Illegible dimensions

A misread dimension can cause thousands of dollars worth of excess cost in a matter of minutes. Errors due to misread dimensions are a daily occurrence; your job is to make sure illegible dimensions don't happen.

Drawing errors

As common as keystroke errors in typing, yet millions of times more costly, drawing errors will hurt your operation. Engineering drawings often go to production unchecked. Set up a system for error-proof drawings.

Too-tight or too-loose tolerances

Most engineering departments use a standard tolerance on the drawing title block. It is very common to leave the standard tolerance in effect even when it does not apply. For example, the shop might be expending great efforts to maintain a plus or minus 0.001 inch tolerance on a hole diameter that would function perfectly with a plus or minus 0.030 inch tolerance.

Just as often, engineering departments forget about the effects of tolerance buildup. The most absurd example is one in which the engineering department specified a lid of 18 inches (plus or minus $1/16$ of an inch) to fit inside an opening of 18 $1/8$ of an inch (plus or minus $1/16$ of an inch) with two $1/32$ of an inch (plus or minus $1/16$ of an inch) hinge bushings to fill the remaining gap. For this example to be workable as specified, the real tolerances would need to be plus or minus absolutely zero — an expensive tolerance to maintain.

Bills of materials (BOM) errors

A bill of materials (BOM) documents the content of a product. It helps assure that a product contains the correct materials. It aids the cost accounting department to calculate the cost of a product. The BOM is valuable in the case of product litigation.

BOM errors cause horrible ripple effect errors like work orders and purchase orders for incorrect parts, or too many or too few parts to support the real needs of production. The result is excess inventories and administrative labor. Materials requirement planning can send a manufacturer into total chaos due to a few minor errors in BOMs.

Make only one BOM per product and structure it as simply as possible. Test it for accuracy. The product engineering department should be responsible for creating, maintaining, and controlling all BOMs. The following illustration shows an ideal BOM.

Bill of Materials (BOM) Example

Bill of Materials	Part Number: *12-0034-1*			
	Description: *Corner Post, Painted*			
	Prepared by: *R.P. Johnson, Engineer*		Date: *Feb. 20, 1990*	

Part Number	Description	Quantity	Unit of Measure
10-0012-0	Steel, Cold Rolled, 12 gauge	3.60	lb.
11-0029-0	Bolt, NC, 3/8 x 1.0	4.00	ea.
11-0030-0	Nut, NC, 3/8	4.00	ea.
11-0031-0	Washer, Lock, 3/8	4.00	ea.
15-0006-0	Paint, Epoxy, Pearl White #222J	.006	gal.

Process instruction errors

Lack of or erroneous process instructions causes wasted time to determine correct methods, sequences, and tools. The more costly condition is one in which employees do not take the time to investigate correct methods, sequences, and tools. Process instructions are normally called routings. Routings should contain enough information — the sequence of operations, machines or tools to use, proper fixtures, and special instructions and techniques — to enable an employee to make a part correctly. A standard time for each operation should be included. Inadequate routings result in:

• Excess setup times;

• Setup errors with resultant scrap or machine breakage;

• Excess training time for new employees;

• Errors leading to warranty claims and liability exposure; and

• Errors in sequence that cause excess material handling and scrap.

Routings are used to facilitate production and to calculate product cost. A manufacturing or industrial engineering department creates, maintains, and controls routings. Cost reducing or otherwise improved methods are communicated via routings. Examine the following routing example. Notice the date and the sign-off by the engineer that prepared the routing. Both aid in keeping routings current and accurate.

Routing Example

Routing

Part Number: *12-0034-1*

Description: *Corner Post, Painted*

Prepared by: *R.P. Johnson, Engineer*   Date: *Feb. 13, 1990*

Op No.	Work Center	W.C. Desc	Task Description	Std. Hours
10	SH	Shear	Shear to drawing specs	0.001
20	LA	Laser	Laser cut to drawing See spec. 23-A	0.012
30	BR	Brake	Brake to program #456 Use small die	0.100
40	PR	Prep	Prepare for epoxy paint	0.100
50	PA	Paint	Paint to current color Dry 24 hours	0.100

Develop a User-Friendly Part Numbering System

A part numbering system has a subtle impact on costs. You probably have never heard of a manufacturer that assigns responsibility for a cost-incurring error on a part number. But rest assured, an inept part numbering system will cause errors that are frequently attributed to human failings. You will avoid four common errors if you develop a user-friendly part numbering system.

Order entry errors

Part numbers that exceed eight digits are difficult for the human brain to process. Alpha-numeric combinations require change-overs from the numeric keypad to the alpha keyboard. Every change invites error. Varying lengths of part numbers violate the rhythm developed by data entry personnel. Part numbers should all be the same length, even if zeros must be used as placeholders. One order entry error can cause an incorrect shipment. If you calculate the accompanying customer dissatisfaction, return, and reshipment, you will find a costly and inefficient result.

Order picking errors

Part numbers that exceed eight digits lead to order picking errors. Look at the following example of a proper stock code format. This example simplifies the mental image of the part number, vastly reducing the opportunity for normal human errors in processing. The number of digits in any of the prefix, body, or suffix may be modified to suit the needs of your business. Try to keep the total number of digits at seven or less.

Stock Code Format Example – 92-012-0

Major Group: **9**2-012-0. The major group is a large grouping of like types of stock items. Finished goods is an example of a large grouping. Ten major groups (0–9) may be assigned.

Subgroup: 9**2**-012-0. The subgroup is a subdivision within a major group. Finished goods may be subdivided into subgroups. Ten subgroups (0–9) may be assigned within each major group.

Body: 92-**012**-0. The body of the stock code is assigned in numeric order as items are created, with no significance attached to lower or higher numbers. Up to 999 items are available within each major group/subgroup designation.

Revision Code: 92-012-**0**. The revision code is changed each time the item is revised significantly. A change that disallows indiscriminate mixing of new and old items requires an update of the revision code. Ten revisions are allowed by the system.

Engineering change orders and revisions

Dealers who stock service parts are often in total dismay at the difficulty of handling a revised service part. The new and old parts are often physically separated by rows of intervening part numbers. In such a case, most dealers don't even try to maintain an orderly system. Multitudes of errors in ordering and stocking result. Unless aided by a friendly part numbering system, sales personnel in your own plant may be stymied by engineering change orders (ECOs) and revisions.

In plants plagued by frequent ECOs, sales personnel may simply enter an order for whatever they remember and hope for the best — not a guarantee of perfect customer service. Service parts are often different from the same parts used in production. For instance, a replacement blower motor may be packaged with instructions and new fasteners to assure proper installation. A user-friendly part numbering system will assist order entry personnel in ordering the packaged component rather than the raw component used in production.

Two part numbers for the same part

Duplication of part numbers might happen when an engineer can't quickly locate a number for a specific item, so a new number is assigned for an existing item. When that happens, you have one more stock keeping unit (SKU) to control — and double the inventory of that item. A systematic technique described in the previous stock code format example will prevent double entries.

Each time a new stock keeping unit is introduced, assign a part number. Document the assignment in a log similar in design to the one located at the end of this chapter. Divide the log into orderly sections — one section per part number prefix. As you properly divide the sections, you group like items together for quick visual reference. Quick visual reference allows a design engineer to determine at a glance whether an item already exists as a part number. If not, an engineer can write the new description in the log in the next available space.

Write descriptions so that the dominant noun is the first word of the description. The dominant modifier should be the second word. Such description-writing techniques result in like items grouping together in computer searches by description. For example, the description of a half-inch diameter, four-inch long, stainless steel bolt should be written as:

Bolt, stainless steel, .5" $\times$ 4.0"

Computer reports and searches based on such a descriptive technique will:

- ▶ Group all bolts together;
- ▶ Subgroup all stainless steel bolts together; and
- ▶ Further subgroup all 0.5 inch stainless steel bolts together.

With such grouping techniques, finding a specific bolt on the list is very quick and error-resistant.

You can use a revision log to record revisions to a base part number. The base number will always end in a hyphen followed by a zero. Then, as necessary record the first revision to the base number as -1; the second as -2, and so on. This revision technique groups all revised parts together with the base part in all reports, on warehouse shelves, and on dealer shelves. An example of such revision grouping looks like this:

Revision Group Example

51-1234-0   Bolt stainless steel, .5" × 4.0"

51-1234-1   Bolt stainless steel, .5" × 4.0", Type 304

51-1234-2   Bolt stainless steel, .5" × 4.0", Type 316

Samples of a completed revision log and a stock code log are located at the end of this chapter.

Most of your competitors will never dedicate the resources to set up such a system. Further, they will have an internal resistance to the disciplines required to perpetually maintain such a system. It follows that they will experience errors in customer service, internal errors, and excess costs. When you develop an orderly, user-friendly, error-prevention system, you will have a competitive advantage.

Chapter Recap

The energy that you put into reducing labor costs will provide your company with multiple side benefits. For example, you will find that your cycle time from order to delivery of your product becomes quicker. Shorter cycle times result in lower inventories, improved customer service, and ultimately, higher profits.

You will also discover that the orderly procedures you have aimed at labor cost reduction have a quality-enhancing effect: you will experience fewer errors, less rework, and a lower scrap rate. The result is lower costs of materials and fewer warranty claims.

Further, shorter cycle times and lower inventory result in reduced requirements for total floorspace. Companies that have implemented the recommendations of this chapter have been able to increase production by as much as 50 percent while reducing total square footage by 50 percent.

Most businesses are a complex and interrelated set of systems. You will find that, as you organize and improve in one area, other areas become more efficient. When you have made multiple improvements in multiple areas, a synergy will evolve that results in a self-perpetuating spiral of benefits to costs, quality, productivity, and employee morale. Management tasks will become simpler as company processes smooth into a continuous flow of product and cash.

Stock Code Log Example

Group: _51_

Types of items in this group: _BOLTS, STAINLESS STEEL (SS)_

Group	Body	Rev.	Description (maximum ___ characters)	Rev. Date
51	001	O	BOLT, SS, .25 × .75	8-16-97
51	002	O	BOLT, SS, .25 × 1.00	
51	003	O	BOLT, SS, .25 × 1.25	
51	004	O	BOLT, SS, .25 × 1.50	
51	005	O	BOLT, SS, .25 × 1.75	
51	006	O	BOLT, SS, .25 × 2.0	
51	007	O	BOLT, SS, .375 × 1.00	
51	008	O	BOLT, SS, .375 × 1.25	
51	009	O	BOLT, SS, .375 × 1.50	
51	010	O	BOLT, SS, .375 × 1.75	

Revision Log Example

Group: _51_

Old Stock Code	Description of Change [Use as much space as necessary.]	New Stock Code
51-001-0	Use Type 304 alloy. Add "Type 304" to description.	
	Reason is to prevent varying alloys in purchasing.	51-001-1

CHAPTER 9

REDUCE MATERIALS COSTS

Twenty percent of all gold is on the surface. The greater wealth is found by looking where others have stopped looking.

You are probably spending more money than is necessary for materials. When you find and eliminate a dollar of excess costs, that dollar goes straight to the bottom line — profit. Even better, every dollar saved in materials costs is saved repeatedly every time you buy.

Most businesses, including your competition, believe that they are keeping materials costs at the lowest possible level. By doing this, they are usually thinking of the purchase price as the only component of materials costs. You can best understand the "other-than-purchase-price" components of materials costs by asking a series of questions. Ask yourself:

- ▸ Is the material really needed in our product or service? In other words, can we redesign to eliminate the material, reduce the quantity of material, or substitute a less costly material?

- ▸ Do we waste material? Material can be wasted by freight damage, damage in storage, errors in processing, or by raw materials sizes and quantities that lead to discarded leftovers.

- ▸ Do our materials specifications induce extra internal processing costs? Are we saving $1.00 in materials costs only to add $1.25 in additional processing costs? Are we buying expensive capital equipment that would be unnecessary if we paid a few cents more for material?

► Does our purchase price include price add-ons that result from our own demands on our suppliers? Do we require suppliers to hold large inventories from which we can draw on short notice? Do we place other costly demands upon our suppliers that can only result in price increases?

► Do we overstock material? Overstocks result in escalated storage costs, spoilage, loss, obsolescence, and additional handling.

► Do we understock material? Understocks induce cost increases in nonmaterial areas. Understocking interrupts the production flow, which ultimately results in premium freight costs, overtime, missed deliveries, and lower total production flow. If understocking is deliberate — deliberate understocking is in vogue as a method of keeping inventory investment low — you will have escalated overhead costs of planning and administration to order small quantities at the last minute.

► Are we buying components that we can make in house at a lower cost?

Keep the above questions in mind as you read this chapter. The goal is to recognize what cost-causing conditions you may be able to rectify. Your task is to create a set of conditions that will minimize the burden on your suppliers — which will result in lower purchase pricing — and to eliminate costs that are caused by inadequate materials flow, storage, transportation, or specifications.

Implement Total Quality Management

Profit Pointer

◆ 49 ◆

Total quality management (TQM) is a set of disciplines that will provide you with results that exceed "just" quality. TQM requires you to look deeply into your processes and practices. When you take that deep look, you will find many opportunities to reduce costs associated with materials. You will also find the practices that improve quality will frequently reduce the costs associated with materials as a happy byproduct. You can expect to reduce several materials related costs with a TQM program.

Reduced inspection cost
TQM will eliminate the need for most inspections of materials. As you eliminate the causes of quality defects — both internally and from suppliers — you will find that inspections are unnecessary because they will find no defects.

Prevention of scrap and rework

As you improve the quality of incoming material and of items produced internally, you will prevent the cost of losses due to scrap and rework.

Avoidance of defective product

You will experience reduced costs as a result of reduced warranty claims. Reduced warranty claims mean that you will realize a reduction of the associated costs of return freight, processing of claims, and the subsequent costs of the recovery of customer goodwill.

The goal of TQM is to reduce total manufacturing costs while increasing your level of customer satisfaction. Direct materials costs and materials-associated costs are the prime cost benefits of TQM. Numerous books exist that explain the details of total quality management. Get a good one — thin and concise — and begin a total quality management plan right away.

PROFIT POINTER

◅ 50 ▻

Reduce Associated Costs

Price is the most noticed and the least controllable factor in materials costs. Most of your competitors place their efforts on controlling materials costs by attempting to manipulate the prices they pay. Manipulating prices can — and usually does — backfire. Consider the following true story.

"I just saved this company $52,000 this year alone." The excited announcement came from a novice buyer who had negotiated a deal with a new steel supplier. The price was about seven percent lower than the company had been paying. There were only a few difficulties, that were easy to overcome, such as:

- *Larger order requirements with a two-week leadtime;*
- *A shed to house the larger inventories that costs $28,000;*
- *Racks to keep the steel off the floor that cost $12,000;*
- *Another forklift to handle the heavier shipped weights that costs $12,000;*
- *Additional material handling time to transfer steel into the main shop;*
- *Carrying cost on the additional $50,000 of inventory due to larger order requirements and longer leadtimes;*
- *A little extra labor to grind the rust pits out of the steel that costs $15,000 annually; and*
- *Some extra time in the shot blaster to remove the grind marks.*

*Beyond those few predicted and unpredicted costs, a few prob-
lems cropped up. An engineering change made one size of raw
steel obsolete. With a two-week leadtime, the order could not
be cancelled.*

*The company struggled for over a year to figure out an eco-
nomic way to use $5,200 worth of steel. In addition, the pre-
vious supplier announced a five percent price reduction a few
days after the purchasing manager had negotiated the seven
percent lower cost. So the savings from the new supplier
amounted to only two percent, or $15,000. The cost to "save"
that $15,000 amounted to $67,000 in the first year — a net
loss of $42,000!*

Every decision made by the novice buyer seemed perfectly reasonable at the time it was made, with the information at hand. However,
there are more factors to successful purchasing that just unit price. You
are far better off to establish a close, lasting working relationship with a
local supplier.

Anytime you consider changing suppliers, make a detailed analysis of unexpected impacts on costs in unpredictable areas. Check the following list of specific cost concerns when switching to a new supplier to
see how a change would affect your business.

Inventory
You will need to ask yourself if suppliers will deliver in such a
timely manner that your own inventories can be kept low. High
inventories equal higher costs.

Freight
If a new supplier offers you a lower unit cost, look to see if it
will make up the difference in freight charges.

Flexibility
Make sure the supplier can respond to your normal scheduling
fluctuations. If not, the price you pay for overtime and premium
freight can quickly override any savings. If you have schedules
that change quickly, you need a local supplier who can respond
at an equally fast pace. Otherwise, you will be plagued with
excess inventory and missed deliveries.

Quality
You need to be able to use run-of-the-mill product from your
supplier without the need for a piece-by-piece inspection. In the

example cited earlier, the new steel supplier would slip in occasional batches of undersized steel. As a result, the company had to inspect every shipment piece-by-piece. The supplier always replaced the steel, but the cost of inspection and the delays to production were not reimbursed.

Too many suppliers

The standard purchasing practice of shopping around for the best price will always lead to a large number of suppliers — some active, some inactive. Reducing the total number of suppliers will both increase supplier goodwill (due to increased dollar volumes) and reduce the administrative workload in the purchasing, receiving, and accounts payable departments. Incoming freight costs will trend downward also.

Long pipelines

If your supplier is located somewhere across the country, you will have to support what is called a pipeline inventory. You pay the cost of the inventory whether it is officially in your ownership or not. Plus, you have the increased threat of late deliveries, loss, or damage. Sooner or later you will incur the cost of a late delivery, loss, or damage due to an interrupted schedule. Keep your pipelines as short as possible to avoid extra costs.

Purchasing for lowest associated cost means that you must be aware of all the elements of cost; the price being only one of those elements. Many of your competitors will always attempt to control only the price and will overlook those elements of materials costs that are more controllable. Focus on reducing associated costs and you will have a competitive advantage.

Optimize Product Design

Most companies are likely to overspecify components or materials. The reasoning used is that the cost of an overspecified material is less than the cost of warranty claims due to widespread product failure as a result of insufficient testing. This reasoning is correct — so do the sufficient testing rather than overspecify the material. You can easily pay 50 percent more than is necessary for materials and components that are failure-proof.

If such perfect longevity is not required by the customer, take the time to find and test the componentry that will provide the proper service life. The savings are worth the effort.

Further, don't release a product with failure-proof componentry and then downgrade. Your customers will complain because of your penny-pinching ways. The bigger cost is in the engineering changes required to change components. You should also think of the service part inventories you will create. The correct way to optimize materials specifications is to provide enough leadtime for the product engineering department to fully test and refine a design. Let someone else be first to the market with a product that is overspecified, undertested, and too costly.

Product design can increase materials costs in a variety of other ways. The parts count, for example, increases cost. Every part that is eliminated through a design refinement results in an elimination of the part itself, plus the costs of ordering the part, monitoring the status of the order, receiving the part, paying the invoice, and all the costs of controlling the inventory. Most product designs can be simplified to require fewer and less costly materials.

Control Capital Expenditures

PROFIT POINTER

◄꙲► 52 ◄꙲►

The issue of unjustified capital expenditures needs significant attention in every small business. Unjustified means that the expenditure is made without calculating a payback. The kind of payback calculation that you should prepare is a careful analysis of all the costs of the proposed expenditure compared to all the real benefits. A blank Capital Expenditure Justification form is located at the end of this chapter for your use. The initial payback calculation is best made by someone who has the time, analytical ability, and motivation to do a flawless job. That person is normally not a business owner or top manager. Such calculations are normally the task of an industrial/manufacturing engineer. Once the calculations are complete, the justification should be reviewed by a higher authority. The final review should ◆ be made by the person who is responsible for making the final decision to write the check, such as the president or top manager.

You may already understand the need to do an excellent job of justifying capital production equipment. But what about a roof repair or a computer? Do you justify a new warehouse or new factory building? How about an additional staff person? American manufacturers add staff personnel based on uncalculated justifications. An increased workload may not mean you need another employee. Any major expenditure should be justified by calculating a payback. That rule includes new staff additions, more computers, new software, bigger warehouses, and roof repairs. A cost-to-savings ratio should be calculated for every proposed expenditure. Examine the cost calculations in the following CNC laser justification example.

CNC Laser Justification Example

Initial Costs

New CNC metal-cutting laser	$385,000
Freight	5,000
Installation	5,000
Operator training	3,000
Liquid oxygen tank and other hardware	10,000
Programming and setup	3,000
Total	$411,000
Multiplied by 110% for contingencies	$452,000

Annual Operational Costs

Expendable supplies [$22 per hour per 1,500 hours]	$33,000
Engineering support [estimated 300 hours]	6,000
Routine maintenance and repair (manufacturer's estimate)	5,000
Operator's wages (per year)	22,000
Total	$66,000
Multiplied by 110% for contingencies	$73,000

Annual Savings

Subcontract charges for Laser cutting [22 items x 6,000 pieces x $2 each]	$264,000
Purchasing and receiving costs	4,000
Incoming freight	6,000
Total	$274,000

Overall Payback Calculation

Annual savings	$274,000
Annual operational costs	73,000
Total Annual Savings	$199,000
Less corporate tax on additional profit (50%)	99,500
Total Annual Savings	$99,500

In this example, the calculation would be $452,000 divided by $99,500 for a ratio of 4.54:1. It would take 4 1/2 years of operation to begin seeing real profits from the investment. Understanding the full meaning of payback time can have a sobering effect on the heady excitement of buying a new technical masterpiece. For instance, you must ask yourself whether the purchase will conflict with preexisting plans for the timespan in question and whether the products that generate the savings will still exist in 4 1/2 years. Consider whether the machine will need a costly overhaul during that time or whether it will become obsolete.

After you have determined a payback ratio, compare the payback to other capital projects under consideration. See the Capital Expenditure Prioritization form at the end of this chapter. When you list the proposed projects in payback order, you can decide at a glance how many projects you can finance and stay within your budget. You will gain the maximum payback per budget dollar spent using this method.

Make More and Buy Less

PROFIT POINTER

◆ 53 ◆

"We can't afford to make it ourselves. It is cheaper to buy it." This comment was made by a manufacturing engineer who regularly authorized make-buy decisions. Notice the deeper meaning behind this comment. The implication was that even with a substantial profit, plus freight, an outside source could make the part at a lower cost than the engineer's own plant.

You can make a theoretical comparison to see if this assumption is correct. The average manufacturer in America might have a cost breakdown like this on a $10.00 part:

Cost Breakdown of a Typical $10.00 Part

Materials	$6.50
Overhead	$2.00
Labor	$1.50

An outside shop will incur nearly the same materials cost as your own shop, so little or no savings is available on the $6.50 materials cost. If the outside shop is more efficient than your own shop, then it may be able to spend only $0.75 on labor. Also, the outside shop can possibly save on overhead costs and spend only $1.00 per part. The total cost for an outside shop might be as low as $8.25. The outside shop will then add a markup! If it makes a normal 40 percent profit on the work, then the price you will pay will have to be $13.78! Even with half the cost of labor and overhead, an outside shop will charge more for the part. You can even try to refigure the cost with dramatically lower costs to see the same scenario. Assume the outside shop is so efficient that it doesn't have any labor or overhead costs. The total cost to the supplier is the $6.50 materials cost. But, then if you add a 40 percent profit, you will get $10.86 — still not cheaper than your cost of making the product.

For an outside supplier to be able to provide a component at a lower cost than your own cost for a $10.00 component, then it must be able to buy the materials for only $6.00 (eight percent lower than your cost), provide labor and materials at no cost, and then deliver it for free! This is not a likely scenario. If you find that your internal cost is higher than the cost of buying the component made by an outside supplier, then either:

- ▶ Your labor and overhead functions are desperately inefficient, and your purchasing practices are costing more than your supplier; or
- ▶ Your methods of assigning costs are wrong. You mistakenly think that your costs are higher than they really are.

Both situations are so common that you would be wise to assume that you have both desperate inefficiency and incorrect costing. If you have many items made by outside shops because you believe that their price to you is lower than your internal costs of producing the items — you are probably wrong and it is probably costing you.

You should make anything that is required for your product that you have the equipment and skill to do. Also, make anything for which you can develop the skill and justify the equipment. A rule of thumb is that anything that is unique to your product is something that you should make in house. Exceptions are items that are low in cost and volume and require expensive equipment or skills that are difficult to develop. Your best bet is to restrict your purchases to:

- ▶ Commodity items, such as tires, resistors, bolts, ballpoint pens, tape, nails, bearings, v-belts, pulleys, shafts, hoses, fittings, boxes, wheels, terminals, cylinders, and rivets;
- ▶ Materials, such as welding rods, sheet metal, paint, glass, wire, paper, rope, tubing, composites, adhesives, chemicals, gaskets, insulation, raw plastic, and steel;
- ▶ Low-volume parts requiring high-cost capital equipment, like a laser-cut part if you only use such a few that you cannot justify buying your own laser; castings; plated parts, and sometimes, injection-molded parts; and
- ▶ Low-volume parts that require unique operations, such as printed labels, engines, or motors, or parts that require expensive capital equipment or special facilities to produce.

Entirely too many American manufacturers buy components that they should be making in house. An emerging trend is to make only what is easiest for you and buy the rest. Don't believe it — every item that is unique to your product that you buy costs you 40 to 50 percent more than if you make it in house. You should develop the skills and buy the equipment to make the things that may be difficult to master. Doing well what others fail to attempt is a competitive advantage.

Chapter Recap

You can achieve a significant competitive advantage by reducing materials costs. Most of your competitors are either ignoring materials costs entirely or they are focusing on the purchase price and failing to consider the more controllable costs in other areas that are influenced by materials. Further, many of your competitors will follow the trend of outsourcing — buying rather than making components.

When you have developed pro-profit suppliers, as described in Chapter 4, you and your suppliers can work as a team to bring down the total cost of materials. Remember, you may actually pay a higher purchase price to bring down the total cost of materials.

Capital Expenditure Justification

Fill in the blanks to determine the annual return on a planned expenditure. Attach backup documents to explain the details. Planned expenditures must be approved by top managers.

_____

Project Description

Describe the project: _____

_____ Date of planned purchase: _____

Installation Capital Required

Equipment price: _____

Freight to plant: _____

Installation labor (subcontract): _____

Training of operator(s): _____

Other: _____   Total installation capital: _____

Annual Cost Savings [attach details]

Labor savings: _____

Materials savings: _____

Outside services savings: _____

Production and sales increases [show the anticipated sales and profits]: _____

Utilities savings: _____

Maintenance and repair savings: _____

Tooling savings: _____

Supplies savings: _____

Other savings: _____ _____   Total savings: _____

Annual Repetitive Costs [attach details]

Annual tooling costs: _____

Annual utilities costs: _____

Additional staff support: _____

Operator(s) wages: _____

Annual depreciation: _____

Maintenance costs (labor): _____

Maintenance costs (parts): _____

Special supplies costs: _____

Cost of money (interest): _____

Other: _____ _____   Total costs: _____

Total Gross Annual Savings [subtract total costs from total savings]   _____

Corporate tax of _____% from total gross annual savings [subtract]   _____

Net Annual Savings   _____

Return on Investment [divide net annual savings by total installation capital]   _____%

Capital Expenditure Prioritization

Prioritize expenditure proposals based on return on investment (ROI). The project with the highest ROI goes at the top of the list. The rest are ranked in descending order. The capital available for projects should be utilized to attain the highest ROI. The result is that you will maximize profits for the least possible cost.

Project	Savings	Cost	ROI
Example: Make part #66-0123 in house	$118,000	$17,500	674.0%
Example: New layout for assembly	55,000	9,500	579.0
Example: CNC laser	62,000	398,000	15.6

Project	Savings	Cost	ROI

PART IV

ACTION ITEMS

The greater load is no relief to the faltering beast. The wise master has thought for tomorrow and lightens the load of today.

Action is the heart of turning around business profits. More important than action, however, is the ability to predict the results of a given action. A common error in business management is to initiate a lot of action, keep doing what works well, and quit doing what doesn't work well. Such an approach is called reactionary management. Reactionary management waits for a crisis to present itself, then works overtime to apply corrective measures until one of them works.

Reactionary management wastes resources and demoralizes employees. It is inefficient and costly. If you use reactionary management, your business' costs stay high and final pricing of products must stay high to cover those costs. A business under reactionary management is highly vulnerable to recessions or other unfavorable business world events. Such a business is volatile and unpredictable.

A more effective method of managing your business is called planned response management. In the mode of planned response management, you will initiate action only after you have predicted the full range of results. The full range of results includes what happens immediately as a result of your action (the primary effect) and the permanent changes that ultimately affect the profits of tomorrow (the secondary response).

When you incorporate planned response management, you will realize two advantages. First, you will predict and plan your actions many months ahead of your competitors, who are most likely using reactionary management. Second, you will chart a business path that is different from your competitors, all of whom are locked into reactionary responses to the business environment. Since they are all reacting to the same sets of stimuli, their responses will be similar and their business paths will be similar.

Parts I through III of this book have given you a foundation of knowledge of human nature, organizational principles, and profit concepts. Part IV details specific dollars-and-cents actions that you can take to enhance profits or turn around a business that is unprofitable. The actions of Part IV are actions that are reliable — they will enhance your profits with little or no risk.

Chapter 10

PRICE FOR MAXIMUM PROFIT

Answers abound. The more glorious the answer, the greater the fanfare. Correct answers, however, are lonely; rejected for their commonality.

Pricing that is too low stimulates great sales volumes but delivers little profit. Pricing that is too high delivers great per-item profit but will cut into sales volumes and will ultimately erode total profit. Your task is to discover the right price for your product that will deliver the maximum total profit.

Since pricing affects the volumes of your product or service that customers buy, pricing affects the volumes that you produce as well as the volumes of materials and parts that you buy. Higher volumes generally equate to lower costs, which result in higher profit.

Pricing, sales volumes, costs, and ultimate profit have an imprecise relationship. It follows that they are probably the most difficult-to-manage aspect of your business.

One company, for example, initiated a marketing campaign aimed at doubling market share. The marketing campaign was a huge success, with sales doubling as predicted. But, its profits did not double. The marketing campaign was enormously expensive. The doubled sales volume overtaxed the production facility resulting in inefficiency, quality failings, high scrap rates, and excess overtime. When all the costs were accounted, the company had not only failed to show an increase in profits, it had realized a substantial loss. The profit pointers in this chapter will help you price your products and services for maximum profitability over the long term.

Use Function-Driven Costing to Provide Real Costs

Across the nation every day, companies are making more products than ever before, making more sales than ever before, and working more hours than ever before — yet they are making lower profits than ever before. They cannot determine why, so they cannot take remedial action. The fundamental flaw is their use of standard accounting practices to drive manufacturing decisions. To understand the flaw, consider the power of correct cost information.

Costing products independently will provide you with a competitive advantage. Today, very few businesses use any type of correct product costing. As a result, incorrect decisions are made on the basis of incorrect costing. These businesses are operating at a competitive disadvantage — they are flying blind. To arrive at correct cost data, use the cost of the functions — machines, facilities, and workforce — that are actually required to manufacture each product line.

Consider the costs of each part of each function; then, think in terms of the secondary effects of the costs.

- ▶ A thousand square feet of building area costs more than a hundred.
- ▶ A CNC punch press costs more per hour than a hammer.
- ▶ A machine that requires engineering support costs more than one that doesn't.
- ▶ Highly skilled operators cost more than manual labor.

Conventional costing loads every hour of direct labor with an overhead figure — whether the actual function being performed requires a higher-than-average or lower-than-average amount of the real overhead is disregarded. Overhead per working hour loading does not give a correct cost picture for components nor for completed products. Incorrect management decisions are the inevitable result!

Using the actual, functional costs to calculate product cost is called function-driven costing (FDC). Function-driven costing means that you cost a product according to the costs of the functions required to make it. Take a close look at the differences between function-driven and conventional costing in the following illustration.

Function-Driven Costing versus Conventional Costing

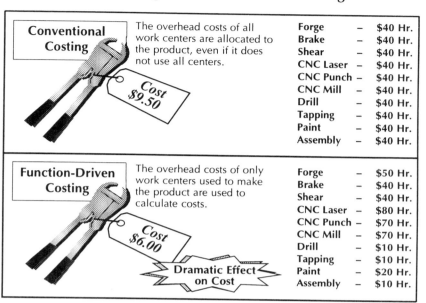

| Conventional Costing | The overhead costs of all work centers are allocated to the product, even if it does not use all centers. | Forge – $40 Hr.
Brake – $40 Hr.
Shear – $40 Hr.
CNC Laser – $40 Hr.
CNC Punch – $40 Hr.
CNC Mill – $40 Hr.
Drill – $40 Hr.
Tapping – $40 Hr.
Paint – $40 Hr.
Assembly – $40 Hr. |

Cost $9.50

| Function-Driven Costing | The overhead costs of only work centers used to make the product are used to calculate costs. | Forge – $50 Hr.
Brake – $40 Hr.
Shear – $40 Hr.
CNC Laser – $80 Hr.
CNC Punch – $70 Hr.
CNC Mill – $70 Hr.
Drill – $10 Hr.
Tapping – $10 Hr.
Paint – $20 Hr.
Assembly – $10 Hr. |

Cost $6.00

Dramatic Effect on Cost

Function-driven costing will allow your business to calculate product costs in a manner that closely approximates reality. Conventional costing can lead to significant costing miscalculations. In addition, function-driven costing allows you to learn what products are truly profitable and what products are not profitable.

The knowledge will lead to pricing changes and changes in your sales and marketing strategies. Calculating the true effects on costs that results from additions of capital intensive high-technologies can be revealing using FDC. Management decisions are highly affected by FDC.

Integration of FDC is simple if you have a good computer-based manufacturing control system. In such a system, you simply load the real cost of running a work center into the work center file. The system uses time standards (or reported actuals) to calculate a function-driven cost for every component and product. You should use FDC as a base for making decisions of what to do to increase profits.

You will find that as you begin to do a few things correctly, each decision or process begins to complement the other. Subsequent improvements get easier and they contribute more profit with each effort. Remember the discussion on routings from Profit Pointer 47? Function-driven costing is based on routings. Good routings make FDC a snap. To arrive at a function-driven cost, answer the following questions.

▶ What is done? Know every move and operation. Good routings answer this question.

▶ How many minutes of each function are required? Routings answer this question.

▶ How much do those minutes cost? You must calculate this. But, once it is calculated, it stays the same until there is a measurable change.

Then, determine the wage and benefits of the employee who normally performs the function and the actual cost of operating the machine. What percentage of the facility cost is dedicated to the machine? To calculate the percent of facility overhead to allocate to a given machine or work center, use the following logic.

▶ Measure the square feet of floorspace required to operate the machine or work center.

▶ Divide that number by the total square feet of the facility. The quotient is the percent of total floorspace required.

▶ Use the percent figure to multiply your total facility costs to learn the dollars per year required for the machine or work center in question.

Percent of Facility Overhead

% of total square feet of facility = the same % of total facility cost

When you have arrived at the dollars per year required to operate the machine or work center, divide that total by the number of hours you expect to operate the machine or work center. Your answer is the dollars per hour of cost that you should allocate.

Because it will change your understanding of your real costs, function-driven costing will make dramatic reversals in your decision making. For example, once you know your real cost of making a component, you will have a better idea of the real cost of not making the component. This knowledge will vastly improve your make-buy decisions. Your competitors rarely use anything that approaches the decision making support offered by function-driven costing. With an imaginative effort, you can use their lack of costing know-how to your advantage.

Function-Driven Costing Compared to Activity-Based Costing

If you have studied activity-based costing (ABC), you will immediately see similarities between ABC and FDC. The foundational concepts are the same. Activity-based costing is more detailed than function-driven costing.

FDC properly assigns manufacturing costs. ABC assigns all costs of all functions, including things like administrative overhead and travel. While ABC provides a more perfect cost picture, its implementation is more demanding than you may care to attempt. FDC is a great first step for businesses that wish to implement ABC in the future. FDC may prove to provide all the cost detail you may ever need.

PROFIT POINTER

❧ 55 ❧

Diagnose Insufficient Pricing

In today's tough business environment of escalating prices, you may find it hard to believe that any company has products with prices that are too low — but it does happen. To find out if your prices are too low, look at your order backlog. Determine whether your orders are backed up for a period that exceeds the leadtime of your incoming material. Look for a factor of at least one and one-half times your leadtime. If this condition currently exists, then your pricing may be too low.

You can also look at your incoming order rate. Calculate an average for the past year to smooth seasonal variations. If your history of incoming orders exceeds your demonstrated capacity to produce, you have pricing that is too low. Question your salespeople to find out if they experience customer complaints due to a long leadtime before delivery. If so, consider it as an indicator of pricing that is too low. Do you have order cancellations due to long leadtimes? If so, you should consider that as another indicator that your pricing is too low. Further, insufficient profits indicate pricing that is possibly too low.

Insufficient profits, long leadtimes, and an incoming order rate that exceeds production capacity are all tell-tale signs of pricing that is too low. However, before you raise prices make sure you know why your pricing is low. Before you hike prices, read the rest of this chapter. You need to fully understand why your prices are low before you take action.

PROFIT POINTER

❧ 56 ❧

Diagnose Excessive Pricing

Insufficient profits can be an indicator of pricing that is too high; excessively high pricing cuts into sales volumes, thereby reducing your economy of scale and, in turn, escalating costs. You might think that the indicators of excessive pricing would be the opposite of insufficient pricing, but such is not always the case. For example, if you have a very short backlog of orders (less than your component leadtime), the condition could be because you have insufficient pricing while concurrently running at less than full capacity.

Pricing that is too high can be best recognized by two comparisons. First, compare your sales levels to what they were before your last price increase. If your sales levels have dropped you may have reached a point of buyer resistance. Second, compare your profits to what they were before your last price increase. If the net result of your last price increase is falling profits and falling sales volumes, then you have excessive pricing.

Avoid the error of increasing your sales and marketing effort when sales and profits begin to drop. Such increased efforts are costly and produce unpredictable effects. At best, you will experience roller-coaster swings of sales with swings in production schedules. Efficiency levels will decrease, inventories will increase, and your error rate will escalate. Two proper approaches to diagnosing excessive pricing exist.

The Preventative Approach

An ounce of prevention is worth a pound of what-do-we-do-now. You should stay close to your customer base so you can predict the response to a given price increase. Maintain a focus on cost control so that you are last in line to increase prices. Once your costs are out of line and you escalate prices to cover out-of-control costs, you have started a cycle that will consummate in high prices, buyer resistance, high sales costs, and faltering profits. Customers will accept price increases that mirror the effects of inflation. Price increases that stay within the bounds of inflation are acceptable.

The Reactive Approach

When you are losing profits because of excessive pricing, the remedy is to lower prices. Be careful — your first response is to get your costs under control so that you have an adequate margin that will allow a price reduction. When you reduce prices, you will gain sales and total profits. You will find that control of costs is the foundational remedy again and again.

Listen to Customer Complaints

You may be sensitive to customer complaints about pricing. As discussed in Chapter 3, you should always be aware of the attitude of your customers. But realize that customers will always try to press prices down. If you are the lowest-priced contender, you will still have complaints about pricing. If you have kept pricing low due to customer complaints and you have the indicators of insufficient pricing, then you should raise prices. Before you make any pricing adjustments, be sure to read about pricing rules and strategies in Profit Pointer 62 at the end of this chapter.

PROFIT POINTER

⊰ 57 ⊱

Remedy Poor Quality

Poor quality irritates and repels customers; they will expect a price concession to make up for poor quality. You must provide a high-quality product before your customers will be receptive to a price increase. Your competitors are quick to declare that they have excellent quality. For you to have a unique competitive advantage, adopt the opposite attitude — assume that your products' quality needs significant improvement.

The precision alignment of what you produce and what customers want — called external quality — is defined by your customers. You don't have input when it comes to external quality. Customers see your products and they perceive a level of quality. You don't have much of a second chance. Customers notice things that you may not consider to be important, such as a run in the paint, an erratic gap between two parts, a noisy motor, dirty fingerprints, a footprint on a shipping box, or a stray spot of glue. Customers regard the little things as important indicators of the care that you give with the critical components.

If your customers perceive that the quality is substandard, then they will refuse to buy the product. You may be offering lower pricing to overcome customer buying resistance due to footprints on a shipping container. Correct whatever real or perceived quality problems you have before you take the price increase.

Adapt to a Shrinking Market

Your product may be part of a declining market. Sales of the general type of product may be in a decline in your entire market area — the pie is getting smaller. You may be keeping prices low to maintain stable sales — cutting your margins to keep sales up. This tactic works if you are buying time to bring out a new product that will revive your sales.

Cutting margins to keep sales up for any other reason is an error. Sooner or later, a declining market will shrink your sales and margins to the point of bankruptcy. Price cutting may keep you in business longer than some of your competitors, but that doesn't qualify it as a good management practice.

Your best alternative is to have a new product in the wings — ready for introduction when the market decline tells you to phase out your current line. If you do not have a new product on line, but do have a backlog and long leadtimes, you may still be able to slightly raise your prices — maybe one or two percent. Then, invest everything you can into developing new products to replace the ones that are dying. Resist the temptation to press for a crash program. A product introduction that happens too fast is fraught with costs and plagued with errors. Make sure that the design is ready for production and use without a flood of engineering change orders right after introduction.

There is another alternative action if you are in the right market. If you are involved in markets that are destined to decline into a state of near-zero sales, new product introduction is your only alternative. However, if you are in a market that is destined to decline to a lower level of steady replacement sales, then your alternative is to become the low-price, high-quality leader in the marketplace.

A hot market of today that is destined to decline into a low level of steady, replacement sales is the personal computer industry. There is a yet unknown price and performance level at which designs will stabilize. Immediately thereafter, market saturation will occur — everyone who wants a PC will have one. The hot market will cool quickly and the shake-out will occur. When the shakeout occurs, the low-price, high-quality producers will be the only PC manufacturers who will remain.

The best market that exists is the market of steady, replacement sales where forecasts are reliable. The stress of beating your competitor to the market with a new design is mostly gone. Distribution, sales patterns, and cash flow are predictable. Your business will be easy to manage. If you find that you have the opportunity to become a leader in the stable marketplace of steady, replacement sales — then go for it.

Become the Efficient and Established Producer

If you have a competitor who has low prices and you have lowered prices to meet that low-price standard, become the low-price, high-quality producer. Low price and high quality should always be a prime goal. You know that by now. But, there are some other tactics to meet the low price challenge.

First, remember that your prices qualify as too low only if you have a backlog and your incoming orders exceed production capacity. If you have an inconvenient abundance of orders, but your profits are too low, raise your prices. Your price increase will reduce your incoming order rate but will increase your per-sale profits. Since you are producing at capacity, you will see no decrease in total shipments, only a decrease in customer complaints and order cancellations.

The alternative to raising prices is to keep prices the same and increase production if:

PROFIT POINTER

⊰ 60 ⊱

> ► You are able to add capacity by adding a shift;

> ► Your incoming order rate can justify another shift; and

> ► You project your sales to stay high long enough to justify another shift.

If your situation meets these three conditions, then add more capacity via a second shift. Keep your per-unit price low and sell 150–200 percent of your current volume. Economy of scale alone will drive your per-unit cost down and your per-unit profits up. With more production volume flowing through the same facility, the real (function-driven costing) manufacturing overhead cost per unit will decrease. The real cost of selling per unit will decrease also.

At this time, you may realize the significance of the early warning system mentioned in Chapter 7. If you are varying production volumes, your real cost per unit will change at every level of production. As volumes go up, manufacturing overhead per unit always goes down. As volumes go up, the cost of selling per unit usually, but not always, goes down. The cost of selling will go up if you have to increase your selling efforts (costs) to move overproduced inventory. In such a case, if you discount your price to make sales, then count the dollar amount of the discount as a cost of selling the product. If you set up systems to show (chart) your real costs, then you will be able to see which costs go up and which costs go down in response to your decisions. You can quickly reverse bad decisions and learn from the effects of all your decisions.

Combat the Price-Slashing Competitor

PROFIT POINTER

❧ 61 ❧

If you were asked to pick the most dangerous competitor between the two following examples, would you choose:

> ► The well-managed, low-cost, high-quality, established producer; and

> ► The poorly managed, seat-of-the-pants, high-cost, low-quality newcomer?

The most dangerous competitor is the poorly managed newcomer. The reason is that the established producer will keep margins high enough to cover all contingencies; even if the product cost is kept low, the price will be kept high enough to keep the company healthy. The poorly managed company is dangerous because it is apt to fixate on sales volume only due to the mistaken belief that large sales volumes will ultimately generate profits. Such a competitor is often referred to as market-driven. Since all manufacturers are ultimately market-driven, it is more accurate to call companies that are fixated on sales, sales-oriented companies.

The sales-oriented company pursues sales at any cost. It will literally sell below cost forever, if that will make the sales goals. Such a company often has no idea of costs. It often views its substantial losses as bookkeeping errors.

The day-to-day tactics of the sales-oriented company are volatile and unpredictable. You can, however, predict that there is a good chance that it will elect to compete by slashing prices. Since the sales-oriented company doesn't know its costs, selling at a loss doesn't bother it as much as it might bother you.

Don't count on this type of business to quickly bankrupt. The sales-oriented company has an uncanny way of attracting investors just before the doors close. With a new influx of cash it can maintain the price war until the new money is gone. Then, it will seek another investor. The toughest, most dangerous competitor in the world is the sales-oriented company without reliable cost data. Your alternatives against such competition are based on a set of conditions your business is facing.

If your business is experiencing a set of conditions that includes a low order rate, low profits, and a price-slashing competitor, then phase out the product line very quickly. Low profits and low orders mean that you can neither raise prices (and reduce sales) nor lower prices (and reduce profits). In such a case, let your competitor have all the losses.

If you have the opposite set of conditions — a high order rate and a backlog of orders — the implication is that you have already cut prices to meet your competitor's price-slashing tactics. Your customers are proving that they like your product better. You very likely have an advantage in quality and service. You can safely raise your prices and be assured that you will lose very little business. Those extremely cost-conscious customers that you may lose are the ones that you would most likely choose to surrender anyway.

Don't become lax just because you may have an advantage through service and quality. Make sure that you have products that are available or are being developed that your price-slashing competitor does not offer.

Use the Product Positioning Map at the end of Chapter 6 to determine where your price-slashing competitor is located. With rare exception, it will be in the low-price, low-quality quadrant. Make sure your product has a unique nature that will position it at a distance from the price-slasher.

You want to avoid head-to-head battle with a suicidal competitor. When faced with the price-slasher, there are two avenues to destruction and two avenues to success.

Avoid the Path of Destruction

First, beware of price matching. A price-slasher will simply reduce prices. Then, you must follow suit. One price cut leads to another — no one wins. It becomes a war of attrition. Even the company that thinks it is the winner is sometimes irrevocably damaged.

Second, don't wait. A well-managed firm will often believe that the price-slasher will soon self-destruct. Don't count on it. The sales-oriented company is spectacular in its ability to attract investors, build more facilities, open new territories, and attract more investors. It will buy and sell assets, open and close facilities, and borrow and repay in such complex methods that it is hard for anyone to know who owns what and whether anyone is making a profit. A sales-oriented company can go on for 20 years. During that time, someone may develop an effective cost-control system and start making real profits from production.

Choose the Path of Success

First, you can diversify. Chart a course of new products that will carry you completely out of the realm of the market of the price-slasher. Be careful that you do not diversify too much or too quickly. Stay within the realm of your strengths. Stretch the boundaries of your own abilities to move toward more stable and different markets. A side benefit may be that, once you let the price-slasher have all the sales of a product, self-destruction may indeed occur. If so, be prepared to move quickly back into the market. If you keep your tooling, prints, and specifications, no one can move more quickly than you to recapture the market.

Second, while you are still in the market with the price-slasher, aggressively attack your own costs. Review the cost-control techniques in chapters 8 and 9. You can probably reduce your real costs to the point where you can compete at any reasonable price. Even the most unthinking of price-slashers has a bottom limit to product pricing. Even without cost data, there is a lowest price. If you can become the true low-cost producer, then you can make a profit at a price where the price-slasher is losing big money. If you can manage to do that, then you can keep right on selling. Make sure that you keep your quality and service levels high. Price-slashers rarely have good quality and service.

PROFIT POINTER

❧ 62 ❧

Apply Wise Pricing Rules and Strategies

A course on basic economics teaches that when the price of a product goes up, the number of qualified buyers goes down. In common business terms, that means that every time you raise prices, you will lose sales.

Since the phenomenon is psychological in nature, it is impossible to predict how much a given price increase will decrease sales.

American managers have grown to believe that this basic economic rule is invalid. During the last two generations, the total world market has grown explosively. The sales potential of all products has increased regularly, without letup, for as long as most us can remember. We have witnessed price increases followed by sales increases for our lifetimes. Despite evidence that implies otherwise, the rule is valid.

To understand the rule, consider the following scenario. Imagine that the sales potential for your product is exactly 22,500 units for next year at a price of $15.00 each. Last year, you sold 17,000 at $15.00 per unit. If you choose to raise the price to $17.50 and sell 18,500 — have you lost or gained sales? All your records prove is that you sold nine percent more of your product at the higher price. There is no evidence that you lost any sales. There is no way to prove to the skeptic that sales were actually lost! Suppose the price increase was accompanied by a magnificent sales effort, mass advertising, imaginative promotions, and new colors and models. You might sell 22,500 units — the theoretical potential total sales at the lower price of $15.00 per unit. The skeptic could make a pretty good argument that there is no connection between total sales and total price.

Don't be a skeptic. You must understand the basic rules — that price increases equal lower sales and price decreases equal higher sales. It is difficult to predict the precise effect of price adjustments on sales quantities. Your goal is to match demand with production capacity over the span of a year. If your incoming order rate exceeds your production capacity by 15 percent, for example, try to estimate what kind of price increase would inhibit sales by 15 percent. This is not the kind of estimate you want to make off-the-cuff. Ask your key salespeople for their opinions. Ask your key customers for their opinions. Eliminate the extreme estimates from the formula then average the rest of the answers. If you get an average answer of a seven percent price increase to decrease sales by 15 percent, don't be tempted to immediately raise the price by seven percent.

Try a five percent hike first. Then, monitor the results. You don't want to lose any more orders than you are losing already through a lack of capacity. If a five percent price hike equals a three percent drop in orders, you are safe to try another five percent, or more, price hike. However, if a five percent hike gives you a 14 percent drop in incoming orders, then stabilize your price at that level. If you are within one percent of your goal in the pricing game, you have done very well.

Different product lines respond differently to price hikes for uncounted and usually unknown reasons. If a five percent price hike on widgets equals a three percent drop in orders, you cannot assume that a five percent hike will equal the same drop in orders for computers. It follows that you must handle price increases of separate products separately. Make your best guess increase on each product, independently. Monitor the results and follow up on each product, independently. It is unwise to adopt across-the-board price increases — the same percentage increase for every product line.

Remember, one of the elements of maximizing profits via pricing adjustments is to influence sales so that your capacity to produce and your sales volume match. For example, if you can produce 5,000 home heaters per year when you are operating most efficiently, then your pricing levels should be set so as to keep sales volumes at 5,000 heaters per year. This means that you may actually raise prices for the sole purpose of discouraging orders. Discouraging orders through increased pricing should only be practiced when you are certain that the long-term demand for your product or service exceeds your long-term capacity to produce.

You can assume that few of your competitors will dare to escalate prices in order to match demand with production capacity. They will, instead, take the orders and miss delivery dates. Your wisdom to manage demand via pricing will result in a high level of customer service, maximum profits, controlled costs, and a unique competitive advantage.

Chapter Recap

Product pricing will affect sales volume and total profitability. Excessive pricing and insufficient pricing can have identical effects on profits, so you must diagnose your pricing level by noting indicators. A unique competitive advantage is to view your pricing from a totally objective perspective and to be willing to take action that your competitors would not consider.

Chapter 11

STIMULATE QUICK CASH FLOW

Electric shock and chest-pounding are acts of mercy for the dying.

The heart of any profit-enhancement project is the stimulation of short-term cash flow. Cash flow is absolutely necessary for short-term survival, and cash for investment is necessary for the inventory, tools, and payroll that are the foundation for long-term profitability. The necessity of generating cash flow will cause you to take actions that would be rare or even unwise during more ordinary times. The actions that make a rapid profits turnaround possible are significantly more aggressive than normal.

Actions that are good for generating immediate cash flow may or may not work for everyday operations. Each one of the actions can have a place in everyday business when applied with thought and caution. However, the intensity and aggressiveness of turnaround management are too demanding to be applied daily. Further, expedient answers are inherently risky — they often trade off enormous long-term benefits for a few bucks today. In short, the decision that is made to save the company during a financial crisis will not automatically bring on the secondary responses that support long-term survival.

If the heart of a profit turnaround is cash flow, its soul is long-term corrections — the foundation upon which continued success can be built.

Its spirit is the spirit of simplicity. Its rule of conduct is unrelenting upward pressure on revenues; unrelenting downward pressure on costs. Both the short-term and the long-term actions should be initiated concurrently. The short-term actions create the cash to initiate the long term. If the long-term corrections are not initiated, the cash from the short-term sacrifices will do no permanent good! Long-term corrections are discussed in Chapter 12.

Close Down a Product Line

Most manufacturers have several product lines — portable widgets, built-in widgets, and quick-change widgets, for example. If you have several product lines, identify the least profitable one. You can increase your immediate cash flow and improve profitability by stopping production on that product. Cash flow is stimulated because you are selling product and you are not replacing inventory as you sell. Every dollar of closeout sales behaves as if it is pure profit. You should, however, consider four things before you actually stop production.

1. Know which product line is the least profitable. It is very dangerous to assume that you already know. Use function-driven costing to arrive at cost figures for each product line. It is not critical to be precise or accurate in your costing. What is critical is that you know, with certainty, which product is the least profitable when compared with other products using the same method of costing. If you use conventional methods of overhead distribution — loading per working hour — you will likely pick the wrong product to phase out. Use the Product Profit Worksheet at the end of this chapter to determine your annual profit per product. The product at the bottom of the list is your prime candidate for phaseout.

2. Balance your inventory so that all inventory is consumed in the phaseout. Balancing inventory means that you will make and sell the most final product possible, thereby maximizing your cash flow.

3. Keep necessary tooling, fixtures, and drawings. Once your business regains health, you may wish to reintroduce the product.

4. Keep valuable people. You may have another product line that needs a production increase. Transfer your best people to your best-selling product line. You may have someone with a particular talent for cost reductions or efficiency improvements. If so, assign that person to a special project.

PROFIT POINTER

◄► 63 ◄►

Keep the purpose of short-term cash flow in the front of your mind. The reason that you want the cash flow is to keep the business viable until long-term corrections begin to take effect and generate real profits. Your financial statement will likely continue to show no change in profits, or even diminished profits, as you phase out a product line. Remember, your total inventory is being sold down. Total sales revenues will likely drop as the last of the product line is sold.

You may be frightened by decreasing sales figures accompanied by a steeper decline in profits that you see on paper. Do not be concerned by these pretenders of doom. Decreasing the sales of money-losing products is a valid goal; your reduced sales figures indicate that you have achieved the goal. Inventory shows up on financial statements as profit, so reduced inventory may reveal itself as reduced profits for a short time. Real profits (cash) will increase as you convert sold-off inventory into goods that can be sold at a profit.

Keep Your Investors Informed

If you have investors, this can be a time that is especially unnerving. Most people will find it difficult to understand that declining sales and more rapid profit erosion are really indicators of a turnaround. You may be harshly criticized. Education is your ally. Write a letter to your investors predicting that sales and profits may nosedive as you initiate corrections to save the business. Your best chance of keeping your investors calm is to make reliable predictions of what will happen next in the project.

PROFIT POINTER

❖ 64 ❖

Cleverly Price a Phaseout Product

As you phase out a product, you have two options for pricing — you can lower prices or raise prices. Rarely should you leave pricing constant as you cease production.

You should lower prices if your product is late in the product life cycle — where sales are declining. Lower pricing will stimulate quicker sales, bringing in cash faster than it is leaving. This tactic is especially good if you have a major cost-reducing project that needs the capital, or if you are on a C.O.D. basis with suppliers and need to expand production on a more profitable line.

You should raise prices if your product is in early or mid-position on the product life cycle curve — where sales are stable or even on the increase. Higher pricing will generate more gross revenue per sale and may even make the product profitable.

Focus on Collections

You can improve cash flow by increasing the turnover of accounts receivable. If your turnover exceeds 30 days, you can gain additional cash flow if you can get your typical turn to less than 30 days. Thirty days is the magic number because your own payables are normally due in 30 days. If your receivables are turning in more than 30 days, your cash flow is hindered. If they turn in less than 30 days, your cash flow is assisted.

Remember that your goal is to generate immediate cash. You want to close the gap between what you have paid out to make the product and what you are collecting from the sale of the product. There are three categories of collections. You should deal with each differently.

Negotiate Past-Due Accounts

Past due refers to accounts that are unacceptably slow in making full payment. For most businesses, these accounts are 90 days past due. To collect these monies, you will need to negotiate. You can offer discounts for an immediate payment of the full (discounted) amount. If you fear that some accounts will never be able to pay in full, offer substantial discounts — 50 percent immediately is better than tiny dribbles forever.

Some people may get snagged by the idea of giving away 50 percent to slow accounts. Don't worry about it. Get your 50 percent, put them on a C.O.D. basis, and go about saving your business. You can sell past-due accounts to collection agencies. They usually will give you 50 percent upon collection. Do it quickly and don't worry if you make a couple of errors in judgment.

Frequently Communicate with Almost Past-Due Accounts

These are the accounts that may continue to be excellent customers once they have caught up on their accounts. Be imaginative and tactful. The method that offers the best results is to communicate frequently. If you communicate more frequently than other creditors who are vying for their cash shortage, you will get the largest chunk in the quickest time. Never intimidate, offer constructive solutions, and be a buddy. People respond to those who understand their situation and are helpful.

Offer Incentives for Current Accounts

Just because an account is technically current doesn't mean that the cash is turning quickly enough to satisfy your needs. You need your cash back before your own bills come due. You may be able to arrange short-term financing on current receivables.

A more customer-friendly idea is to offer discounts for immediate payment. Make the discount equal to your cost of short-term financing — maybe slightly more. The customer wins and you win. Current accounts cannot be badgered into early payment. Offer something of value in a fair trade for a quick turnaround of cash.

When you are initiating new ideas to speed up collections, be sure that the precedents you set are conditions you can live with after your own crisis is over — something that is palatable for both you and your customers on an everyday basis.

PROFIT POINTER

❖ 66 ❖

Stimulate Immediate Sales

You may have the opportunity to enhance your cash flow by stimulating immediate sales. Remember that your goal is to get cash moving in quickly — a positive cash flow. Most manufacturers put their first efforts and their greatest efforts into increasing sales any time profits decline. Sales stimulation can be a trap if it is not done exactly right. Know how increased sales can be an error so you can avoid it.

The common error is to indiscriminately sell everything you can. Every sale you make generates a need to build more product — sometimes for stock or sometimes built-to-order. In either case, you must buy materials and pay for labor to build the product. If you are operating at a loss, then every time you increase sales, you will increase your losses.

If you dramatically increase sales, you will dramatically increase the need for materials and labor to support the additional sales. You pay for the labor and materials before you receive payment for the increases in sales. Indiscriminate sales increases can actually retard cash flow. You can use the following safe methods of increasing sales that will have the best effect on cash flow.

Sell obsolete inventory

You may have inventories of discontinued products, damaged goods, or seconds. You can sell these products. You will probably have to price them below your theoretical cost, but that is okay. Selling below cost on old inventory brings in cash. Trying to sell at a profit will result in no sales. If you have substantial obsolete component inventory, you may even want to build more obsolete product to sell below cost; it is your method of getting money out of the obsolete component inventory. If repairs or upgrades must be made, spend the time and money if it means you can sell off some old stock. If you spend $100 to repair a second, but you can sell it for $300, you have made $200 — even if you sold below cost. Without the repair, the item is unsaleable.

Offer substitutions

You are probably overstocked on a slow moving model. Offer speedy delivery and a discount if your customer will accept a slower moving model as a substitution. You can offer a premium product as a substitute and charge the customer for the lower priced model. The customer wins and you win.

Discount overstocked items

You may be overstocked on a fast-moving item — maybe it is a seasonal item and you are in the off-season. Discounts can generate sales now — when you need the cash. Just remember, every unit that you sell now is one that you won't sell when the season arrives, so plan accordingly.

Overcome resistance

There may be some specific customer resistance to your product, your company, or your sales techniques. Make sure you have a close rapport with your customers so that you will know their reasons for resistance. Many are easily remedied, such as calling at the wrong time of day, billing errors, or rude salespeople. A distributor of a major brand of American-made chainsaws alienated the entire dealer network by selling directly to large retail customers. A simple "don't-do-that-anymore" command to the field sales representatives changed the dealer's attitude. Major corrections are often simple and free.

Fill backorders

Check your backlog of backorders. You might be delighted to discover that you have an enormous backlog. Find out why backorders are stalled and fill them now. Service parts are often the source of backorders. You would be wise to attach importance to service parts. Shipping backordered service parts accomplishes three things with one effort: it helps cash flow and (usually) profits; it enhances customer goodwill; and, it lays the foundation for future sales.

You can probably think of more tricks to get immediate sales moving. Just remember, your challenge is to do the unconventional. Sell the odd stuff, the old stuff, and the things that you won't have to replace.

Upgrade Quality

You understand the significance of quality. Your future depends on quality. If you have not been actively managing quality, you may be surprised at how quickly a quality program can provide cash results. Upgrading quality is of double importance because it accomplishes two things with one effort.

1. It increases cash inflow through higher levels of customer satisfaction and repeat business.
2. It reduces cash outflow through lower levels of loss and improved shop efficiency.

Below are tips to get a quick cash flow improvement via both internal and external quality.

Internal Quality

Start your attack on internal quality problems by going to your scrap and rework reports. Find the number one (measured in dollars) cause of scrap and rework and assign an employee to solve the problem — now. You can predict the cash results by looking at the dollar value you are losing through your number one scrap and rework problem.

If you don't keep records of scrap and rework, you need to begin charting these items as part of your early warning system. Record losses by part number, cost at the stage of completion, work center and operation that caused the loss, the quantity lost, and the total cost of the event. A clerk can post the data to a database every week. Then, you can pull up whatever information you need, such as work center with the most losses, part number with the most losses, or timeframe with the most losses. You need this kind of information to predict and solve problems. If you do not have a formal scrap reporting method, begin one now. The better formal manufacturing control systems have built-in systems for scrap reporting. You can get sorted reports that are very helpful in determining causes and remedies of scrap problems.

Every quality problem that you solve not only saves materials and labor, it saves in complimentary ways as well. For example, if you eliminate the cause of the most repeated loss, you probably just eliminated the cause of many near-losses that are time consuming to prevent. You have probably made parts fit the next operation more reliably, which will reduce labor there. The ripple effect may save you more than you saved by correcting the problem. Remember, too, that correcting a root cause will always provide unexpected and free side benefits.

External Quality

External quality means that your customers get what they expect or more than they expect. Happy customers refer your product to other customers. Products that exceed customer expectations don't generate complaints, warranty claims, or lawsuits. Find out the number one cause of customer complaints, then correct it.

Reduce Overstaffing

PROFIT POINTER

⋙ 68 ⋘

Overstaffing is reduced by laying off people — a measure that should be approached with much thought and consideration. Indiscriminate layoffs are normally an error. There are two prerequisites to a staff reduction layoff. First, develop a function-driven organization. A function-driven organization assigns responsibility. You know who is responsible for what achievements. No one can deceive you. You don't have to ask who did what. Who-does-what is assigned and measured.

As discussed in Chapter 7, a maximum of one person is required to head each of the four functional areas: manufacturing, product engineering, sales and marketing, and finance. As you develop functional assignments, you will discover that you have staff left over. Second, you must discriminate between talkers and doers. There is a very subtle difference between the doers with communicative abilities and the pure talkers. The way to tell the difference is to observe results.

For you to make the decisions regarding layoff of managers, you must be able to discern the results achieved by each person under consideration. The popular, but erroneous method of learning what managers have accomplished is to simply ask them. There is a built-in hazard in trying to discern between the talkers and the doers by asking them to tell you what they have done. Talkers can keep on for hours, delighted with the opportunity to enhance their own credibility. Doers, however, tend to be conservative. They will understate their achievements. They will be anxious to leave the interview and go back to work. The early warning system is a charted record of performance for every functional area. If you don't have an early warning system in place, you can do two things that will help you evaluate the real performance of staff employees.

Ask employees

Don't target the talkative employees, but the head-down-no-time-for-talk working employees. They know who is supporting real achievement and who is spending company time feathering a nest. Your employees will tell you, but only if you ask in an unthreatening manner.

Observe

Look for indications of work. Look at whose name is at the bottom of analyses, reports, and recommendations. Determine who has initiated new programs and who spends the least time in your office. Who is unafraid to associate with a failed project — to pick up the pieces and make the best of it? Who takes on new responsibilities even if they are drab and routine? The person who does these things is the doer. Beware of the employee who never fails — the one who delights you with frequent visits to your office and belittles the mundane tasks — the one who directs your attention to the failings of others.

The talkers do not produce results. They create illusions of results. The illusions that they create are for your viewing. Often, you will be the only person in the company who sees the illusion. Ask around — others do not see the illusions created for your benefit and can help you understand who is producing and who is creating illusions. You may not believe that you have a problem with too many talkers and not enough doers. If you do not have such a problem, then you can be counted among the well-managed few in American business. You most likely have entrenched deadwood — nonperformers who justify their existence with glib talk. Elimination of one such employee is like hiring two hard working employees. The importance of identifying your deadwood and getting it out of your company cannot be overemphasized.

Lay Off Selected Production Employees

Lay off the employees who have the poorest records of efficiency or losses in scrap and rework. Employees with poor attendance or records of other objectionable work habits are candidates for a layoff. You can only lay off selectively if you are not constrained by rules of a union contract. If you are, then ask the union for help in rooting out the poorest performers. If you have a good rapport with your union leaders, they will help you.

Check your overtime. To achieve the highest possible output per-dollar spent on labor, a small amount of irregular overtime should show up. Look for an average of 5–10 percent overtime in surges — a day here, two days there. No overtime means that your workforce is idle during the lulls in production. Regular overtime — as in one hour a day, every day — may imply that overtime is being scheduled blindly, whether or not it is actually required. Adjust your workforce until you have sporadic overtime to compensate for contingencies. Keep the average overtime per employee at two to four hours per week.

Bring an Outside Operation In House

PROFIT POINTER

◈ 70 ◈

You may have amazing opportunities in this realm. If you phase out a product, you may have highly skilled employees who can develop the procedure to build a challenging part. Imagination and innovation can use the resources you have to save you a lot. An actual example involved bringing an outside machine shop operation in house. The company paid $47.15 for machine shop services on a component common to every unit of production — a total of $707.00 a day, or $177,000.00 per year.

Pure imagination brought the operation in-house. An obsolete tape-controlled mill was jury-rigged to function as a heavy-duty drill press. Fixturing was built in house to turn and locate the part. Within 30 days, an operator could produce the 15 per day requirements in one hour on a Just-in-Time basis. The net savings was $14,500 per month after the in-house labor was paid. Ripple benefits included reductions in inventory and freight costs, total control of the process, no stockouts, and no production slow-downs due to a late delivery of parts. Refer to Profit Pointer 53 in Chapter 9 for guidance in making your make-buy decisions.

Produce and Sell More

PROFIT POINTER

◈ 71 ◈

Even if you do not have a backlog of sales, you need to find out if the sales department is intentionally holding back on some product lines. Your sales-people may discourage orders because they may think that a higher order rate would result in backorders and cancellations. Your sales department may be losing orders if leadtimes surpass a given limit. Some customers for some products will simply buy somewhere else if your leadtimes are too long. If you are losing sales due to your rate of production, you must increase production or raise prices. (See Profit Pointer 56 in Chapter 10.) Do not increase production across-the-board; increase it only on the right product line. If you have a situation where your customers don't mind wait-ing for portable widgets, but you can't ship built-in widgets in two weeks and so they buy somewhere else, then increase production on the built-in widget line, but not on the portables line. Even a one or two percent increase in production and sales helps your cash flow. Remember, you will not nor-mally get a great big result from one, single action. Your turnaround of cash flow is dependent upon the total of a large number of small contributions.

Reduce Inventory

PROFIT POINTER

◈ 72 ◈

All purchased components have a leadtime — the time lapse between the date the order is placed and the date the components arrive. A six-week leadtime means that if you order 100 units of a product today, you receive the 100 units six weeks later. What happens if the production schedule changes during the interim six weeks? If you reschedule to run 80, then you will have 20 components of surplus inventory left over. If you reschedule to run 120, then you will see a production shortfall of 20. There will be the attendant missed shipments, backorders, and production schedule reshuffling.

The way employees compensate for such unplanned schedule changes is to stock excess inventory. A fluctuating master production schedule is the cause of excess inventory.

Stabilize Your Master Production Schedule

Stabilize your master production schedule (MPS) within the span of the longest leadtime item and you will remove the cause of excess inventories. Stabilizing the schedule is based on managing demand. (See Profit Pointer 84.) Once your MPS is stabilized, assign an employee to manage your biggest inventory dollars.

Pareto's Law, or the 80/20 Rule as illustrated below, states that 80 percent of your problems comes from 20 percent of your situations. The reverse is true also: 20 percent of your situations causes 80 percent of your problems. The basic idea is that you can achieve 80 percent of your desired results with only a 20 percent effort — provided you learn the 20 percent of situations that are the offenders. An example is that 20 percent of your inventory items constitute 80 percent of your inventory costs. Improved controls on that 20 percent of items will improve the controls over 80 percent of your inventory investment.

Pareto's Law – the 80/20 Rule

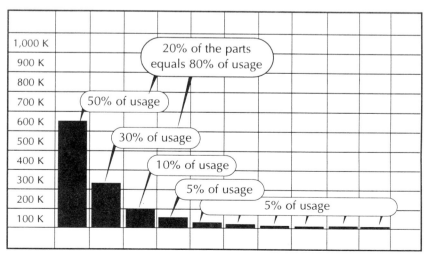

You can estimate your savings from intensely controlling the top five percent of your inventory. Start with your inventory dollar amount — work in process (WIP) and raw materials. If your company has $25 million in sales, a 40 percent profit margin, an average (70 percent) materials content, and four inventory turns per year, your WIP and raw materials will be $2.6 million. If you have 1,000 stock keeping units (SKUs), then managing only 50 parts will control $1.3 million in inventory very precisely.

In the case of an erratic MPS, you will need a minimum 20 percent excess inventory to keep production from stopping. Intense management will cut the excess in half easily. By intensely managing $1.3 million in inventory, you can make a 10 percent — or $130,000 — reduction in inventory easily in 90 days. The $130,000 will go directly into your cash flow. You make your product and sell your product like always. But because you are managing your schedules and inventories intensely, you do not have to replace $130,000 of inventory. You can use the cash to support cost reductions and new product development.

Assign a resourceful, energetic person — or more if your business is large enough to justify more than one person — to control the top five percent of your inventory to precise standards for use and replacement. Don't wait for systems, education, or any other reason of why it must be deferred. Intense control of the top five percent can be done with a pencil, a calculator, and a resourceful person.

Eliminate Waste

You will want to try to eliminate the waste of time. Every minute that an employee is doing something useless is a minute of wasted payroll dollars. You can reduce wasted minutes without resorting to whip-and-chair tyranny to squeeze unrealistic performance out of your employees. Your goal is to eliminate employees doing things that look like work, but don't add value to the product. Any act that does not directly add value is waste.

You may be paying for large amounts of wasted time and energy. You should find and correct the biggest time wasters. They are predictable. Following is a list of typical time wasters. It will help you to think of similar time wasting tasks in your own company.

Setups

Changeover time from one task to another is classified as waste. All companies have waste in the form of setup time. We usually think of setup time as something that happens in the shop — changing a machine over

PROFIT POINTER

❧ 73 ❧

from running part A to running part B. Think of your setup time in broader terms, such as changeover times in the order entry, warehousing, production control, and payroll departments. Do people in these areas have to fumble and search for the tools and materials to start the next task? Are they stored in the next office or down the hall? Do they have to call the data processing department for permission to run the next task? All changeover time can be reduced.

Material Handling

Moving materials is wasted effort. You will never get rid of all of it, but you can make significant reductions. In Chapter 8, you learned how departmental layout can cause excess material handling. You will find that five percent of your layout causes 50 percent of your wasted material handling costs. A well-designed layout of one or two work centers will usually make a dramatic difference in efficiency. You can expect a 50 percent reduction in material handling with one or two well-thought-out moves.

Lack of Tools

Every work area should have instant access to every tool that is required. Use racks, belt holsters, overhead tool balancers, or custom holders to place tools within an arm's reach. Be imaginative — build special holders. Do whatever is necessary. The savings available via tool accessibility is measurable.

Use a stopwatch to measure how long an employee is detracted from adding value to the product because of stepping away to get a tool. You will be amazed — tool searching is such a subtle waster of time. Your casual observations will miss the 30 seconds in 10 minutes lost for a tool search. It adds up over a day — 24 minutes per employee per day — that is five percent efficiency lost. Five percent doesn't sound like much until you realize what it means in total cost. If you employ 150 people, 7 1/2 of them are being paid to do nothing. That is $125,000 down the drain because tools are not readily available.

Inaccurate Drawings, Routings, and Instructions

The time wasted by inaccurate documents can best be understood by observing your employees as they work. Look around your business — within 60 seconds you will see two employees talking and pointing. You can bet that they are trying to clarify some error or unclear document. All it takes is a few minutes per person, per day to multiply into a lot of dollars that you can save by creating accurate and clear documents.

Simplify the Product Line

Every manufacturer will grow to the level at which it offers too many products. Too many products complicate a product line and a production schedule to the extent that added people and facilities are required to administer, plan, build, and store the additions to a product line. More inventory is required for the new products, plus added inventory is required to compensate for a more complex and frequently changing production schedule. The ultimate result is a lot more cost to support not-so-much-more sales. Consider the experience of this boat manufacturer.

Imagine a company that builds boats. Early in its life, the firm features a product line that includes ordinary flat-bottomed fishing boats at 12, 14, and 16 foot lengths. A few years later, the company discovers that it is losing some sales. So it begins to expand its product line to include deluxe vee-bottomed fishing boats at 12, 14, and 16 foot lengths. Boat sales double so it adds supreme pleasure boats, upholstered and carpeted, at 16, 20, and 22 foot lengths.

At this point, sales are good and the product line is a reasonable size. Options and accessories are offered to compliment the boats. The marketing department figures that the company is offering a full market basket — that is, no sales are being lost due to a lack of product offering. Controlling schedules for materials and production is simple; production is on time and costs are controlled. Customer service is near 100 percent. Profits are good and the dealers are happy and stable.

The sales and marketing staff reports that additional sales may be possible by adding a larger pleasure boat and by tripling the number of options and accessories available. The product line grows by adding a super supreme pleasure boat, leather and velvet trimmed, at any length over 26 foot, custom-built to order with hundreds of options and accessories.

The example is simplistic, but you get the idea. The last addition to the product line probably doubled the overhead required to control production schedules and inventory. Additional factory space is necessary to build the custom product even if there are no orders. Every option and accessory is stocked to prevent backorders. Ultra-expensive inventories of raw materials are stocked in anticipation of orders. The additional product line may have added 30 percent to overhead costs and added two percent to sales volume. It may have added nothing at all to profits.

Consider Correct Costing

If the boat manufacturer used conventional costing techniques, what would be done with the additional overhead generated by the new product line? It would be evenly allocated on a per-working hour basis. Specifically, an example would look like this:

Overhead Allocation via Conventional Costing

Before the New Product:

An employee building ordinary flat-bottomed fishing boats at an hourly rate of $8.00 plus overhead of $8.00 equals a cost of $16.00 per hour.

After the New Product:

Same employee building ordinary flat-bottomed fishing boats at an hourly rate of $8.00 plus overhead of $10.00 equals a cost of $18.00 per hour.

All of the additional overhead caused to the new product line should be allocated only to the cost of the new product. Conventional costing will allocate some of the added overhead to the old product line, causing an illusion of higher costs for the old line and lower costs for the new line. In the example, function-driven costing would immediately identify the new product as a loser. Management would quickly identify the source of the added costs and eliminate the new line.

However, if conventional costing is used in the example, the ordinary flat-bottomed fishing boats would be identified as the losers and they would be eliminated. Conventional costing will always identify the low-cost models as losers and the high-cost models as winners. It is the nature of the technique.

This type of simple costing error has caused a plague of management errors in American manufacturing. Countless times you will see a manufacturer drop a popular bottom-of-the-line model and keep a top-of-the-line model.

In the example, the complex, custom-built line of boats should be dropped. It adds to numerous costs and contributes little, if anything, to profits. Not all examples are so obvious, so you will have to do some analysis. Pareto's Law (the 80/20 Rule) applies to your product line — the top 20 percent of your items sold are generating 80 percent of your sales. Reverse that to gain a full understanding of the potential of simplifying your product line — 80 percent of your product line is generating 20 percent of your sales dollars, or 50 percent of your product line is generating a scant 10 percent of sales dollars. The bottom 20 percent of your product line is generating nearly nothing.

To know which items are winners and which are losers, follow these three steps.

1. Calculate the profit on every item. You must use function-driven costing to arrive at costs and profits. Otherwise, your figures will mislead you.
2. Multiply the profit per item by the number of items sold annually. This will give you the annual profit per item.
3. List your by-item profits with the highest profit figure at the top. Rank all items from the top down in descending order.

Profitability Ranking

Rank	Item	Profit per Item	Annual Sales	Total Profit
1	Painted basic widget	$122	540	$65,880
2	Gold plated widget	202	110	22,220
3	Complex widget	107	92	9,844

This type of profit charting is illustrated in the following diagram.

Pareto's Law for Profits Charted

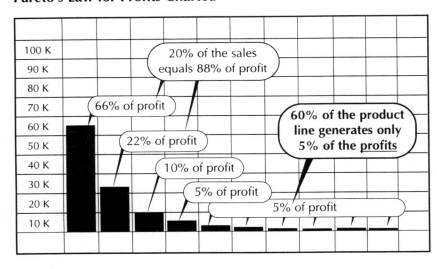

Examine Your Product Line

Examine the sales records of the bottom-selling 30 percent of your product line. Look at accessories, options, model variations, and color and trim offerings. You might find a surprising number of offerings that nearly never sell. Yet, you bear the expense of inventory, storage facilities, handling, sales brochures, and a myriad of other costs of simply offering the item for sale.

As you work through this simplification process, ask your production control employees to tell you about products that they believe should be dropped. You may be surprised at the massive effort that is required to move infrequent orders of one or two items through a shop that is accustomed to the faster-moving items. Avoid selling products that exploit your weaknesses. A reasonable guideline for product line simplification is to count your number of items offered and try to reduce it by ten percent. Even one percent helps noticeably.

Remember the full market basket concept. To entice dealers to sell your product line, you must offer a full line. At the same time, remember that an item that nearly never sells is not a legitimate part of the full market basket. Your competition sees the potential of losing any sales as a negative. Learn to look at losing the bottom one percent of sales as a positive. By intentionally losing that bottom one percent, you will lose five percent in costs. Five percent less cost is a positive in your favor.

Chapter Recap

Short-term actions are meant to create a positive cash flow. You should be able to achieve a positive cash flow in the first 30 days. Creating that positive cash flow is the most critical single element of rapid profits turnaround. Cash is what enables you to survive long enough to turn around profits.

If you apply all of the short-term actions described in this chapter, you may quickly generate impressive results — impressive enough to lull you right back into practices that got you into your mess. Remember that your short-term actions are mostly one-shot opportunities; they generate cash and maybe profits. But their effects will soon go away. It is the long-term corrections in the next chapter that provide substance and staying power to your turnaround.

A quickly stimulated cash flow is vital to establishing a foundation for future profits. Use the following list to help you make sure that you are on track in generating short-term cash flow.

- ► Cost your full product line using function-driven costing. Compare cost to selling price. Identify your least profitable product line and schedule it for phaseout.
- ► Begin the phaseout of the product line. The first step is to balance all inventory so that it will all be consumed in production.

- ► Develop a pricing strategy for the phaseout that will generate the most sales dollars in the shortest time span.
- ► Initiate a collection procedure for slow accounts that will collect cash within 30 days. Expect to discount, but get the cash.
- ► Offer incentives to current accounts for near-instant cash turnaround.
- ► Sell inventory that is obsolete or damaged.
- ► Offer substitutes of slow-moving inventory items. Discount pricing if required.
- ► Offer incentives for early purchases of off-season inventory.
- ► Ship backorders.

Product Profit Worksheet Instructions

Use this worksheet to determine which products are most profitable.

When you have annual profit figures for every product, then prioritize the list with the most profitable product at the top. The bottom ten percent of the list should be evaluated for phaseout.

Simply plug in the actual dollars spent for the four main cost categories: materials, labor, overhead, and cost of selling. Use function-driven costing to calculate overhead costs. Use your routing forms to allocate operation-by-operation overhead. Cost of selling is the cost that is dedicated to selling a specific product. Realistic estimates are okay, assuming that you allocate costs as they are really driven by the specific product. For example, OEM replacement parts require nearly no cost of selling. A new standalone product may require extensive marketing and advertising.

Product Profit Worksheet

Product	Materials	Labor	Overhead	Cost of Selling	Annual Profit/Loss

CHAPTER 12

BUILD A FOUNDATION FOR PROFITS

Tomorrow's harvest is the result of planting seeds today. A plentiful harvest is preceded by seeding and by meticulous toil.

The goal of a successful turnaround is a plentiful future harvest. If you were a farmer in danger of starving, you would buy or trade for enough food to sustain you for the present. The cash flow actions of Chapter 11 will sustain you for the present. The cash flow prevents immediate starvation, but will do nothing for the future. A smart farmer tills the soil and plants immediately to sustain life before the temporary store of food has been consumed. The long-term corrections recommended in this chapter will provide harvest and sustenance indefinitely. The sooner you plant, the sooner you harvest. You would be wise to plant the seeds — your foundation for profits — as soon as you possibly can, concurrently with the short-term actions. A foundation for profits will require an investment of time and capital to start the processes — like planting a crop.

Many of your competitors are overwhelmed by the need to react to crises. They look for results on the bottom line at the end of the current month. Mature, effective management works during the current month to provide results for the subsequent month, following quarter, or even a year down the road. Mature management will even sacrifice profits this month to achieve a fuller harvest later.

Do you favor the short-term effect at the sacrifice of long-term good? If you have end-of-the-month shipping rushes, then you are sacrificing profits so that you can have quick fix results on the financial statement for the current month. The majority of your competitors will squeeze all the dollars they can out of the current month and will worry about the following month later. When you orient yourself toward the long term you will be in the minority. You will attain a competitive advantage. Your competition will be mostly oriented to the short term — like a farmer buying food every month and never planting. Every month is a crisis. Long-term success is not in the crystal ball for the farmer who never plants — nor is it in the future of your competitors who never build a foundation for the future.

Initiate Morale Improvements

You learned about the costs and remedies for low morale in Profit Pointer 10 in Chapter 2. High morale is a prerequisite to building a foundation for profits. Your employees will do much of the work; their attitude must be pro-profit for you to realize long-term success. Morale enhancements require time. Your first action of building a foundation for profits should be to assure that you place a top priority on your employees' morale. Be sure to follow up with frequent how-are-we-doing interviews with your employees to know your progress.

PROFIT POINTER

◈ 75 ◈

Improve Long-Term Quality

The quality issues discussed in Chapter 11 are primarily aimed at providing immediate cash flow benefits and at providing you with a jump start toward long-term benefits. Those cash flow benefits will merge into your long-term profit picture as a permanent contributor. The mother lode of benefits is in a major quality overhaul — an overhaul that will provide a competitive advantage forever.

High quality is an advantage over your competitors. Many of them are permanently stuck in the mode of increasing-sales-at-any-cost. Their cost of selling their inferior products will someday terminate their business. Your high-quality products will sell themselves. Go back to the Product Positioning Map discussed with Profit Pointer 36. Notice the characteristics of the low-quality, high-price producer. Some of the characteristics that your competitors face are:

- ► High marketing costs
- ► Heavy competition
- ► Unpredictable profits

PROFIT POINTER

◈ 76 ◈

There are three avenues that improve quality while reducing costs. You can pursue all three concurrently. All three should be initiated as soon as possible.

Improve processes

For example, envision a machine that is able to hold a tolerance of plus or minus a 0.010 of an inch under normal conditions. Then, envision a part that has a required tolerance of plus or minus a 0.010 of an inch, the same as the normal capability of the machine. If anything goes wrong — dull tooling, machine wear, operator fatigue, unnoticed changes in procedure, or unnoticed variations in materials — the part will be out-of-tolerance. However, if the machine is capable of holding plus or minus a 0.001 of an inch tolerance, then the same variations in other places will not push the part out-of-tolerance. The same variables will produce a quality part.

Design for quality

Design new products with a respect for the capabilities of the available processes. For example, specify new parts at one-half of the tolerance holding ability of the processes (and people) in your shop. The design-for-quality goal is to prevent scrap and rework costs. Avoid designs that press your processes and people to the limits of their capabilities.

Revise for quality

Minor design revisions in existing products can deliver surprising reductions in scrap and rework while improving efficiency. Most products have dozens, if not hundreds, of opportunities for design-for-quality revisions. Ask your employees if they know the causes of the problems. The cause will be either the process or the design. Your employees will know the answer and are waiting for someone to implement it.

Internal Quality

Internal quality is the assurance that the product is made correctly the first time. Top-notch internal quality can dramatically affect the overall cost of production. Complete every item on this list and you will have a firm foundation for quality control.

▶ Set up a system to identify every occurrence of scrap and rework.

- ▶ Assign one person to analyze scrap and rework and to correct the causes. Begin with the 20 percent of items that constitutes 80 percent of the scrap and rework costs.
- ▶ Assure that incoming material is consistently adequate to support your desired quality levels.
- ▶ Assure that your machines and processes are capable of consistently holding the tolerances required for your product and quality.
- ▶ Assure that your employees are properly trained in the use of tools and know how to read drawings and routings.
- ▶ Assure that all tools are adequate and in good repair for the job.
- ▶ Assure that routings are correct and accurate.
- ▶ Assure that bills of materials (BOMs) are correct and accurate.
- ▶ Assure that drawings are correct and accurate.
- ▶ Implement a system to assure that only correct and current drawings, routings, and BOMs are available to the shop.

Introduce a New Product

PROFIT POINTER

❦ 77 ❦

No matter how tempting it may be, wait until you have a positive cash flow and profitability before you attempt a new product introduction. New products carry with them a number of uncertainties — market acceptance, service reliability, and the real cost of manufacturing, to name a few. Introduce new products from a position of relative strength — a position that will forgive errors. You can, however, begin preparations for a new product immediately. That way, you can introduce the new product as soon as you are financially strong enough. There are rules to follow when introducing a new product.

Meet a Recognized Market Demand

Do your research. Find out what the market wants that is not available in your market area — the unsatisfied demand. Design a product that will precisely fill that demand. Resist the temptation to introduce a new product that you think is a great idea unless it fills an unsatisfied demand. The reason for finding the market void is that it will save untold dollars later in the cost of selling. There is little buying resistance to overcome. Don't make assumptions; rather, find out exactly what the market wants, how much it will pay, then provide it.

Maintain Market Channels

Your new product should use the same channels of distribution and sales that you currently use. Setting up new channels will cost you. New channel costs are unpredictable with results that are unpredictable. Use the channels that you have established for predictable results. You will find that there is more safety in working with people and systems that you already know.

Slightly Diversify

The ideal new product will be slightly diverse — as diverse as you can make it and still use existing facilities, skills, and market channels. The ideal diversification example comes from a company that manufactures wood stoves.

The new product was pellet stoves. The two products used similar technology, identical processes, and the same market channels. But the two products were diverse enough to appeal to totally different target markets, with a small overlap. The customer base doubled.

The two products were affected by different environmental rules; difficulty in meeting regulations in one line would have no effect on the other. The geographic distribution of potential customers was diverse; wood stoves sell in areas with available firewood. Pellet stoves sell in areas of limited firewood availability; pellets are manufactured and transported. You buy pellets in grocery stores. The back-to-basics customer is more likely to buy the wood stove. The more prosperous customers with two working household members are more likely to buy the pellet stove.

The factor that made such a diversification ideal is that the market for wood stoves was beginning a decline while the market for pellet stoves was new.

Design for Manufacturability

Your new product should be simple in all regards. Production control and scheduling should be simple. Components should be simple to build with the process and skills available to you. Purchased parts should be simple for your suppliers to provide. Assembly should be straightforward. The objective in keeping a product universally simple to produce is to keep two numbers low:

1. The number of parts; and
2. The number of operations.

By keeping the number of parts and the number of operations low, you will automatically keep costs low. You can use a technique to promote manufacturing-friendly designs called concurrent engineering. Concurrent means that your manufacturing and product engineering staff is concurrently involved in designing a product and the processes to make the product. The result is that the product fits the processes and the processes fit the product. Close proximity and constant communications are the hallmarks of concurrent engineering.

Concurrent engineering also involves customers and suppliers in product design. Utilize materials from professional organizations to help you design for manufacturability. The Society of Manufacturing Engineers (SME) and the American Production and Inventory Control Society (APICS) have excellent materials to help develop designs that are manufacturable. To learn how to contact either of these associations, refer to Chapter 2.

Document a Plan

If you want to set yourself apart from your competitors in new product introductions, then be on-time and on-budget. Most of your competitors cannot achieve either goal. The way to do it is to develop a budgetary plan and a timetable. Make sure that both are realistic. Document each plan in graphic form and post conspicuously. Plot progress against each plan regularly — usually monthly. Each plan should highlight milestone events, such as:

- ► Completion of specs
- ► Completion of preliminary drawings
- ► Completion of first prototypes
- ► Testing of first prototypes
- ► Completion of second prototypes
- ► Testing of second prototypes
- ► Revision of specs and drawings
- ► Completion of production drawings
- ► A pilot production run
- ► Revisions of production drawings
- ► The first full production run

▶ Shipment to distributors

▶ The date when the product will be available for sale

When each event has a date attached to it — and a cumulative expenditure total — it is easy to see if you are going to be on target very early in the project. You can take corrective action early, instead of after you have missed a promised introduction date. The key is to take action. Your competitors may use progress charting techniques; yet all they do is graphically display how far the project is behind schedule. As soon as the project shows evidence of falling behind, take immediate action.

Design for Quality

By now, you know the basics of how to design for quality. The key is to make certain that your designers know how to design for quality and you actually do it. Professional organizations, such as the ASQC, APICS, and SME offer books and training to help you design for quality.

Use Existing Facilities

To get the most profits from a new product, design it to use existing facilities as much as possible. The definition of facilities includes buildings, machines, people and their skills, management organization, and tooling. If you must diversify as part of your competitive strategy, then you may have to expand your facilities. If so, keep your expansion moderate. Stay within the abilities of your people and your finances.

PROFIT POINTER

≈ 78 ≈

Implement Significant Cost Reductions

Cost reduction is the biggest area of opportunity for most organizations. If you have not had an ongoing effort to control and reduce costs, then you have opportunities to save a large percentage of your product cost. Even if you reduce costs by one percent, you will see positive effects on your profits. Consider this example:

Cost Reduction Example

Before a 1% Cost Reduction		After a 1% Cost Reduction	
Sales:	$1,000,000	Sales:	$1,000,000
Costs:	990,000	Costs:	990,000
Profit:	10,000	Cost Reduction	−9,900
		Profit:	19,900 (profits up by 99 percent)

A one percent cost reduction in this case increased profits by 99 percent — nearly double. A one percent cost reduction is not hard to find if you know where to look. Start your search for cost-reduction opportunities by looking at materials costs. Purchasing records will reveal those costs. Materials costs are driven up by practices that are often totally within your control as the customer.

Control Materials Costs

Materials costs are often secondary responses to primary actions that seemed like the thing to do at the time. Chapter 9 has discussed many of the causes and remedies of high materials costs. The primary actions that may get you into trouble with materials costs are predictable.

You can avoid driving materials costs up via secondary responses if you avoid:

- ► Misleading costing techniques;
- ► Buying via subcontract services;
- ► Seeking the lowest per-unit prices;
- ► Adverse supplier relations;
- ► A rapidly changing master production schedule;
- ► Rapidly changing product design;
- ► Over or under-specified parts and materials;
- ► Inconsistent parts or materials; and
- ► Low priority on internal quality.

All of these actions are the results of expedient decisions. For you to have a competitive advantage, you should look to the secondary responses of your decisions and always make decisions that will provide profit-enhancing final effects.

The Subcontracting Option

Much is written in favor of the virtual corporation — the company that subcontracts all work. The virtual corporation does little or no actual work, but simply administers and coordinates. Current writings extol the great reductions in overhead that result from the practice of subcontracting everything. Be cautious of becoming a business that depends on subcontractors.

Subcontractors have overhead built into their own pricing. When you buy their services, you are paying for their overhead. You are additionally paying for their profits and for additional transportation costs. When you buy subcontract services, you are frequently paying a super premium price compared to the cost of doing the task in house. Your overhead as it appears on a financial statement will be dramatically reduced. However, you still incur overhead costs; they are simply transferred to the cost that you label as materials.

If you have competitors that are moving in the direction of becoming virtual corporations, write them letters congratulating them on their wisdom. Then, expand your own operation. Who knows, you may wind up making their products for them. If you develop high skills in the areas that your competitors find difficult to master, you will have a competitive advantage.

PROFIT POINTER

◈ 80 ◈

Reduce Overhead Costs

Overhead is the catchall phrase that collects all the costs of manufacturing except for the direct costs of labor and materials. Included are supplies, facility costs, support personnel, maintenance, management, and staff. Some companies wisely break down overhead and allocate portions to prominent functional areas. A manufacturing company, for example, will proportion overhead to the four main functional departments — sales, engineering, manufacturing, and finance. Unfortunately, the breakdown usually is not sufficiently detailed nor is it accurate in its representation of the real costs of each functional area. Overhead costs should be assigned as accurately as possible to the function that creates the cost. When you know which area is generating which costs (and why) you can begin to precisely attack overhead costs.

Some of the remedies for excess overhead costs are the same as the remedies for excess materials costs. Some remedies are the same as remedies for poor morale. One action will correct many business ills. In addition to the numerous actions you can take to reduce overall costs and enhance your business' profits as discussed in previous chapters, you can do two things to help reduce your overhead costs — systemize and reduce technology dependency.

Systemize

Systemization in all areas amounts to prescribing a simple, repeatable method for achieving daily tasks. It reduces errors (and subsequent corrections), training time, and the time required to achieve the task. Systemization allows computerization of such tasks as billing, pick lists, order entry, inventories, accounting, payroll, and production control. If properly used, a good computerized system requires entry of data one time only. It detects errors in some cases — prevents errors in others. Whether or not systemization helps you depends upon your own resourcefulness and discipline. Systemization has enabled companies to reduce overstaffing by as much as 80 percent. Use the concept of the function-driven organization to determine what organizational tasks absolutely need to be done; eliminate the rest.

Reduce Technology Dependence

You already know to prepare a detailed capital expenditure justification before you purchase any new technology. The discipline required to prepare a written justification has some valuable cost-reducing side effects.

High technology is fine if it is indeed the cost-reducing way to more efficient production. Always remember the subtle costs like maintenance, programming, additional fixturing, closer tolerances, a constant flow of materials, and precise placement. Further, a full-front assault on a new technology can be overwhelming to people who are accustomed to a low-tech workplace. New technology can be a costly stumbling block. Use technology as a method to simplify other processes. A new technology should be able to pass two tests:

1. It should simplify what it does.
2. It should simplify what is required to make the technology work.

If either side of the new technology breeds complexity, then the result may be an increase in overhead rather than a decrease.

The underlying concept to remember is that overhead costs tend to be pushed upward as managers attempt to reduce costs in other areas. The primary cost reduction will often cause a secondary response that bloats overhead. You will find that pressing costs back where they belong will press overhead downward. Lower overhead is part of the foundation for profits.

Develop Accurate Forecasts

All forecasts are wrong. You may have heard that statement until you repeat it as an accepted truth. Everyone in manufacturing has agreed that all forecasts are wrong; however, forecasts don't have to be wrong. A technique called forecast commitment will make your sales forecasts substantially accurate. Forecast commitment means that you sell what you have predicted you will sell and then you sell what you have forecast. When you

PROFIT POINTER

◆ 81 ◆

develop forecast commitment, you will have laid an important block in the foundation for profits. You can expect four results.

Inventory reductions

Inventory is reduced by forecast commitment. You know what you are going to sell, so you know what you need to build and when to build it. Finished goods inventories stay lower. Forecast commitment causes a stable MPS; a stable MPS requires lower total work-in-process and raw materials inventories. Remember the following cause-and-effect chain: lower inventory is enabled by a stable MPS; a stable MPS is enabled by predictable demand; predictable demand is enabled by forecast commitment.

Improved service levels

A predictable demand and a stable MPS enable production to build according to plan — near 100 percent is normal. It follows that near 100 percent customer service levels will result. Forecast commitment is the foundation.

Supplier partnerships and Just-in-Time

An integral part of supplier partnering is the sharing of the MPS. For your suppliers to build and deliver according to your MPS, they must have confidence that you will not make last minute changes. Stability that begins with forecast commitment is the root answer.

Reduction of direct labor

A stable MPS enables higher labor efficiency. You don't lose time from runs that are too short or incorporating unscheduled changeovers.

Motivate for Forecast Commitment

The key to developing forecast commitment lies in how well you motivate your salesforce. Your salespeople should reap their highest total commissions for exactly selling to the forecast. Any quantities over or under should earn progressively lower total commissions.

Design for Forecastability

Design model variations as add-ons so forecasts can be developed for the base units rather than for final variations. If your product is designed in such a manner that it must be built uniquely from the beginning, then you will have great difficulty in forecasting. You will also have higher inventories and costs.

Simplify for Forecastability

Complex product lines defy successful forecasting. Complexity in this area causes other costs as discussed in Profit Pointer 74 in Chapter 11. Simplification of your product line will give you a quick shot of cash and the substantial cost reductions attributable to an accurate forecast.

Manage Demand

You can use any of the great mathematical techniques to manipulate historic data to help develop a forecast of future sales — averaging, moving averaging, and exponential smoothing. All these techniques assume that the forecaster has no knowledge nor control over impending demand. You can and should manage demand. However, you will want to note the difference between demand management and demand manipulation.

Demand Manipulation

Most of your competitors manipulate demand. To understand the difference between management and manipulation, you must first understand the difference between natural demand and artificial demand. Think of natural demand as the demand for a product that occurs without the stimulation of any aggressive selling tactics — things like normal advertising or a price that allows normal profits and normal availability. Given these normal conditions of marketing, what will be the sales life cycle of a given product?

Assume that natural demand will allow you to sell 1,000 units a month. If you stimulate a demand greater than 1,000 units a month — say 1,500 a month — you may be pleased with the results. But look at where the extra sales came from. They came from the following month. So, the natural demand for the following month will drop to only 500 units. Now you might use another promotion to stimulate more demand. The result — you borrow another batch of demand from future months; this time, you have to double the stimulus. You have to borrow a demand of 500 units to bring demand up to the normal level, plus another 500 to get your 1,500 units-a-month goal. Stimulating artificial demand is a heady, addictive experience.

Sooner or later, you will not be able to artificially stimulate demand. You will come down hard — cold turkey — to a natural demand pattern that has been violated by your own manipulations. Unpredictably, your demand will fall to near zero. Then, it will zip back up, equally unpredictably. If you keep on trying to manipulate demand, it will zip up and down like a yo-yo — only with less predictability.

Now, run the figures on 10–15 products with varying degrees of maturity in their life cycles. The demand for each is zipping up and down unpredictably. Sometimes you will have multiple upswings that occur in the same week. You pull out all the stops and work double overtime through the weekend. Then, you may get multiple downswings that coincide the next week that result in no work. So, you build something for stock. Efficiency goes in the trash can. Inventory stacks up and quality goes out the window. The answer to the desperate chaos that results from a manipulated demand is to manage the natural demand.

Smooth the Natural Demand

Natural demand has fluctuations. However, they are nothing like the out-of-control roller-coaster ride of manipulated artificial demand. Managing demand means that you smooth out the fluctuations in the natural demand pattern. The prerequisite to demand management is to become a reasonably low-cost, high-quality producer. Low cost and high quality provide you two advantages. First, low cost provides you with higher margins. Second, high quality provides you with a higher level of natural demand. From that foundational advantage, you can apply a strategy that is not available to your competitors.

Aim for Level Production

Level production means that you produce the same quantity every day. Another aim is to keep your schedule frozen — that is, unchanging during the leadtime of your longest leadtime component. Two strategies work together to help you achieve those aims.

First, develop an intent to sell less than the projected natural demand. American firms err often by intending to sell more than their projected natural demand. You can only manage demand if you have some surplus demand. Remember, the goal for your business is to make all the profit you can. Making all the sales you can will often erode profits.

Second, use two tools — leadtime and price — to smooth demand. Your goal is to achieve a stable master production schedule and level production quantities. If demand exceeds what your level and stable production plan can produce, you may either raise the price or quote longer leadtimes. If demand falls below what you intend to produce via a level, stable production plan, you may lower prices; this is the right time for discounts or promotions. You don't want to build to stock and then try to move the product via discounts or promotions. Being the low-cost producer offers a substantial advantage if you have to lower prices. You can still make a profit at the lower price; your competitors cannot.

Benefits of Managed Demand

Managed demand and the resulting stability provide excellent reductions in total cost. For example, if you know that you will produce exactly 1,000 portable widgets next month, you will provide no more and no less than 1,000 sets of parts. You will not have excess inventory.

The trend in modern inventory management is to arrive at a constant scheduled flow of inventory. Such a flow — called Just-in-Time or Demand Flow — is considered the ultimate in inventory management. Some businesses dedicate teams of people, large budgets, and much time in an effort to attain a constant scheduled flow.

You don't have to dedicate a team of people or a large budget to realize the savings and efficiency of a constant scheduled flow of inventory. A level, stable master production schedule will catalyze a level, stable flow of inventory. Managing demand is the first step toward such a level, stable, scheduled flow of inventory.

Chapter Recap

Building a foundation for profits requires time. You should start the building process immediately so that you can begin to reap enhanced profits as early as possible. Most of the foundational issues of business have to do with long-term control of total costs. Morale, quality, product design, organizational structure, and general philosophy all contribute to higher costs.

CHAPTER 13

PREPARE FOR SECONDARY RESPONSES

For every problem, there exists a solution that is self-evident, convenient to implement, plausible, and disastrously wrong.

E very action has at least two effects. Your competitors are probably good at predicting the first effect — called the primary effect. They are probably dismally poor at predicting the aftereffect — or the secondary response. The success of their businesses — and of your business — is determined by a complex interaction of secondary responses. The primary effect of a business decision fades away quickly. The secondary response hangs on much longer, often forever. The end result is that the secondary responses run your business. Your job as a leader is to be able to predict secondary responses. All of your business planning should revolve around a predicted interplay of those long-term effects. At this moment, your competitors are concentrating on the primary effects of primary actions. The following pages contain the most common errors your competitors make. Knowing these errors is useful to your profit picture in two ways:

- ► You can predict the secondary responses of your competitors.
- ► You will know what primary actions will cause profit-robbing secondary responses.

Be very aware of the competitive advantage that you will have by practicing this kind of long-term thinking.

Know the Effects of Raising Prices

Raising prices is the most common first response to declining profits. Although pricing strategies are thoroughly discussed in Chapter 10, you still need to know how to anticipate the results of a price increase that is made in error.

The Primary Effect

Because most manufacturers sell through distribution channels, distributors and dealers that normally handle a product will continue to order after a price increase. The primary effect for your company in the case of a price increase is that you will see an increase in cash flow and profits. A ten percent price hike goes straight to the bottom line. The primary effect on profits is great: you may double or triple profits for a short time — then what?

The Secondary Response

As you know, a price increase will cause some lost sales. For every incremental price increase, there are fewer qualified buyers. The result is that fewer final purchasers will buy your product. You won't see the change in sales for several months due to the fact that distributors and dealers reduce their purchases long after a reduced demand is noted. When sales at the factory drop, most manufacturers do whatever is necessary to regain the lost sales — promotions, more models, coupons, rebates, new sales territories, new products, and parking lot sales — whatever it takes. Although these responses are invariably expensive, the driving necessity is to get the sales figures back to where they were. Until sales go back up — if they go back up — production volumes will be lower. Because of the loss of economy of scale, per-unit cost will go up. If the sales forecast did not predict the loss of volume, then inventories will increase and labor efficiency will go down. When costs go up, profits go down. When profits go down, your competitor will predictably react the same way as the first time the profits went down: prices will increase. You can predict the secondary response cycle: sales fall off, costs go up, profits down, prices up, sales down. Your competitor is locked in a position that requires an increase in sales efforts and attendant costs. You have an advantage.

What You Can Do

Resist the temptation to follow the price increase. Keep your prices stable. In a few months, you will begin to see increases in sales as customers begin to choose your product more frequently. The resultant production increases will improve your economy of scale and your per-unit costs will decrease. Your per-unit profit will increase and your total profits will increase.

There is an exception. Raising prices works well in cases of rapidly increasing demand. In all cases, maintain pressure toward reducing costs and increasing revenue. Often, raising prices does the opposite. Keep in mind, the consumer shift to your product will come slowly — one individual choice at a time. The shift will begin months after your competitor raised prices. It may not register as a measurable increase for much longer. Be patient and work on your own projects of increasing quality and reducing costs.

PROFIT POINTER

❦ 84 ❦

Know the Effects of Borrowing Money

Resist borrowing money in times when profits turn to losses. If you have pressing obligations for payroll, inventory and the like, use the techniques you learned in Chapter 11 to raise the cash. The best alternative is to monitor the future of your business by using an early warning system. Monitoring your future allows you to predict dips in profits or cash flow and to take preventative action before adversity strikes. Your competitors will likely respond to a shortage of cash or profits by going into the respond-to-the-crisis mode. They will borrow money to meet current obligations and press to sell more product. The results are predictable.

The Primary Effect

A business manager who negotiates a loan from a position of receding profits is normally thinking only of primary effects. The thought is to get caught up on some important tasks: catching up on past-due bills, making payroll, finishing an important project, granting past-due pay raises, increasing inventory, introducing a new variety of options to boost sales, or increasing promotions. Once the loan funds are in the bank, human nature will normally allow a harried manager relax. Watch a business that you know is struggling with profitability. Watch what happens when it secures a major loan or a cash investment. All problems are deferred. All sense of urgency goes away. Free spending takes over until the cash is gone.

The Secondary Response

If actions to correct the basic problem are not taken, when the cash is gone, the business conditions that brought on a decline of profits still exist, with some important additions:

> ► Interest costs increase the costs of operation. With higher costs, the profit picture will be worse than before the loan.

> ► Payment on the loan principal increases the pressure to perform after the cash proceeds of the loan are gone. Increased pressure encourages seat-of-the-pants decision making — not good in times of crisis.

The time that was bought with the proceeds of the loan allow preexisting profit-robbing conditions to entrench and to get progressively worse. Cash in the bank imparts a sense of security that defers facing the task of turning around a business.

What You Can Do

Remember that if one of your competitors secures a windfall of cash, the respite is likely temporary. Watch for signs of serious changes in the management of the business. You likely have distributors that handle the products of your competitor. They can tell you if the funds are being used for competitive improvements, such as quality enhancements. If your competitor keeps on doing business as usual, then you can simply wait until the cash is gone. Then, your competitor will be at a disadvantage because payments will be due. Your competitor may embark on a major expansion project with the new funds. An expansion from a position of weakness is often an error. If your competitor was losing money before a size-doubling expansion, then the expansion will double the losses. The reason is that the basic problems of excess costs and, more than likely poor quality, were never addressed. Even an expansion from a position of strength can cause bankruptcy, as illustrated in the following true story.

One business used the proceeds from a loan to build a $2 million expansion. The expansion was dedicated to a single major project — a project that the estimating department indicated would lose money. The company hoped — but did not calculate — that the expansion would help efficiency to the extent that the project would be profitable. The project still lost money. The company had to repay the $2 million. It was bankrupt within a year.

The foundational problems of the business were:

- *A lack of a system to report costs as they were incurred (no preventative cost-management measures were taken); and*
- *The organizational structure allowed people to make project management decisions who were not held accountable for their results.*

There was bickering and finger-pointing, but little management of the project.

The $2 million expansion did nothing to address the causes of unprofitability. If the company had been forced to make do with the resources it had, it might have faced its foundational management shortcomings.

Distressed companies are sometimes fond of automation. They will invest new money into a project to modernize or automate. They will gain nothing if they automate a process that is laden with waste, nor will they benefit from automating a process that is generating defects. The only thing that changes in automating such a process is that the defects can be generated with splash and dazzle — and at increased cost-per-defect. So, if your competitor just became cash-rich and is making a display of spending it — be patient. Listen for the sounds of self-destruction.

PROFIT POINTER

◈ 85 ◈

Know the Effects of Investors

The first effect of new money coming in from a cash investor is usually the same as new money from the proceeds of a loan. However, there are times when an influx of investment cash brings with it an investor who gets involved with the day-to-day management of the business. In the latter case, the primary effect will likely still be the same as in the case of cash from a loan.

The Primary Effect

An injection of cash from an investor is often misused in ways similar to the proceeds of a loan. In short, the cash will be spent on operating expenses. To the outside observer, the fresh cash has the same primary effects as if the company had suddenly become profitable: past-due accounts are paid, inventories become fatter, employees get pay raises, and the advertising budget gets a boost. The big difference that an investor may make will be seen in the secondary response.

The Secondary Response

A new voice in management may cause significant changes. The investor may have simply bought a plush management job in the competitor's business. Watch for indicators of real change, such as improvements in quality. Usually, however, a new voice in the midst of established management will make a lot of noise for a time, then usually settle in to the established way of doing things. The most intriguing secondary response to the addition of a major investor is that the company will either:

- ▶ Engage in infighting and neglect the foundational problems of the business to an even greater extent; or
- ▶ Subdue the newcomer and continue business-as-usual.

The exception to watch for is the case in which the investor has acquired majority control of your competitor and has made major management changes. In that case, the business may assume new and possibly successful strategies.

What You Can Do

If your competitor is distressed because of a lack of cost control and poor quality, then the proceeds from investment will dwindle away. When the cash is gone, your competitor will be the same high-cost, low-quality producer it was before the investment. If the new investor is actively changing the management of the company, watch for indications that the management philosophy of the company has changed for the better. If it has, then you will see refinements (simplifications) of product design, simplification of the product line, elimination of nonperforming employees (the talkers), and improved quality. If you see such indicators of higher performance, immediately employ the cost-controlling, quality-enhancing ideas you find in this book.

Recognize the Error of Downsizing

Profit Pointer

⋐ 86 ⋑

"What is downsizing?" "Why would you downsize?" "When do you downsize?" The questions were pointedly antagonistic. The questioner was an experienced manager of a successful manufacturing business. The victim was a younger manger who had just given a speech about downsizing techniques. The experienced manager was making a point at the expense of the speaker. The contention was that a company should be aware of its own business volumes to the extent that any resizing of the company should take place spontaneously. Additions or deletions of personnel should follow incrementally — or even precede — changes in business volume. Why wasn't the company managing demand so that dramatic resizing never became necessary?

Dramatic layoffs are evidence that management was asleep at the wheel. Downsizing is a red flag that indicates mismanagement. If you have a competitor who is downsizing, rightsizing, or restructuring, watch for the secondary response.

The Primary Effect

Downsizing happens when managers look at the financial statement and see that their company is in the red. Financial wizards check the financial statement and declare that sales and production are down by 15 percent; the obvious decision is to downsize by 15 percent. A little multiplication and the primary action is crystal clear — lay off 40 people and sell off 15 percent of assets. Forty layoffs and an auction later, the downsizing is complete. The immediate effect is $640,000 in lower costs and $30,000 in revenue from sales of assets. Of course, the assets were worth ten times what they sold for, but that is the reality of selling dedicated production equipment. So the company takes its downsizing lumps and goes on with business. Things are more or less corrected. Profits are back, although a little lower. In total, the first effect of the downsizing looks acceptable.

The Secondary Response

When a company engages in a mass layoff, who gets terminated? How do the layoff instructions get carried out? Whatever happens, the layoff results are typically dismal. There are two possible outcomes:

- ► The deadwood is canned; the best workers stay.
- ► The best workers are canned; the deadwood stays.

You can guess that the latter outcome occurs most often — the deadwood stays in a downsizing frenzy. The fact that a downsizing was necessary indicates that management was not paying attention. A lack of an early warning system, poor internal communications, and probably a chaotic organizational structure were all contributors to the need to downsize. Nothing changed within the inept management system the moment the layoff order was issued. In a poorly managed organization, the talkers rule. The doers are at the bottom of the social order — unpopular. The layoff gets the doers first and the deadwood stays.

Downsizing may cut some costs, but most overhead costs remain unchanged; some things cannot be downsized. Buildings and parking lots stay the same — so do the grounds, air conditioning, heating, insurance, data processing systems, fixturing, and warehouse shelving. The costs for these unchangeables stay the same. That means that your downsized competitor just increased the overhead cost per-unit of production — costs upsized, profits downsized.

What You Can Do

If you have a competitor who is downsizing, watch what is being cast off. The unthinking slash-and-burn downsizer will often get rid of products, machinery, and people that can be of great value to your business. (See Profit Pointer 88.)

If, for example, a competitor shuts down a product line and auctions the surplus, you may be able to buy tools and machinery that are set up for your type of product for ten cents on the dollar. There are even cases in which a business has bought an entire competitive product line, including designs, patents, and special tooling at highly distressed prices. Drastic downsizing is often an unthinking, faddish response to business distress. It does not address core problems in any way. If your competitor is downsizing, be patient and stay on your own course. You have the advantage.

Use Real Costing to Beat the Competition

By now, you are aware of the importance of using costing techniques that provide you with real cost figures. Correct costs lead to correct management decisions. Correct decisions lead to higher profits. Most companies use conventional costing techniques: overhead costs equally divided among all functions, allocated on the basis of direct labor per working hour. It is rare to encounter a business that uses any technique of costing other than conventional overhead distribution. The chances that your competitors are basing decisions on conventional costing are nearly 100 percent. The chances that your competitors are making errors in management decisions are also nearly 100 percent.

The Primary Effect

If your competition is using conventional costing techniques, then products and parts that have a high-labor content will show a high cost because of overhead loading per working hour. Low-labor items show a low cost; high-labor items will show a high cost, even if their consumption of overhead cost is, in reality, minimal. Look at the following example to understand this primary effect.

A firm located in the Pacific Northwest made small stainless steel tanks. All operations were manual, using simple machines and tools. The building was small and the equipment was fully depreciated. There was no depreciation overhead attributable to the small tank product line. Average labor was six hours per tank — 1,000 tanks per year required 6,000 hours — which equaled three full-time employees.

The firm entered the market of heavy steel custom fabrications. A custom-made four-inch capacity plate roll was installed in a new building. The total cost of the facility was close to $500,000. Depreciation alone was $71,000 a year on a seven-year schedule. The plate roll was used about four hours per project, 20 times a year — which equaled one employee for 80 hours.

Conventional costing techniques evenly distributed the new overhead load to all working hours at $11.68 per working hour — whether at the four-inch plate roll or on the small tank line. The new overhead figure added $70.08 to the cost of the average small tank — more than the previous total cost of labor ($60.00). This resulted in $70.08 that was taken out of the profit of an item with a previous profit of $300.00 per tank.

The overhead attributed to heavy projects on the four-inch plate roll averaged $46.72; nearly nothing for a project that would sell for $30,000.00. The result: $46.72 out of the profits that averaged $7,500.00 per project. Function-driven overhead allocation would have attributed all of the $71,000.00 depreciation to the plate roll projects. That would be $888.00 per hour or $3,552.00 per project out of the average $7,500.00 profit. Conversely, the small tank line would have seen no increase in costs or decrease in profits under function-driven costing techniques.

The Secondary Response

Eventually, the firm in the above example acquired more heavy fabrication equipment. Overhead on the small tank line continued to increase until the line was no longer profitable. Prices increased to cover costs until the small tanks were no longer price competitive. Sales and production dropped. Finally, production of small tanks was closed down because the line was uncompetitive.

The $300,000 a year in real profits that were generated by the small tank line dropped as sales dropped. The profits ceased totally with the closure of the line. The decision was founded on conventional cost data. The closure was a slash-and-burn cost-cutting error. The overhead that was being absorbed (in error) by the small tank line was gradually redistributed to the heavy projects. As real costs were attributed to the heavy projects, the bid prices went up to maintain the target 25 percent profit margin. As bid prices went up, the number of contracts that were won diminished. The number of working hours diminished. As working hours went down, the overhead allocation per working hour went up, bid pricing went up, and new contracts went down. Three years later, the company was bankrupt, all resulting from erroneous management decisions based on incorrect cost distribution.

What You Can Do

If your competitor is using conventional costing techniques, the decision making quality of management will be affected much like the example of the Pacific Northwest fabricator. Those decision errors will manifest themselves as price increases in low-end, labor-intensive products. You will find this is especially prevalent in manufacturers that have a relatively wide diversity of product types. When you see price increases in your competitors' low-end products, compete! Keep your prices down. Offer better service and upgrade quality. When your competitor is focusing on the high-end products and taking their focus off the low-end, that is your indicator of improper overhead distribution causing bad decisions.

You can take all of your competitors' low-end business and all the profits that go with it. Just make sure that you have function-driven costing in place so that you know how to price your low-end products.

Upgrade Your Workforce via Competitors' Errors

A slash-and-burn cost cutter will tend to make the first cuts in direct labor. Usually, these cuts are not the result of well-thought-out projects to reduce labor requirements. Rather they are direct, across-the-board cuts. The reasoning is the erroneous belief that labor is the most versatile and flexible element of cost. That simple-minded belief purports this: if you need to cut costs by ten percent, then terminate ten percent of your workforce. The rest of your employees will work harder to protect their jobs. There are some serious problems with an attack on direct labor.

The Primary Effect

The slash-and-burn cost cutter is correct in the assessment that the remaining workforce will work harder to protect their jobs, but only at first. The primary effect will be exactly as expected: a ten percent reduction in workforce results in ten percent less labor costs with nearly the same production. The dollars can be tacked directly to the bottom line. Profits go up and everyone is happy — everyone except the ten percent of employees who were terminated and the 90 percent who are left doing ten percent more work.

The Secondary Response

For the remaining 90 percent of the employees to produce at 100 percent of scheduled production, they must work at a pace that is beyond their normal capacity. Within a few weeks, they will drift back down to normal. Production will be at 90 percent. Orders will be late; backorders will increase. The master production schedule will be altered to satisfy irate customers. Overtime will increase. To catch up the ten percent shortfall in production, new employees are hired to fill in the crisis spots.

Before long, the workforce will be back up to 100 percent — back to what it was before the layoff. The difficulty is that the new ten percent of employees are inexperienced. The firm will experience the typical errors and inefficiencies that are typical of new employees. For months, production will be a few percentage points short. Add this type of management-induced layoff cycle to the real requirements that sometimes dictate seasonal layoffs and you have two layoff-rehire cycles that give rise to confusion in management and in the workforce.

Manufacturing thrives on stability and predictability. Confusion always adds costs. The cost-cutting company will experience a production shortfall at the same direct labor cost that it had a few months earlier. Per-unit and total profit will be lower. Management will start considering an across-the-board layoff — again. A post-secondary response of the layoff-rehire cycle is demoralization of the workforce. People rely on their jobs as the source of the essentials of life. If their lifestyles are threatened every six months, the effect is demoralization. The work-harder-to-compensate-for-mismanagement condition is also demoralizing.

What You Can Do

Pick up experienced and talented employees when your competitor goes into a layoff frenzy. Don't be too concerned whether you have a specific opening — quality people who are experienced in your type of business are of great value. You can find the ideal spot after you have them employed.

Work on your own internal policies and procedures to help yourself establish a level production plan. Level production prevents you from entering a layoff-rehire cycle that can endanger your own workforce.

Remember earlier lessons. Direct labor represents only ten percent of the product cost in most American manufactured products. The opportunities for cost reductions abound in overhead and in materials; you will find 90 percent of typical manufacturing costs in overhead and materials. Those are the costs that are least frequently attacked with cost-reduction projects.

An influx of high-quality, experienced people can help you press down the costs of overhead and materials. Work on reducing the costs of overhead and materials. Keep your labor force stable and make sure to boost employee morale. You will have a unique competitive advantage.

PROFIT POINTER

❧ 89 ❧

Predict Effects of New Products out of Weakness

New products are exciting. Managers like to think of the new markets that will open up, such as hot demand, a seller's market, or pricing that will cover the excess costs of the business and turn a new profit. Talk of a new product will:

- ▶ Add life to staff meetings;
- ▶ Be the topic of reports;
- ▶ Excite dealers and distributors; and
- ▶ Break the monotony of trying to turn a profit with the old products.

On the other hand, a new product from a position of weakness can be a terminal burden. Before you consider a new product introduction, your business should have the following strengths.

- A positive cash flow with some reserve of cash in the bank;
- Past-due accounts that have been paid up-to-date;
- Employee morale that is on the upswing;
- Corporate priorities placed on cost reductions with several projects nearing completion; and
- Simplification as an accepted guiding principle of management.

Conversely, if your competitor introduces a new product from a position of weakness, you can expect the following primary effect and secondary response.

The Primary Effect

Excitement will be high. People will be motivated and optimism will abound. The product engineering staff will be willing to work extensive overtime to beat the introduction deadline. Manufacturing will scurry to set up for new production. Talk of the new product will permeate the dealer-distributor network and your dealers and distributors will be primed to buy. Your customers will quickly consume the first production run and orders will come in for more. The product will be an obvious success. Management will relax and turn its focus on other projects.

The Secondary Response

The raw cash requirements of a new product introduction are enormous: development labor, additional inventory, and direct labor at all stages to fill the pipeline with parts. Also, there are costs for agency approvals, prototypes, field trials, scrap and rework to prove and modify components, promotional literature, and crisis overtime; it all adds up. The bills come due long before cash comes in from the first round of production. Cash flow goes from slightly negative to a total disaster. Orders for the second round of raw materials are deferred due to cash flow problems. Production of the second round is postponed because of parts shortages. Shipments are missed and customers are irate.

Further, a crash development program may overlook a few functional flaws in the product, which can result in returned units for warranty work. The result: engineering change orders (ECOs) are issued to correct the flaws and parts become obsolete and are scrapped. The changes require more testing and more ECOs. The result is more production inefficiency and more missed shipments. Established products suffer due to the focus on the new product. Costing of the product — if any was attempted — is an early estimate before the final details were filled in. The cost was based on conventional costing techniques, so any additional overhead caused by the new product is absorbed by existing products.

All factors work together to make the cost of a new product optimistically low. Data from the first production run show enormous over-runs. The second run is better, but costs still indicate that a price increase will be required. Dealers scream in protest of the price hike. They extract promises to hold the price line for six months. Your competitor is locked into production of a new product at a loss — from a position of negative cash flow and scant cash reserves.

What You Can Do

Prepare for an orderly introduction of a new product when your business is strong. Resist the temptation to beat your competitor to market with a new product. First-to-market is rarely a long-term advantage. Even in the short term, first-to-market is not a reliable advantage. Wait until the market is proven, then introduce a higher quality product at a lower price, from a position of strength. In the long term, you will have a competitive advantage.

PROFIT POINTER

❧ 90 ❧

Avoid the Sales-at-Any-Cost Syndrome

A common reaction to lost profits is to promote sales-at-any-cost, whether it be by adding new products, new options, or new levels of diversification. The hope is to secure every sale possible. The objective is to fill the marketplace with such an array of models, variances, options, and accessories that customers will look no further. A complimentary element of the sales-at-any-cost tactic is to offer discounts and expand sales territories. The total philosophy is to fill the marketplace — a tactic that will not work in the long term.

The Primary Effect

Adding a product adds to total sales. The same is true for model variations, options, and accessories. In every line of products, there are always potential sales for one more model, accessory, and option. Those potential sales represent a demand void that cries out to be filled. The accepted truth that more sales equal more profits cannot be denied.

The Secondary Response

A competitor that embraces the fill-the-marketplace philosophy probably has a complex product line. Inventories are already high. The master production schedule is ripped apart with interruptions and shortened runs. Expediting and premium freight are the order of the day, every day. The production control department is overstaffed for the dollar volume of the business. Backorders abound because there is always a hole in the inventory. Product engineering is overloaded with product documentation chores and ECOs. Engineering errors are prevalent. Corrections come late due to the overload. Scrap and rework are high because of the high numbers of parts and the short runs. Labor efficiency is low; total manufacturing costs are high.

A competitor with a complex product line will seek out an automated system to help control the excess inventories of consistently incorrect items. Such systems are commonly referred to as materials requirements planning (MRP). MRP systems are notoriously difficult to implement. A business with a complex product will have higher-than-average difficulties with MRP. The system implementation will stall because the complex product line cannot be adequately identified and documented. If it ever runs, MRP will be plagued with errors. More production control personnel are required to make MRP work.

The company has no idea of per-product costs. Complex product lines are seldom costed on a per-product basis. When they are costed, the effort is frequently quick-and-dirty because there are so many items with which to deal. Salespeople will equally promote the losers and profitable items. One more product further overloads an already overloaded system. The effect of one more product on sales can be unpredictable.

Companies that have full, complex product lines will commonly introduce a new product that has no clear, definable advantages over competing products. But the new item may have a clear, definable advantage over its own line-mate. The sales of the new product do just fine. The older product loses the sales volume gained by the new product. The business experiences higher costs with little added sales volume.

What You Can Do

If your competitor has a full product line, you have no immediate advantage. Offer high quality, low prices, and dealer support. Produce and sell the mainstay products: the top 20 percent that comprises 80 percent of sales. Your competitor will eventually falter due to pure overload. Costs will go out of control. Product prices will soar as your competitor withdraws dealer support and compromises quality. Every manufacturer who tries to fill the marketplace follows the same chain of cause and effect. You will win in the long term. You have a competitive advantage, but it is subtle. You must simply stay aware of your advantage and stay on your course.

Know the Strength of the Giant

Head-to-head competition with a large, powerful, established producer is normally an error. Four reasons that lead a company to believe that it can successfully compete with the giants include:

1. Tantalizing sales leads. The customer who promises to buy a product if your business would just make it available.
2. Oversights. Sometimes a company is unaware that there is a giant dominating the marketplace.
3. Mistaken beliefs. The belief that the giants are too big to be efficient. The too-big-to-be-efficient theory may be correct, but don't bet the farm on it.
4. Costing errors. Don't rely on inaccurate initial cost estimates that imply you can make enormous profits at the going market price.

The Primary Effect

In most cases, the first effect is costs that exceed selling prices. High volume producers experience an economy of scale so great that a small producer is at a marked disadvantage. Sales will be to customers who are disgruntled with the big producer — not an ideal customer base. Opportunities for significant sales are few.

The Secondary Response

The small producer will try a number of tactics to regain the start-up costs of the product — price discounts, impressive sales efforts, and quick response to custom configurations. The giant may ignore the small producer completely. Any competitive response made by the giant will be devastating. The large, powerful producer can maintain a below-cost marketing position until the small producer is out of business. The only possible ways to survive competition with a large producer is to:

▶ Offer low-volume, custom configurations that the giant will not accept.
▶ Serve a small territory that is very expensive for the big producer to serve.
▶ Serve dealers that the large producer uses its size to manipulate.

What You Can Do

If you are an astute businessperson, you may know of cases in which a small producer successfully kicked a giant out of the marketplace. It does happen, but it is the exception. There is a set of circumstances in which a small producer can outcompete the giant. Simply stated, it is a case of the lean and quick outmaneuvering the fat and slow. In such a David-and-Goliath showdown, the following circumstances should prevail for the small producer to succeed.

▶ The small producer will be efficient, well-managed, and focused. Focused means that it will be dedicated to a limited, well-defined product line.

▶ The small producer will be very well-capitalized. Introductory pricing may well be below-cost for months — years in some cases — to gain market acceptance over the large producer. State-of-the-art equipment is required, even though initial production volumes cannot justify the investment.

▶ The large producer will be overconfident. The giant will be convinced that the new competitor is not a threat and will initiate little or no competitive response.

▶ The large producer will be high-cost, bureaucratic, and slow to move. Quality defects, customer distancing, and coercive marketing techniques all will work to the disadvantage of the large producer.

Remember that the small producer has few inherent advantages; the large producer has few inherent disadvantages. A successful small-over-large upset depends on advantageous circumstances and on sharp, quick management. The lean and quick manufacturers in the Pacific Rim nations are very good in finding the fat and slow producers. They have staged a series of small-over-large upsets that continue today. They have proven that it can be done regularly. If they can do it, so can you. Nevertheless, there are less dangerous ways of making profits in manufacturing.

Diversify with Low Risk

PROFIT POINTER
◈ 92 ◈

In Chapter 12, Profit Pointer 77 recommended slight diversification when you design a new product. Slight diversification lends stability to a manufacturer. Too much diversification, on the other hand, is volatile and hard to manage. A diversification rule of thumb is: great diversification equals great risk; small diversification equals small risk. If the position of a company is weak, it should keep diversification small. In other words, it should do what it does best until it is profitable and has a good cash reserve. Diversification requires entering unknown territories with unpredictable costs and uncertain results. Also, take a look at the effects of diversification on the four major functional areas.

Product development

Development of a new type of product involves techniques and tools that the company may not have available. Waiting time, learning time, and cash are required. The primary effect is that the introduction timetable will fall behind schedule and will go overbudget. The secondary response is that management will require shortcuts in an attempt to get back on schedule and within budget. Design quality will suffer. The cost of manufacturing will be higher than projected; quality will be lower than expected. The introduction will likely be behind schedule, which will plant seeds of trouble for the sales department.

Manufacturing

Manufacturing will be inexperienced with the production techniques required to produce the new product type. The primary effect is that new machinery and processes will take unplanned time and money to master. The first production run will start later and take longer than anticipated. The cost of start up will exceed estimates. Per-unit costs will likely exceed initial cost estimates. The secondary response is that promised deliveries will be late. High costs will cause cash flow shortages — a serious difficulty for an already weak business. Customers will be irate.

Sales and marketing

A greatly diverse new product requires different selling techniques. It appeals to different demographic targets. The primary effect is that marketing personnel must learn the subtleties of the new sales process. New strategies and tactics must be developed. New market channels must be established. The secondary response is that something in the new marketing effort will produce results that are less than expected; marketing is an inexact science. Initial sales volumes will be erratic and lower than expected. The costs of market experimentation will be high. Revenues and profits will be lower than anticipated.

Finance

Costs will accumulate at unexpectedly high rates and revenues will be erratic and lower than expected. Cash flow will be lower than expected and profits will likely be negative. New dealers will offer unproven credit risks. The unpredictability of the results of the new product will keep the finance department in disarray. Cash flow will be difficult to predict with accuracy. Financial planning will be hampered.

What You Can Do

When any company introduces a new product that is significantly diverse, the odds are that suffering will follow. If the financial position of the company is weak, then introduction of a significantly diverse product can be terminal. Gambling that the product will be successful is a long shot. If your competitor introduces a diverse product that happens to be well-accepted, then learn from the situation and consider entering the same market. You can redesign to eliminate the hurried flaws and serve the market with a lower-cost, higher-quality product.

Chapter Recap

The ability to accurately predict secondary responses is among the most valuable of management skills; it is also among the most rare. Primary-effect thinking is what drives most businesses. Since secondary responses often cancel out the primary effects of yesterday, managers run from one primary crisis to another. Your competitive advantage is to avoid the perpetual crisis of managing for primary effect only.

The primary effects of some decisions may initially contribute to the success of your business. Those first effects soon fade. What is left are the seeds of permanent secondary responses that plague most businesses with excess costs that will not go away. You need to remember the primary effects that are so appealing. You need to remember the inevitable secondary responses that are so withering. Predict and manage the interactions of secondary responses and you will build a business that is easy to manage and consistently profitable.

PART V

TURNAROUND SEQUENCE

Every act of significance has been achieved by people with desire and conviction — except in the case of slavery, which precedes rebellion.

A turnaround is a rapid-fire series of decisions and directions that are simple in concept. To successfully turn a company around, assume that nothing is right. Scrutinize everything with a criticism that is eager to change or to cast out. Your goal is to terminate activity that does not add value. Seek opportunities to redirect the activity of your business. While you are making decisions and giving directions, keep in mind these four concepts.

1. Simplification. Any revised activity will be easier to comprehend, involve fewer steps, and not be as subject to error.
2. Revenues. Any revised activity should have an upward pressure on revenues.
3. Costs. Any revised activity should have a downward pressure on costs.
4. Secondary responses. Any revised activity will have a respect for the power of secondary responses — effects that are usually permanent.

The real turnaround winners excel at making single decisions that will simplify, press revenues up and press costs down, while creating beneficial secondary responses.

To gain knowledge that supports business profits is one thing. Making it happen in the real world is another. A turnaround of profits is a people project. Everything that is done — every decision, every action, every reversal of a profit-robbing practice — gets done by people. As the leader of a turnaround effort, your job is entirely people-oriented. Even when you intensely analyze cost data or perform some other lonely chore, you do it so that you can help people work more effectively. Your job is to organize, instruct, and motivate. The role of people in the success of a business is vital.

The first four parts of this book have provided you with the knowledge to make the correct decisions — knowledge that will help you transform chaos and conflict into activity that adds saleable value to your product or service. Part V is dedicated to guiding you to make those decisions in the most effective sequence.

CHAPTER 14

STEP ONE: BUILD THE FOUNDATION

Knowledge without action is poverty. Action without knowledge is poverty preceded by hard work.

There are three essential steps to a turnaround project — build the foundation, organize and monitor, and achieve your objectives. This three-step sequence has evolved from successful turnaround experiences. Your exact sequence may differ because of differences in your company, differences in your own personality, or differences in the personalities of other people who are involved. You should attempt this sequence first because it is efficient; it reduces the amount of time required to cause a turnaround. A 90-day turnaround is possible.

The turnaround sequence in this book disagrees with the methods used by many well-known turnaround specialists. Those specialists use "big" solutions. Specifically, they will sell off assets and use the cash to buy "higher performing" assets. Such methods quickly enrich the cash position of the business and drive the price of stock up — sometimes a lot. Higher stock prices constitute a "turnaround," so the job is "done." Such a tactic usually results in higher costs — the cause and effect sequence is complex — which in the long term, drive profits further down. The root causes of lost profits are never addressed, so they stay around to erode profits forever. The three-step sequence that your company can use is less risky; it is also far more certain to provide profits in future years.

The three-step turnaround sequence is best engineered from the top leadership position — either the president, owner, or CEO. The turnaround can be accomplished from some subordinate positions if the person leading the effort is an exceptional leader and if that person is capable of helping all departments work together in a mutually supportive effort. Keep in mind, the three-step sequence of turnaround events in these final three chapters is described from the perspective of the top manager.

Some companies will not respond to the turnaround formula. You need to know if your company falls into a group that will not respond. If your company is experiencing one of the following particularly adverse circumstances, then you need to directly remedy that disqualifying circumstance before you attempt the turnaround.

A cold market
If you are building a product line that has lost appeal to the buying public, then completely change your product offerings. For example, if you are building manual typewriters, your sales are essentially dead.

An inept staff
Fast-growth companies in hot markets are apt to develop a management and staff that are unable to manage adverse conditions. Such companies harvest rich profits because the markets will accept pricing that covers any degree of inefficiency. When the markets cool, competition wipes profits away due to high costs. You may find that such a company simply does not have enough basic business skills to reduce costs and simplify. Practical, experienced, resourceful individuals are necessary in your key positions to put a turnaround plan into effect. In a distressed situation, you may not have enough time to recruit and train a staff of professionals. If the majority of the staff and management are poorly skilled, a turnaround manager will be faced with organized resistance and even ridicule.

A closed-minded top manager
The top manager is the key to success. If the top manager's mindset is closed to the practices required to turn the business around, then the business will always continue on the path that brought about distress in first place. In this situation, a new top manager is required to cause a turnaround.

An operation too focused on one product
A company that is dedicated to a single product type and a single market can lose sales very quickly as the market becomes saturated.

This also happens when there is a change in the national economy. The only option is to get into another type of business: an option that may be impossible with highly specialized resources.

Depleted resources

If your business has been depleting resources for an extended period of time, the resources available may be too modest to provide a foundation from which to launch the turnaround. For the turnaround sequence to work, some minimum resources are required, including operational equipment, a reasonable flow of orders, key experienced people, enough parts and materials to continue production, and some cash and accounts receivables.

Most unprofitable companies can be turned around, barring the five extremes cited above. Conduct the project with a confidence that it can be done. Confidence on the part of the turnaround leader is a good as cash in the bank.

PROFIT POINTER

◈ 93 ◈

Adopt a 90-Day Goal

The leader's first task is to adopt a 90-day goal for achieving profits. Another twelve months of followup will be required to fully clean up profit-robbing conditions. The follow-up work is a continuation of the initial 90-day effort. Start with corrections of the worst profit-robbing conditions in the first 90 days. A timeframe of 90 days makes a good project length from the perspective of human psychology. People can get excited about a project that promises measurable results in the near future. Their excitement stimulates high levels of performance.

The 90-day turnaround is vital for immediate survival. However, it is a tenuous condition that is easily reversed as people fall back into old habits. The 12-month followup is the time to solidify profitable practices. After twelve months of reinforcement, your employees will continue the practices that you have initiated. You will establish a set of habits that will promote continued profitability.

PROFIT POINTER

◈ 94 ◈

Start with a Kickoff Meeting

Imagine that you are going to lead a turnaround in a company that is new to you. You are the new top manager. You do not know the people; they don't know you. The people of the company know something big is going to happen, but they don't know what. So, remember the basics of human nature in such a condition. The unknown breeds fear; fear breeds defensiveness.

You will be dealing with a group of people who are defensive. They will be quiet and noncommittal. They will listen and wait. They are waiting for any indicators of insincerity, dishonesty, arrogance, or egotism. If their curiosity of who and what you are is not fulfilled soon, then your employees will become aggressive. They will ask difficult questions. They will demand to know your plan and intent. Your job is to communicate first. You do that with a kickoff meeting with key people. These key people normally include the managers that report directly to the president or CEO. Others may be included if their functions are vital to the project.

Hold the kickoff meeting the first day that you arrive or the first day of the 90-day timeframe — the morning hours are the best. The formal goal of the meeting is to inform key employees of the general plan of the turnaround. One informal goal is to build a foundation of open communications and mutual trust. A second informal goal is for you to learn something about the immediate status of the business; there are likely some problems of crisis proportion that these people must handle immediately. A third informal goal is that you will be gathering information so that you can eliminate the deadwood (talkers) and effectively utilize the people who get things done (doers). The plan for the kickoff meeting will include a topic, list of attendees, and a timeframe scheduled for the meeting.

The topic

You will announce the general plan — that is, to establish profits in ninety days. You will provide some general instructions, concepts, and principles. You will explain the basics of your techniques — things like, press costs down and press revenues up. You will talk about basic, general issues — such as causes of lost profits and excess costs, organizational structure, and morale. You will let the employees know you will formulate a final plan after you have listened to each of them extensively. Let them know that they will contribute substantially to the final plan.

Who should attend

Ultimately, your staff meetings will have five attendees plus yourself. The heads of the four functional departments — manufacturing, finance, product engineering, and sales and marketing — plus an executive assistant. In this first meeting, however, you will likely have eight to ten attendees because you will need to initially involve all key people. Remember, you are gathering information and you are learning who is really doing the work and who is doing the talking. The eight to ten key people will soon be sorted out when you reorganize.

Length of the meeting

Allocate 90 minutes, but schedule an open-ended time so an extended meeting is possible. You want to stimulate open conversation. If you can get 90 minutes of active questions and answers, consider the meeting a grand success. You should talk 40 to 50 percent of the time; others should talk a little more — 50 to 60 percent of the time. This is your prime opportunity to become recognized as a listener.

Attendees should leave the first meeting with a belief that the company has entered a new era; an era of significant change. They should leave with a degree of enthusiasm in support of the changes that are to come. They should leave with excitement. You will be walking a tightrope in the first meeting. You must show evidence of an unshakable strength, without being intimidating. You can do that by knowing the business; by having a certainty that your plans will work. You must also show that you value the ideas of others.

Answer All Questions

The group will ask questions. Your answers lay the foundation for the entire turnaround effort. The answers that you give set the mood: they indicate your attitude. You must anticipate two things about the questions. First, you need to anticipate what questions will be asked. Second, you need to anticipate what the employee really wants to know. The kinds of questions that will be asked are usually going to be specific, such as:

 ▶ What are you going to do about accounts receivable?
 ▶ Are you going to change sales commissions?
 ▶ Will there be layoffs?
 ▶ Will you initiate a quality program?
 ▶ Do you really believe that you can turn this business around in 90 days?

Look closely at the last question for clues to what the employee really wants to find out. The person who asks this question really wants to know whether you intend to make the turnaround an effort that is going to include the people or if you intend to do it yourself and grab the glory. Your answer should assure the employees that they will be involved and will have influence. In general, this first question-and-answer session can be likened to two new dogs in a neighborhood meeting for the first time. They are bristled and prepared to fight. Each stalks the other, looking for signs of weakness and strength. Your delicate task is to exhibit a strength that is sufficient to subdue a challenge. However, you must refrain from beating up potential opponents to prove your strength. Your task is to build a powerful, efficient, well-informed team that can attack and subdue the challenges to the profits of the business.

The question regarding layoffs is the most sensitive issue. Employees are most concerned about whether they will be laid off. If you answer yes this early, you will inspire fear and damage morale. If you answer no, you will create suspicion of your honesty. The right answer is, "You will tell me if there will be layoffs. You will tell me when, how many, and in what departments we need to lay off. We will lay off no more than we have to and we will call back as soon as we can."

Let people know what to expect and what not to expect. Give them as many "knowns" as possible. You want to remove the element of fear as quickly as possible so you can get on with the turnaround. Let them know what to immediately expect. You will be meeting with them individually for several days, asking their opinions of the causes of the lost profits. Then you will have another formal meeting. Schedule the formal meeting in about two weeks. Your employees may want an interim meeting. If so, do it — you can't communicate too much during the critical first two weeks. The topic of the second meeting will be to finalize a list of things to be done to turn around the company.

Conduct One-on-One Q&A Sessions

PROFIT POINTER

◆ 95 ◆

Allow a week for one-on-one question and answer (Q&A) sessions. Most of the time you spend will be dedicated to firming up new relationships and developing a common language. You will meet with each key person at least two times — maybe more. You will ask questions and you will encourage them to ask questions. As people become more comfortable with you, they will give you more direct and honest answers. The answers that you get will fall into two categories.

1. What is wrong. The manager may give you the answer that he or she thinks you might want to hear, or a superficial condition that has no real bearing on profits. You must listen to these answers and continue to probe deeper.
2. What is really wrong. You will learn what is really wrong after you have established a level of comfort with the manager. These are the answers that you are looking for. These are the conditions that will help you discover root causes of diminishing profits.

When you conduct the first round of Q&A sessions, you will gain clues to the real issues. Those clues will help you formulate the questions for the next round of sessions. Keep up with your Q&A sessions until you have a list of root causes of lost profits. You will perfect the list in your next staff meeting to eventually formulate assignments to the top managers of the four functional departments. That list of causes will turn into your final action plan.

When staff and managers reach a point of being comfortable with an honest conversation with you, you will find that they will tend to "dump" — that is, they will deluge you with complaints about what is wrong. Some complaints might sound immature or overly sensitive. Recognize that this type of behavior is typical for employees who may have been overloaded for some time. They are also testing you to find out if you are a willing listener. Listening to what they have to say is an essential part of the turnaround effort. Some of what you hear will be valuable. Most of it is an essential dumping of an emotional load so that they can get on board and be part of the team. After they dump, you can get down to real business.

When you are asking questions, it is your job to be specific and to keep the session on topic. Ask the people to explain their opinions of the causes of excess costs in the company. Then ask them for their ideas of the causes of lost revenues. At first, they will be vague. If they have no responses, be even more specific and ask questions like:

- ► Do we have a problem with errors on drawings?
- ► Do we have a problem with excess scrap?
- ► Do materials cost too much? Why?
- ► Is our product priced too high?

You may want to review chapters 5 through 10 to help you formulate specific questions that you want to ask. It is totally appropriate to ask the finance manager questions about manufacturing or to ask the product development manager questions about finance. There are several reasons to do this. One is that people see errors in other areas much better than they see errors in their own departments. Another is that actions taken in one department may cause excess costs in another department.

During this week of Q&A sessions, take the time to converse with the employees who are doing the work. The employees who do the work suffer the consequences of management decisions. You will find that the distressed company has made a number of management mistakes. Often the only people who know that the act turned into an error are the people who do the work. In short, people in offices theorize about the effects of decisions. Ask questions and listen to the answers. If you have never listened to the wisdom of the employees who do the work, you will probably be amazed. They know the problems and they often have extremely competent and workable solutions. Usually, their solutions are inexpensive and effective.

You will discover that you and your key people will be interrupted by crisis after crisis. You should keep informed of each crisis, but do not try to resolve each one. First, you do not need to get sidetracked into the daily details. Second, you will probably make a worse decision than the person who would normally handle the crisis.

You should only act if you recognize that a disaster-level decision is about to be implemented. Even then, it is best to refrain from overruling the decision. Speak to the people responsible. Instruct them and give them the opportunity to learn why the decision is an error. They will appreciate the opportunity to modify their own decision rather than have you overrule it. Remember, one of your goals is to build a high-morale, competent staff.

Develop a Plan and Consensus

PROFIT POINTER

◈ 96 ◈

The meeting of the top manager and the people who report directly to the top manager is called a staff meeting. You know that the total attendance of a staff meeting will ultimately be six people: the top manager, the top manager of the four functional departments, and an executive secretary. Anyone else in attendance is an invited guest. In the case of a turnaround project, the invited guest might be an advisor or coach to keep the project on track. Staff meetings are normally held once a week at a predetermined time.

Every staff meeting should be preceded by an agenda. The agenda should be distributed at least 24 hours (48 hours is better) in advance of the meeting. Remember that the purpose of the staff meeting is to develop plans, solve problems, and prescribe methods of progress. You never want to put a staff member on the spot. If a staff member will be responsible for reporting on progress of some project, for example, that staffer should have ample time to prepare the details. An executive assistant should prepare and distribute the agenda. For an idea of what to include in the agenda, refer to the sample meeting agenda located at the end of this chapter.

Minutes of the meetings should be recorded by the executive assistant and distributed within 24 hours. Minutes of staff meetings should be simple — no more than one page. Minutes should record important decisions and directions. The purpose of minutes is to verify what was decided and to document who is responsible for what. Sample meeting minutes are also located at the end of this chapter. Minutes should include:

- ▶ The time, date, and place of the meeting and who was in attendance;
- ▶ The status of any project that has been reported;
- ▶ Specific directions or important decisions made by the top manager; and
- ▶ Who is responsible for what assignments, what results are expected, and by what date.

Your task is to make certain that every department has at least one task assigned. It should be a task that is achievable in a short time and it should be easy to achieve with measurable results. One or two easy successes help people believe that the 90-day goal is possible. Early success lends enthusiasm; enthusiasm lends energy. Be sure to offer recognition for the early victories in particular. Early victories are frequently easier than you might think. An example is this following true story.

———————

There was a turnaround manager working for a distressed consumer electronics firm. Cash flow was poor. Backorders were high. The manager — a hands-on, get-involved type of person — browsed the backorders to get an idea of what items were short. Later, the manager toured the finished goods stockroom. There were quantities of items in finished goods that were also on the list of backorders. The manager asked the warehouse manager why the goods did not ship to fill backorders." Give me a shipping release and I'll ship them," was the reply.

The manager wrote down some stock numbers and went to the shipping department. "We have backorders for these items. Why don't you print a shipping release for them?" asked the manager. Shipping browsed the computer and discovered that the available-to-ship quantities were zero. After a lot of legwork and questioning, the manager discovered that every item in finished goods had a safety stock of ten. All the people in shipping had been told that they were to never ship any of the safety stock; it was to be saved for emergencies. The result was that ten of everything was permanently lodged on the shelf. A previous manager had mandated a ten-of-everything safety stock and had never followed up on the results. The solution was easy — just change the safety stock in the inventory master file and start shipping the unnecessary safety stock. How the solution was implemented is the headline story here.

The manager brought the sales and manufacturing managers into a conference meeting. The ten-of-everything rule in finished goods was revealed to them. The manager told them that they were free to do whatever they wished with the ten-of-everything rule. The sales manager and manufacturing manager agreed to abolish the ten-of-everything rule.

By the next day, backorders were shipping and warehouse space was free. By the end of the month, most backorders had shipped, inventory was down significantly, and cash flow was up. At the next staff meeting, the turnaround manager announced what the sales and manufacturing departments had done. All the recognition was given to the two mangers who made the decision and implemented the change.

This case is not unique. Distressed companies abound with such opportunities. Find some potential successes and let your people start succeeding. Simple successes happen when you:

- Discover a work simplification.
- Solve a design problem.
- Reduce setup time.
- Eliminate walk or travel — even one step.

Devise a regular way to recognize the small contributions. Make certain that you give equal recognition to the managers and their employees for their contributions.

Prepare by Advanced Research

Before the planning meeting, you will need to do some homework. You will have a list of causes of lost profits that you have gleaned from interviews with key staff members. You have little idea of the degree of losses that are caused by any item on the list. Neither can you be certain that any item on the list is indeed a cause of loss at all.

For example, an item on your list might read, "Loss of sales of quick-change widgets." But are you indeed losing sales of quick-change widgets? Are quick-change widgets profitable? What is the degree of the loss of sales, if any? You need to do the research to verify the sales history of quick-change widgets and you need to verify the profitability of quick-change widgets. You need to do the research personally.

Your close acquaintance with sales records and financial data will expose you to more subtle causes of lost profits — conditions that only reveal themselves after looking into reports and records. As you seek sales patterns of one product, you will discover sales patterns of other products. You may find, for example, that quick-change widgets are losing sales. You may also find that the quick-change model is costly and sells at a slight loss. Fewer sales should mean that profits will be better, not worse. Questions of real costs will quickly arise.

Costing products via function-driven costing will be one of the assignments of the first planning meeting. The new costing must be a team project, with members from the manufacturing and finance departments. Manufacturing should contribute the estimates of overhead dedication to various products; finance should assign cost figures to the specific overhead functions. Your homework will reveal the sources of real profit-robbing conditions. You will get a reasonable idea of what items on the list should be attacked first. You can establish priorities. Priorities enable you to make assignments with a confidence that you will get the most results from the least effort at the quickest rate. Use the Product Profit Worksheet at the end of Chapter 11 to help you to understand where the costs are. That will assist you in defining priorities.

Chapter Recap

The foundation of a turnaround is to develop a rapport with the people who are going to make it happen and to provide them with a plan. The plan must be of such credibility that the full turnaround team enthusiastically supports it. That support comes from involvement in forming the plan. Meeting with and listening to the people who are the turnaround team enlists their support and involvement.

Sample Meeting Agenda

To: Department Managers

From: L. Smith, CEO

Date: 08/14/XX [one day before the meeting]

The regular weekly profits meeting will be held tomorrow, August 15, at 10:00 A.M. as regularly scheduled. The agenda is:

- ► General Status Report: L. Smith. Two projects are behind schedule.
  - The first prototype of the thermal collapser did not perform satisfactorily.
  - Fifty percent of the collections project is past the 30-day deadline.
- ► Consultant's Report: R. Ad Visor. An analysis has shown that there is an opportunity for cost reductions in the warehouse. The warehouse supervisor should be present for this.
- ► Financial Report: Jane Controller. Discuss what actions are planned to pick up the remaining 50 percent of collections.
- ► Sales and Marketing Report: Kris Seller. Need demand estimates for a product to replace the thermal collapser.
- ► Manufacturing Report: J. Hanks. Report results of the departmental rearrangement.
- ► Engineering Report: M. Zeller. Present alternatives to the thermal collapser project.

The number one issue is to plot a course of action to get a new product on board to replace the failed thermal collapser. Sales should offer major design criteria for two or three alternatives to the thermal collapser.

Sample Meeting Minutes

To: Department Managers

From: J. Higgins, executive assistant

Date: 08/16/XX [one day after the meeting]

Subject: Minutes for August 15 meeting

The meeting began at 10:00 A.M.

L. Smith, CEO, gave the general status report. Profits are up five percent — one percent more than expected on this date. The threats are:

- ► Cash flow. There is over $40,000 in outstanding collections. Some payables are still past due, so the cash is critical; and
- ► The failure of the thermal collapser means that a new product introduction will be behind schedule unless someone has a great idea soon.

R. Ad Visor reported that we can reduce ten percent of labor in the warehouse by rearranging. Warehouse manager will have the task done by August 22.

Jane Controller has turned over collections to a new agency. The new agency will pay in advance even though the rate is ten percent less.

Kris Seller will have a field report of demand for a magnetic collapser by August 22.

J. Hanks reports the new arrangement is working and will have initial efficiency reports on August 29.

M. Zeller reports the thermal collapser may be salvageable and will have revised prototype tested by August 21.

Meeting adjourned at 12:30 P.M. A catered lunch was provided.

Date and time of the next meeting will be August 21, 19XX at 10:00 A.M.

CHAPTER 15

STEP TWO: ORGANIZE AND MONITOR

Things that are constantly in sight are constantly in mind. This is a secret of human motivation.

You know how to organize by functional area. You know why you should organize. How to reorganize people who think they are already organized is more difficult. People object to being shuffled around on an organizational chart. Egos are offended; decisions are questioned. A perfectly good idea can be compromised by irate individuals who feel that they have been unjustly treated.

How you handle people when you are reorganizing is critical to the success of the new organization. There is simply no way that a top manager can reshuffle an organization without breeding resentment.

The motivation and energy that you need to nurture can be quickly neutralized by resentment. So, what do you do if you have a management organization that breeds conflict, duplication, and inefficiency? Do you accept second-best choices — or worse — while you are in the first phases of turning around a distressed business?

The answer is that you can generate a new organizational structure while simultaneously building up the levels of motivation, energy, and enthusiasm in your company. Let your employees make the reorganization decisions.

Let the Staff Organize Themselves

People support their own decisions. You can allow your employees to reorganize themselves and there will be a high level of support and the smallest amount of resentment. If you work according to a plan that follows the traits of human nature, you will get exactly what you have designed.

Start by distributing a copy of a function-driven organizational chart without names — just functions. Let your key people know that there will be a reorganization in a few weeks. Tell them that you want them to study the chart so that they can help in the process of deciding who will fill which roles. It is imperative for the new person in a role to be actively supported by the people who are in subordinate roles. It can be argued that subordinate support is at least as important as the technical qualifications. Remember, you are building a team effort; not an accumulation of one-person shows.

You will need to listen to opinions as they form. Offer your guidance. At this point, you will understand which persons are the real doers. Give clues to the people who will decide. They will appreciate the opportunity to decide for themselves and they will tend to follow your preferences.

From the ten or so key people who are attending your staff meetings, assume that you will have two candidates for each top position, including a manufacturing manager, financial manager, sales and marketing manager, and product engineering manager. Surprisingly, if you let the people involved decide, the people who are the best qualified will get the positions. This is a proven process: the conversation at the time of decision sounds something like this:

- ▶ "Kelley and I have talked about this a lot."
- ▶ "Kelley is more outspoken and I have a lot of technical chores with critical due dates."
- ▶ "We figure it is best for Kelley to take over the department."
- ▶ "I would like working for Kelley."

This will end the competition. Compliment them for their maturity. Take their recommendation and go on to fill the other positions. Be sure to remember the quality of the person that voluntarily forgoes an opportunity for a promotion for the benefit of the company. Honor this person appropriately.

When you are done with the reorganization, document the names of the employees who fit into which positions on the chart. Make copies of the chart. Distribute copies to all key people. Post copies in obvious places. An important benefit of the new organization is that energy is now organized to perform essential tasks only once. Knowing who is responsible for what is important to the more efficient organization.

Some people will end up with new supervisors. Physical moves of people may be desirable in order to group similar functions in close physical proximity. Close proximity works to encourage communication and mutual support. Physical change works to underscore the message that the company is no longer doing business as usual: change is happening.

Let the department heads of the four functional areas coordinate most of the change. Your job is to plan the next change. Resolve disputes when you must, but float above the details as much as possible. Maintain a "big picture" perspective of the changes in the company. Complete the organizational change between the second and third weeks. The new organization is a prerequisite to implementing the rapid-fire changes that are going to begin soon.

Keep Charts and Graphs

You should have a team developing function-driven costing. You have a function-driven organization forming. You have a list of suspected profit-robbing conditions with some ideas of priorities. You have assigned specific tasks. You have told your staff that you expect measurable results.

The best way to keep your business sharp is to know what is happening at a glance. Charts and graphs give you that ability. Consider the example of backorders. Remember the story of the consumer electronics firm with the ten-of-everything safety stock rule from Chapter 14? This firm's backorders were high. Eliminating the safety stock dramatically improved backorders. Charting backorders gives all key people instant visual reminders of the condition of backorders. Further, charting gives people an instant historical comparison. For example, a chart will define high backorders. A chart might indicate three percent of sales as a high backorder rate. If your backorders have been ranging from 10 to 15 percent for years, then three percent is great. If your backorders have been stable at 2 1/2 percent, then zoom to three percent, you can immediately see that a problem is developing.

In the beginning, chart every assigned project. Monitor progress in charted form. As your project matures, you will drop some charts as being redundant or misleading. You will find that your management team hovers around a few charts that are the key indicators of the condition of the business. Keep those charts updated carefully and discontinue the rest.

When your team has settled on a group of charts that keeps tabs on the pulse of the business, that is your early warning system. It is also the way that you can keep up with the performance of your management team. Charts eliminate the emotionalism that often governs decisions and directions. You will use facts and figures to support decisions. Charts keep you focused. Computer reports are too easy to close up and stick in a closet. Charts get you involved in whatever crisis is at hand. Charts keep your attention on the key indicators of the business at every staff meeting. Scrap is stable, but high. Backorders are good and declining. Profits are stable. Shipments are up. Purchasing variances are up. Labor efficiency is down, but still better than standard.

You get the idea. Begin charting as soon as you assign the first projects to team members. By the third week (second staff meeting) you should have some key charts in place. (See examples of early warning charts at the end of Chapter 7.)

Charting is not new. Many of your competitors already use a system of charts to monitor business performance, usually on a monthly basis. They update monthly because they use figures directly off the financial statement to update the charts. Such a practice merely restates the financial picture after the statement is complete. You should use a more effective practice.

Some key indicators should be updated weekly or daily. Shipments are a common example. Scrap and backorder rates should be posted weekly. Working hours per unit of production should be posted weekly or biweekly. You will also be monitoring business indicators that do not normally show up on the financial statement. You want to be able to use your charts to predict, in advance, what the financial statement will ultimately show.

Your charts are not legal financial records, so you do not have to calculate them using the same rules and precision that apply to your financial statement. Your charts are guides to decision making. They can be somewhat imprecise, yet will still provide you with correct information regarding trends and causative factors.

Are you getting a little concerned about the numbers of reports and charts? Are you thinking that a turnaround should be filled with more dynamic action and fewer projects of writing and reporting? Do weekly staff meetings seem like a waste of time?

Anything that your management team does that does not add to the profits of your company is a waste of time. If your company is currently unprofitable, all the activity of management has been a waste of time. A method is required to direct management so that its activities become profit-adding. Charts, reports, and staff meetings are part of the method to make sure that management is working on tasks that will result in added profits. Charts direct management's efforts. Managers focus on the area of greatest need and make preventative corrections. When used correctly, charts prevent wasted effort.

Reports are subtle stimulators of action. Managers who know that a monthly progress report is required have a tendency to focus their energies into the projects that are going to be reported. Those managers who must write reports also tend to do research to ensure the accuracy of their findings. Thus, they tend to be constantly aware of important figures like efficiency rates, scrap rates, product cost and utilization of capital equipment. People who keep such knowledge in their heads make better decisions.

Further, reports constitute a series of commitments. Reports contain projected completion dates of projects and promised benefits. A published report puts pressure on a manager to deliver what has been promised. Staff meetings offer pressures to perform that are similar to reports. They also act as a medium for communication. Properly conducted staff meetings direct management's energies to the areas of greatest potential result. Properly conducted means that every meeting starts with an agenda, sticks to the agenda, makes decisions, and assigns action and due dates. Every meeting is followed up with published minutes. Minutes "lock in" the decisions and directions of the meeting.

Focus Your Action

The purpose of the early warning system of charts and graphs is to provide you with information to focus your actions. Design your charts so that they will tell you in an instant whether all is going according to plan. For example, if your profit plan requires you to ship $2 million during the current month, then you should be able to tell on the first working day of the month whether you are on or off your profit plan: $2 million in shipments equals $100,000 every day.

If your first day of shipping hits the chart at $35,000, you know that you are off the profit plan. Learn the cause of the problem, correct the cause, then watch the chart to see if your corrective action actually had the effect that you expected.

As you use the early warning system, you will find that you are initially charting after-effects. If you are charting shipments, for example, you will quickly discover that the shipments of today are an indicator of the events of yesterday. It is too late to change what happened yesterday. You will learn to chart and control the causative events.

For example, the shipments of today are the result of the production of last week or last month. Production of last month depended largely upon the stability of demand — how closely actual sales met with the forecasted sales. You need to chart events that will ultimately result in shipments, production rates, and order rates. The benefits of careful charting can be fabulous as evidenced by the following story.

One company does not chart shipments at all. It charts actual sales — by product line — on a chart that compares actual figures to forecast figures, day-by-day. It also charts units of production — by product line — compared to units forecast, day-by-day. This company normally has a near-100 percent order fill rate. It has a near-100 percent adherence to the production plan. It ships at a constant rate throughout the month — no end-of-month rushes.

The production supervisor of each line posts the daily production to the chart. The supervisors know instantly whether the line is behind. The standing rule is that production shortfalls must be made up the next day. The result is that the production lines operate in a preventative mode. The supervisors know by 9:00 A.M. whether they are on target for the day. They take corrective action to have shortfalls corrected before the day is over. Often, they have time to plan into the next day and predict shortfalls. In those cases, the cause of the shortfall is corrected before the start of production the next day.

In this example, manufacturing management could predict the moment of a model run changeover to within 15 minutes accuracy, six weeks into the future. Imagine the benefits reaped by the sales, shipping, purchasing, and inventory management departments. The seed of such near-perfect performance is the system of charting daily production and comparing it to a daily plan.

Chart relevant measures. Pick the best measurable unit for that purpose: units, dollars or percentage. Resist the common temptation to pick what is easiest to measure. Chart what is easiest to read — and most meaningful — with a minimum of interpretation. For example, charting scrap in total pieces discarded means little. Nine hundred items scrapped at a value of $0.01 (one-cent) each is $9.00 worth of scrap — insignificant in most companies. On the other hand, a mere 20 items at a value of $500 each is $10,000 in scrap — a major event. Charting in dollars is more meaningful than charting pieces.

Dollar signs carry such a powerful impact that most managers are tempted to chart everything in dollars. Dollars are the ultimate measure of business performance. But, you want to chart the causes of dollar performance. Charting takes you into a world of units and percentages. For instance, in the preceding example of scrap charting, dollars of scrap can be misleading.

If your company has seasonal fluctuations in production — or other conditions that vary the dollar volume of product that flows through the shop — then you should chart scrap as a percentage of production. You see, in a shop that has varying production rates, $5,000 in scrap may be unacceptably high in June but would be a very low rate in December. In such a case, you should chart scrap as a percentage.

In all cases, you should be charting profits as they occur. You can plot actual profits and compare them to the projected profits. A good example of this charting method is found in the Profits Progress Chart located below. Note that the dotted line represents the anticipated level of profits based on the profit project plan. The milestones are key events that have a major impact on profits. This type of chart should be available for the entire management team to see. A blank copy of this form is included for your use.

Profits Progress Chart Example

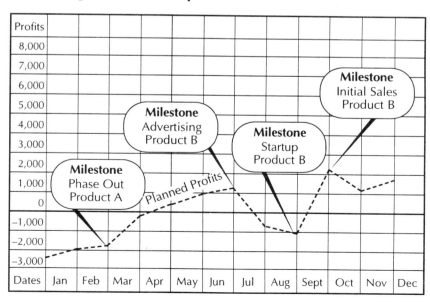

Your charts should always have a line that is called the standard. If you have a standard for scrap that is 0.5 percent, then the line that represents 0.5 percent should be clearly indicated and highlighted. You can tell at a glance whether you are above or below your standard. You can also tell at a glance whether your progress is in the desired direction. If you are at a scrap rate of 2.0 percent, but the trend is toward the 0.5 percent standard line, then do not concern yourself with scrap rate. However, if the current rate is 0.4 percent — better than the standard — and the trend is showing an increase in scrap rates, then you should take preventative action.

When you have a charting system to monitor the causes of profits, you have the most basic set of tools for making profits. You will be in a position to visually see the future of the profits of your company. You can adjust causative conditions to perpetually press for lower costs and higher revenues.

Chapter Recap

The recommendations in this book and the sequence of implementation will work for most companies of most sizes; however, the details will differ. For example, a $6 million company has fewer people, processes, and total number of conditions to correct than a $500 million company. The foundational principles for profits are the same in both sizes of companies: press costs down, press revenues up.

It is possible that more time will be required to turn around the larger company because of the sheer mass of people that must implement the changes. But a large company does not mean a turnaround will be automatically slow. The slowness that is typical in large companies is usually because of an inefficient organizational structure. Organizational structure is one of the first things that you will correct. Then, with an efficient organization, even a large corporation can act quickly.

Organization of the turnaround team enables economy of effort: every person is performing a task that complements and supports the work of every other person. Charting progress intensely focuses the team on the results of its efforts. Organization and progress charting work together to enable a powerful change in the business — a change that moves in the right direction. The enthusiasm that erupts when your team starts seeing positive results may be hard for you to contain and direct.

Profits Progress Chart Instructions

This chart will help you compare actual profits against projected profits. To begin, use the left-hand column to identify the dollar figures you hope to anticipate for a particular product. A profits progress chart should be kept for each product. Then, use a dotted line to show the anticipated level of profits — this line can further indicate the various milestones that you expect the product to achieve. Now you have set the stage to compare this line against the actual figures you will plug in as time goes by.

Profits Progress Chart

Profits												
Dates	Jan	Feb	Mar	Apr	May	Jun	Jul	Aug	Sept	Oct	Nov	Dec

CHAPTER 16

STEP THREE: ACHIEVE YOUR OBJECTIVES

The journey is possible. The destination is desirable. The map is made. The party is prepared. There are no risks. Who will dare to take the first step?

Your third staff meeting will be composed of your new functional department managers. The goal of this meeting, and of all your subsequent meetings, is to begin taking measurable action to enhance the profits of your business. If you have inspired enthusiasm for the turnaround, your staff will already be reporting some wins against profit-robbing conditions. They will also have a torrent of new ideas. Some of the new ideas will represent major steps in the direction of improving revenues and reducing costs.

Many of the ideas presented will address superficial problems or will deal with effects rather than root causes. A staff that is bubbling over with random-action enthusiasm is exactly what you want and need to fuel a spectacular turnaround. At the same time, the bubbling-over characteristic can lead to wasted time, wasted energy, and wasted resources. If you allow too much bubbling-over, the project can end in a quagmire of incomplete, independent projects that achieve little.

Your challenge is this: if you allow the staff to speed off in a self-directed manner, the actions of the turnaround will be sporadic and poorly coordinated. The great increases in profits that you hope for may never materialize. Conversely, if you direct the staff in specific actions, you will dampen the enthusiasm that comes from allowing people to be creative and spontaneous. This chapter tells you the way to achieve a predetermined set of objectives while allowing people to be self-directed and enthusiastic.

Direct Enthusiasm with a Team Checklist

You can direct the enthusiasm of your team by giving each leader a checklist. The checklist will list the types of corrections in each department that offer the greatest good for the least effort. A sample management team checklist is located at the end of this chapter for your use. If you prefer, you can custom tailor a checklist to reflect the exact conditions of your business.

Direct your staff to evaluate its torrent of new ideas based on the checklist. In many cases, your staff's ideas will be simply a differently worded version of a recommended action on the checklist. Your managers will usually be very happy to act on checklist items, simply because they are the same as their own ideas. Remember, keeping enthusiasm high is vital to success. Following is a summary of what to do regarding each of the action items on the checklist. Reading these summaries will help you answer questions that your staff will ask.

Sales and Marketing Action Items

A common attribute to companies that are experiencing declining profits is the effort to make every possible sale. This attribute is common for two reasons. First, the make-every-sale attitude is the root cause of complex product lines that ultimately lead to high costs, low quality, and distressed profits. Second, declining profits stimulate a response to sell more in the belief that more sales will automatically revive profitability. The sales and marketing goals should be related to selling more profitable products and not selling unprofitable products.

The guiding principle for sales and marketing is simplification. Simplification allows for lower total costs and eases the path to higher quality. While you take action, think in terms of simplifying the product, product line, production schedules, and the process of taking customer orders. The top nine action items for sales and marketing are listed on the following pages.

Determine the remaining market life of key products
A key product means a product line that is in the top 80–90 percent of sales. The sales and marketing department will use sales

PROFIT POINTER

◄ӟ 100 ӟ►

histories to make a life cycle chart of each product. It will be able to very accurately chart past sales — by units, not dollars — which will help to predict the future sales of the product. You will use the projected product life cycle to make decisions of what products to drop when the product line is simplified.

Initiate a product for phaseout

This can only be done after the life cycle chart is completed for all products, and after function-driven costs are compiled. With the correct information in hand, the phaseout approval is a rubber-stamping of the decision made by the facts.

Implement techniques to immediately improve sales

Immediately means that you are looking for sales increases in the next 30 days to help cash flow. Consider any ideas that will get cash moving. Be very aware of the secondary responses of decisions, such as promotions and discounts. Promotions and discounts tend to cut into sales that normally would occur at a later date. Future sales are compromised.

Ideally, you want to make sales that are additional to regular sales: obsolete inventory and seconds, for example. You can even sell obsolete raw material. Proposing the techniques is important.

Proposals should be made in staff meetings so that all predictions of secondary responses may be considered before a final decision is made. The top manager has the final authority to give or withhold approval. A decision should be made during the meeting in which the idea is proposed. Prompt approval to act bolsters enthusiasm.

Propose a new product

Stay within the guidelines of new product introductions. There should be market research that indicates a strong, immediate demand. The new product will use existing market channels and existing facilities that are sufficient to build the product. Be conservative with diversification.

Prepare realistic cost figures (function-driven) after the product has preliminary approval. Calculate a sales price and refigure the market demand on the basis of price. Project profitability for that product. Estimate product development time and cost. Base final approval on the projected timetables and profits. The team should consider several new product ideas before the final approval is given. The top manager gives the final approval.

Design techniques to improve long-term sales volumes

Major projects may be required to secure a bigger piece of the market pie: plant expansions, quality upgrades, on-time deliveries, lower product cost, more products, or new territories. Advance several proposals with the projected costs and returns for each. This is a long-term project. It should be started promptly to reap benefits sooner. Include every departmental manager in the evaluations of these major proposals. Analyze dozens of secondary responses and side issues. Choose the proposal that has the best ratio of costs to profits.

Stabilize the master production schedule (MPS)

Your sales and marketing staff needs to work with the manufacturing department to achieve this goal. The goal is to keep the MPS unchanged within the leadtime of the longest leadtime material, or longer if possible. Report progress at every staff meeting. A key to the success of the sales and marketing department is to create accurate forecasts. A key to the success of the manufacturing department is to shorten the leadtime of the longest leadtime items. In short, the goal is to improve response times in manufacturing and reduce the need for quick response in sales.

Prioritize products by profit-to-selling cost ratios

Function-driven costs and an estimate of the cost of selling each product are required to start a turnaround project. The cost of selling estimate is made by totalling all costs of selling all products. Then, you can estimate which product line consumes how much of the total sales effort. For instance, you may end up with a list like:

Total Cost of Selling by Product Line

Product Line A = 50% of selling cost

Product Line B = 35% of selling cost

Product Line C = 15% of selling cost

Now, multiply the total cost by the percentage. If the total cost of selling is $1 million yearly, then Product Line A requires $500,000 in selling cost. Divide the product line selling cost by the number of units sold. If Product Line A sells 5,000 units yearly, then the cost of selling is $100 each. Compare the cost of selling to the profit per unit. Prioritize a list with the best profit-to-selling cost ratio at the top of the list. See the Product Profit Worksheet at the end of Chapter 11 for more details.

Team with the finance department to develop techniques to more accurately monitor the cost of selling by product line. The goal is to be continually aware of the cost of selling — by product — and to maintain a downward pressure on the cost. Most manufacturers are unaware of their cost of selling. Such knowledge is a distinct competitive advantage. The results of this prioritization are almost always surprising. Companies are dumbfounded to discover that some products are costing more to sell than the markup of the product. The cost of selling is such vital information that it should be charted on your early warning system. Your standard line on the chart should be calculated as some percent of profit, but in all cases, less than the profit. Cost of selling should be considered in decisions to phase out products and in the introduction of new products.

Drop the least profitable products

When you have arrived at a per-unit profit, have subtracted a cost of selling from the profit, and have made a prioritized list from most profitable to least profitable, you will have an excellent picture of which of your products are producing the greatest real profits. Consider the bottom 20 percent of products on your list for phaseout. The most profitable method to phase out a product is discussed in profit pointers 63 and 64 in Chapter 11.

Reduce order entry, picking, shipping, and invoicing errors

All of these areas are sources of frequent errors. All errors are costly. The technique to reduce the errors is to reduce the opportunity for error. Part numbering systems and the part number format are a contributor, as is the physical arrangement of stock in the warehouse. The fundamental rule is to simplify.

Finance Action Items

A financial turnaround is not a financial project. It is a project to improve revenues and control over costs. The finance department will mostly keep the score. A great contribution of the finance department is the ability to look at proposed projects from a different perspective — to see the secondary responses that others do not see. Compared to the other functional areas of your business, the list of action items for the finance department is small.

Implement collection procedures

Develop a plan to collect on all past-due accounts within 30 days. Develop techniques to accelerate cash turnover from regular accounts.

Design methods to generate quick, positive cash flow
The finance manager knows more than anyone how much cash is required to keep the business afloat until real profits can be generated.

Project realistic cash flow for the turnaround period
There will be a number of proposals and ideas that may dramatically affect cash flow. Some will be rendered impossible because of inadequate cash flow. Revised cash flow projections will be required repeatedly to evaluate the consequences of various plans. This is an intense requirement. Projections will have to be regenerated often as new ideas are born.

Develop a function-driven cost for every product
Assign properly allocated overhead to all work centers. Use the routing form to determine hours of use of each work center. In allocating overhead, some businesses apply some portion of overhead directly to a material item. The goal is to develop function-driven costing for each product. The function-driven cost will be used for sales to determine product profit.

Develop a profitability report, by product line
Use function-driven costing techniques only. Expect support from the manufacturing department in developing function-driven costs. To develop a profitability report, first subtract the cost from the average selling price for each product to determine unit profit. Next, multiply annual unit sales by the unit profit to find out the annual item profit. Then, group the like items together for product line profitability reports.

Develop a routine method to calculate the dollar value of work in process without the necessity of stopping production and taking a full inventory count. You may do this by recording additions to work in process when labor and materials are added daily, then relieving the value of labor and materials when items are completed and ready for sale. You should also subtract scrap and nonproductive labor routinely to keep your work-in-process figure relevant.

The size of your work-in-process investment reflects the effectiveness of your efforts to manage your business better. A smooth running, simplified, well-managed business moves products through the shop very quickly, which results in low work in process. It follows that high work-in-process is an indicator of the opposite conditions. Update a work-in-process chart daily or weekly. Keep in mind, fabricated parts that are made and stored for later use are not work in process.

Very well-managed businesses will have less than a week of work in the shop — some run with only a day or two of work. Your work-in-process goal will depend on the amount of labor required to complete an item. Do not count time that the products parts spend waiting to be processed.

For most companies, an initial goal is to have no more than one week of work in process. Your goal should normally be less than 30 days of work in process.

Product Engineering Action Items

Control of cost and quality begins with the design of a product. The design determines the number of parts, the diversity of parts, the complexity of making the product, and ultimately has the greatest influence on the number of errors. It follows that product engineering has a prime influence on the future profits of a company as it designs its products.

The immediate goals of product engineering should be to reduce costs by simplifying designs and processes and to eliminate errors induced by faulty documents or specifications. The product engineers contribute further to profits by assuming the following tasks.

Design one new product

Work closely with the sales and marketing and manufacturing staffs. Design the new product for quality and for manufacturability. Be certain that documentation is complete and accurate. Test and develop the product to assure that post-introduction changes are near-zero. Use a progress chart to assure that the product will be introduced on time. Report progress at each staff meeting.

Improve current product designs for greater profitability

Simplify designs to reduce the number of operations and parts. Establish close communications with manufacturing personnel to solve difficulties with manufacturability. Reduce the opportunity for error in manufacturing. Seek out areas for design improvement. Modify designs to fit with the real capabilities of the shop. Increase tolerances in any area possible. Find and respecify any overspecified materials.

Correct all errors in drawings, BOMs, and other documents

Bills of materials and drawings should be near-100 percent accurate. Any error in engineering documentation can become costly.

Initiate regular question and listen sessions

The people who make the product know more about design shortcomings than anyone. They are willing to explain the shortcomings and to suggest corrections if someone will listen and implement a solution. A key person (or several persons) from product engineering should regularly — at least once a day — visit the production lines to learn how the product is put together in actual practice. Such visits should involve a lot of listening and watching on the part of engineers. You will see a cure to the abundance of errors, rework, warranty claims, and inefficiency with an ongoing practice of visiting the production lines and listening.

Correct design-related customer complaints

You can correct some customer complaints by design revisions. Communicate with the sales department to determine the top design features that cause customer complaints. Learn about design features that inhibit sales. Use what you have learned when designing new products.

Evaluate your part numbering system

Determine if the part numbering format or system are contributing to errors in other departments. Typical errors to look for are keystroke errors in order entry, ordering errors from dealers, order fill errors, and part number assignment errors such as duplication. If the numbering system is difficult for users, then develop a new system using the example in Chapter 8 as a guide.

Manufacturing Action Items

The manufacturing department controls the cost of labor, materials, and a large portion of overhead. In fact, most cost control is the responsibility of the manufacturing manager. The tendency of many manufacturing managers is to reduce costs in manufacturing by "dumping" costs into other departments. You want to prevent that.

First, make sure that manufacturing — and all other departments — are rewarded on the basis of overall business performance. Rewarding one department for its own performance only leads to dumping costs into other departments. The result is unproductive conflict. Second, keep close communications between manufacturing and other departments. Place a priority on close communications with the sales staff. Use your diplomatic skills to build a mutually supportive team attitude. Third, give manufacturing personnel a measure of extra support for the effort required to achieve this long list of action items. A good manufacturing or industrial engineer will expedite results in his or her department.

Close the least profitable product line

Phase out the product selected by the management team. Balance inventories and develop a phaseout schedule. Communicate the quantity that will be produced before materials run out. Close out the line in an orderly, economic manner. Store dedicated tooling, jigs, and fixtures for possible reopening of the product line at a later date. Transfer resources to the best performing product line.

Initiate scrap and rework reporting

Chart the percentage of scrap and rework. Report results to weekly staff meetings. Create error-proof jigs, fixtures, and methods. Repair defective equipment. Assist the product engineering staff in projects to simplify the product designs.

Establish labor standards (per product) to meet plan objectives

If Product A presently requires eight working hours (total), but is unprofitable at eight hours, then establish a new standard for total labor content. Set a profitable standard for each product line. Chart working hours as compared to the standard — by product line. Report progress at weekly staff meetings.

Stabilize the master production schedule (MPS)

This is a team effort with both the sales and marketing departments. The goal is to make no changes to the MPS within the leadtime of the longest leadtime material. Publish the schedule to the sales department and all key manufacturing people. Send faxes of current copies of the schedule to suppliers and train them to read and use the schedule. Report status at weekly staff meetings.

Reduce labor costs

Devise projects to efficiently use labor. Improve parts and tooling. Train employees. Provide correct tools. Improve internal quality. Keep work available at all work centers. Provide adequate material handling equipment. Identify and lay off genuinely unproductive workers. Work with the product engineering department to provide accurate drawings. Develop routings to instruct employees on how to use correct methods and tools. Reorganize departments to reduce travel distances. Reduce setup times. Improved efficiency will show up in the labor standards as discussed above.

Introduce a new product

Your goal is to introduce a new product on time and on budget. If a new assembly or fabrication line is required, design it for work-flow — sequential operations, near-zero travel distances, components and tools within one step, and instant changeover from model to model. Follow the product engineering progress chart to make sure that the product line is ready on time. Order first-run fabricated parts in plenty of time to evaluate fit and function. Allow enough time in the schedule for a small pilot run to prove all parts, fixtures, and procedures.

Reduce materials costs

Bring an outside operation in house. Once the master production schedule is stable, use order stability as leverage to negotiate better pricing. Check specifications for overspecification of materials. Reduce inventory by stabilizing the schedule, then schedule supplier deliveries more closely. Assign a competent person to intensely manage the top five percent of inventory. Check for overspecified tolerances. Communicate with suppliers — ask for ideas to reduce materials costs.

Upgrade quality

Begin with the defects that cause the greatest customer complaints. Work with product engineering to identify elements of the product that make quality difficult to achieve; then, participate in redesigning the product so that quality-reducing design features are replaced with quality-enhancing features. Develop processes that are easily capable of maintaining desired quality. Study the principles of total quality management. Train operators and supervisors these principles.

Implement capital projects

Upgrade manufacturing techniques, including setup reduction, dedicated tooling, and state-of-the-art equipment. Prepare a written justification for every project. Follow up by measuring the cost-reduction results. Report cost reductions at weekly staff meetings. Prioritize projects based on profit-improvement potential. Implement when the finance department and top manager give the okay.

Simplify systems

Eliminate unnecessary steps in preparing work orders, purchase orders, or other documents. Eliminate stockroom transactions via online storage. Practice Just-in-Time principles. Eliminate confusion and duplication of effort.

Ask employees for input — they know of the wasted effort already. Implement an automated manufacturing control system. Avoid custom programs. Report to weekly staff meetings.

Improve morale

Communicate with employees. Involve employees in projects. Offer recognition. Frequently listen and ask questions. Practice justice, fairness, and courtesy. Develop a means to measure morale — turnover is one means — and chart it. Report the status of morale at weekly staff meetings. Another way to measure morale is by recording the number of employee suggestions made. High morale is evidenced by employee involvement; involvement is evidenced by suggestions.

Reduce manufacturing overhead

Team with the finance department to document all manufacturing overhead costs. Documenting the costs is the first step to support function-driven costing, so this step will support two cost-reducing efforts. Prioritize the list from the highest to lowest overhead costs. Team with manufacturing staff and supervisors to devise ways to eliminate the need for each overhead function.

Trying to directly reduce individual overhead costs will backfire; the cost reduction in one function will cause increased cost in another. The trick is to determine why the overhead function is needed, then eliminate the need for the function. Manufacturing overhead should be charted — by product line when you have enough information. Any increases in overhead costs should result in a corresponding decrease in costs in another area. Otherwise, the overhead function is a waste and should be discontinued. Report results at the weekly staff meeting.

Top Manager's Action Items

The responsibility of a top manager is to keep a project moving to a successful conclusion. This person must be able to look to the future, predict the roadblocks to progress, and remove those roadblocks before they affect the success of a turnaround project.

One of the roadblocks that is common to a turnaround is dampened enthusiasm. Thus, a key task of a top manager is to monitor enthusiasm levels often. Regular, face-to-face communication is necessary to know the level of enthusiasm. If enthusiasm begins to falter, a top manager will take steps to allow staff more creativity and self-direction. If you are the top manager, you should provide recognition to every person who achieves a step toward the turnaround. A high dose of recognition stimulates high levels of enthusiasm.

Communicate with everyone. Fear is a disabler of change. Frequent communication dissipates fear. Your regular staff meetings are excellent mediums of communication, but you should communicate one-on-one with many people — staff, owners, supervisors, and production line employees. Take the time to understand their concerns. Let them know the status of the turnaround project.

Chart progress

The most essential single element of a turnaround effort is to know its progress. Profit as a percentage of sales is the number to chart. Team with the finance manager to create a method to estimate profits on a weekly basis. Chart the results. Use the monthly financial statement to verify the weekly estimations. Enthusiasm of the management team is bolstered by quick visualization of the effects of actions on profits. Weekly posting is especially desirable in the first 90 days of the project. Once you develop the technique of weekly posting, it is simple to maintain the effort. Weekly posting of profits — by percentage — keeps the entire team focused on the reason for the existence of the company.

Provide monthly progress reports to the owners

Document the projects of the four functional departments. Explain the results that are expected. Quantify expected results and provide a timetable. For example, you can convey that the sales and marketing department teamed with the finance staff to develop the cost of selling by product line. This information will provide the turnaround team with information to determine methods to reduce the cost of selling. An example of a well-stated goal is to reduce the cost of selling by two percent in 90 days.

Continue to report the progress of every project until completion. Generate a written report, a minimum of once each month. Provide copies of the report to each member of the management team. Use names of persons that are involved in the projects. Regular written reports accomplish two things. First, they commit the management team to a path of action. The public statement of intent contributes to a full completion of every project. Second, written reports to owners are a means of providing assurance to the people who have major personal stakes in the company, but have little control over the destiny of their investment.

The report to owners is a courtesy to people who are concerned about the future of their investment. Reports should be totally objective and honest. If a project is stalled, say so and say why. Explain what is being done to get it moving. Provide a copy of the profitability chart.

Coordinate and motivate

As the top leader, you are responsible to oversee the project, provide the vision, stimulate enthusiasm, encourage communication, and encourage team efforts. Time the start and completion dates of projects to complement the projects. Prioritize projects. Provide whatever is necessary to keep the project on track for a successful conclusion.

Monitor results

When the project is in full swing, many individual projects will be underway simultaneously. Your job is to monitor progress. The weekly staff meeting is the format for reporting progress. The agenda for the meeting should document who is expected to report on what projects. It is appropriate to ask for written documentation of each project's status to help you compile your monthly report to the owners.

Conduct staff meetings

Develop a schedule of regular staff meetings. Conduct meetings to enhance the communication among the management team. Keep all discussions on-track — relevant to the agenda topic. Make decisions at the end of each discussion. Report and evaluate progress on pending projects; make new assignments. Every project should have a person responsible for the outcome, a measurable anticipated result, and a due date. The evidence of successful staff meetings is the level of mutual support and cooperation among departments.

Provide leadership

A management team is a committee. There will be dissension. Your leadership can organize tasks in such a manner as to minimize the opportunity for dissension — the function-driven organization is key to minimizing the negative aspects of dissension. In addition, your leadership can resolve conflicts in a way that will promote enthusiasm in all dissenting parties.

The best method of resolving dissension is instructional: teach parties to find a common set of objectives and prioritize the best acts for achieving the objectives. Remember that dissension is creative — it selects the best ideas. Conflict is ruinous; it pits person against person. Your leadership provides the drive that keeps the project going. Managers will need encouragement. Make strategic decisions promptly. Devise solutions. Keep the project in focus and on schedule. Monitor and evaluate results. Monitor and bolster the morale of your management team and workforce.

Facilitate

Provide the resources to keep the project moving. Bring in an outside expert. Conduct training sessions. Provide instructional materials. Identify obstacles to progress and remove them.

The key to successfully enhancing the profits of your business is to do a lot of things right in a short timespan. You can easily step ahead of your competition by focusing your attention on doing the right things — "right" things contribute to profits — and refraining from doing other things — "other" things rob profits. The way to keep your attention focused on doing the right things is to use charts to reveal what action is needed and to use checklists and staff meetings to make sure that the actions are completed on time.

Do It — The Conclusion

Making a profit consistently — through many years, over the course of economic downturns, and through changes in markets, politics, and regulations — is the result of doing a lot of things right. No one task or discipline will guarantee consistent profits. No giant stride of technology or marketing will provide profits that endure. Financial or legal manipulations don't have effects on true profits. The only reliable method to produce enduring, consistent profits is to implement internal change and discipline. Consistent profits result from a complex interaction of tasks, processes, people, organization, philosophy, attitude, and leadership. Mastery of this complex interaction is the ultimate challenge to management.

Analyze everything; look for opportunities to press costs down, to press revenues up. Ask questions; then ask more questions. Challenge the status quo. Defy tradition — especially the traditions of your own company. Defy conventional wisdom. Be creative, imaginative and totally dissatisfied. Drive for positive changes so hard that no other outcome is possible.

Predict secondary responses of every decision. Avoid expediency. Involve every employee in the success of the company. Involve the company in the success of every employee. Simplify, train, and educate. Make quality a top priority. Remember that the bulk of costs is in materials and overhead. Know what functions cause overhead costs. Distribute overhead proportionally to the products that create the overhead costs. Know how much it costs to sell a product. Make written justifications of capital expenditures. Keep the master production schedule stable. Reduce lead-times. Know what causes increased costs.

Intensely manage the top five percent of your inventory. Organize the company by function. Use charts, reports, and staff meetings to keep the management team focused and mutually supportive. Reduce the opportunities for errors and total errors will decrease. Reward the sales personnel for adherence to the sales forecast. Manage by opportunity. Respect the patterns of human nature. Stay close to your customers, employees, and suppliers. Be humble. Ask for opinions. Listen to opinions. Make a plan and lead in its execution.

Know the common strategic blunders and resist their short-term appeals and recognize their long-term consequences. Make a profit plan; subdivide it among the four functional departments and monitor its progress and results. Develop an early warning system that will predict the future of the business. Take preventative action; detest reactive remedies. Read books and trade journals. Participate in professional organizations. Support employee participation in professional organizations. You can build morale by creating comfort, excitement, and value in the workplace.

Seek a broad spectrum of advantage; cultivate a thousand tiny increments toward higher profits. Resist temptations to make quantum leaps. Progress toward the goal of being the low-cost, high-quality producer. Know the difference between symptoms and causes of business distress. Treat the causes. Remember that increasing sales in a distressed business is fruitless if every sale causes a loss of profits. Reducing a cost reaps 10–100 times the profit of a sales increase. Raising prices inhibits sales. Phase out a product and introduce a new product. Diversify within your own means.

A turnaround of profitability results from doing a lot of little things right (attention to detail) and doing them in rapid-fire sequence. The hope that a turnaround will result from one or two broad, sweeping changes will be met with disappointment. Plodding through details to set right one thing after another is the only reliable route to success. Plodding through details is not exciting; it is work and it is routine. Plodding through the details is not glamorous; it is mundane and demanding. Plodding through details does not grab the headlines nearly so quickly as dramatic downsizing or restructuring. But plodding through details works. Grandiose gestures grab attention and offer the illusion of progress, but they seldom work. Complex techniques or following a fad provide the illusion of modern credibility, but they only add to the confusion and cost. The only thing that works reliably is to go back to the basics — to build a foundation for profits then work on one detail at a time until the business becomes a profit machine.

And remember, do only what needs to be done. The wisdom of efficiency is the recognition of what does not need to be done — and then to refrain from doing it.

A turnaround of profits can be prompt. A turnaround can be permanent. You can attain profitability that is stable, predictable, and consistent — profitability that lets you float above the chaos that your competitors experience during every business downturn. It requires work, knowledge, study, and leadership. It requires top priority, intensity, and a sense of purpose. When you have achieved it, you will have achieved a competitive advantage that is the key to profit power.

Management Team Checklist

Use this checklist to guide the profit-enhancement project. The checklist includes the action items for each major functional area. The purpose of this is so that each team member is aware of the other members' roles in the project.

Sales and Marketing Department

1. ____ Determine remaining market life of key products.

2. ____ Initiate phaseout of product with least remaining life.

3. ____ Implement techniques to increase sales in 30 days or less.

4. ____ Propose one new product that has a strong, immediate market demand.

5. ____ Design techniques to improve long-term sales volumes.

6. ____ Stabilize the master production schedule.

7. ____ Prioritize products by profit-to-selling cost ratio.

8. ____ Use the profit-to-selling cost ratio method to drop the least profitable 20 percent of items from the product line.

9. ____ Reduce order entry, picking, shipping, and invoicing errors. Target 98 percent accuracy.

Finance Department

1. ____ Implement collection procedures that will bring slow accounts up to date.

2. ____ Design methods to generate quick, positive cash flow.

3. ____ Generate realistic cash flow projections for the turnaround period.

4. ____ Develop methods to cost products via function-driven costing.

5. ____ Use new costs to report profitability by product.

6. ____ Measure and chart work-in-process inventory. Publish the chart to all managers.

Product Engineering Department

1. ____ Design one new product.

2. ____ Improve current product designs for manufacturability, cost, and quality.

3. ____ Correct all errors in drawings, BOMs, and other documents.

4. ____ Initiate regular question and listen sessions with production people.

5. ____ Correct design-related customer complaints.

6. ____ Evaluate part numbering system.

Management Team Checklist

(continued)

Manufacturing Department

1. _____ Close the least profitable product line. Balance and consume all inventory.

2. _____ Initiate scrap and rework reporting. Distribute reports to all other managers.

3. _____ Establish labor standards (per product) that will meet profit plan objectives.

4. _____ Stabilize the master production schedule.

5. _____ Reduce labor costs.

6. _____ Introduce a new product.

7. _____ Reduce materials costs.

8. _____ Upgrade quality.

9. _____ Implement capital projects.

10. _____ Simplify systems.

11. _____ Improve morale.

12. _____ Reduce manufacturing overhead.

Top Manager

1. _____ Chart progress.

2. _____ Provide monthly progress reports to the owners.

3. _____ Coordinate and motivate.

4. _____ Monitor results.

5. _____ Conduct staff meetings.

6. _____ Provide leadership.

7. _____ Facilitate.

INDEX

F

forecasts 98, 152, 188–189, 240
  accuracy 115, 188–190, 240
  forecastability 189–190
  Forecast Commitment 188–189
fulfillment
  employee needs 10–11, 31–32, 34, 38, 216
  order 11
function-driven costing (*see also* conventional costing; activity-based costing; real costing) 74, 78, 146–148, 153, 160, 173–175, 177, 201–202, 223, 229, 242, 247, 253
functional business plan (*see* business plan)
function-driven organization 96–100, 166, 188, 229, 249
  organizational chart 91, 93, 96, 227–228
  Organizational Effectiveness Evaluation 90, 105–106
  work teams 100

G

goals 5, 7–8, 19, 29–31, 35, 45, 95–96, 99, 154, 220, 238, 243
  how to communicate to employees 8
  turnaround 3, 8, 95, 179, 215–216, 221, 237, 240, 248

I

in-house operations 31, 73, 111, 132, 139–140, 142, 168, 187, 246
internal quality 69–70, 73, 165, 181, 186, 245
inventory reduction 114, 168, 189, 246
investors 6, 154–155, 161, 197

J

job descriptions 16–17
Just-in-Time (JIT) 62, 68, 168, 189, 192, 246

L

labor costs 36, 111, 113–115, 117, 119, 121, 123, 125, 127, 129, 202, 245, 254
layoffs 28, 166–167, 198–199, 202–203, 217–218
leadership 3–7, 9, 11–21, 23, 25, 37–38, 48, 58, 80, 90–91, 99, 214, 249–250, 252, 254
  distancing, effects of 16, 19
  Mindset Evaluation 16, 21–22
  psychology 3–5, 7, 9, 11, 13–15, 17, 19–21
leadership styles 14
  directive style 14–16
  participative style 10, 14–15, 20
lot sizes, most profitable 112–114
low-cost, high-quality 21, 30, 68, 80–84, 88, 151–153, 180, 191, 200, 203, 206, 251
lowest total cost 60–61
lowest unit cost 60–61

M

make-buy decisions 138, 148, 168
Management by Opportunity 34–35, 74–75
management ineffectiveness 92
market demand 182, 239, 253
market saturation 79–80, 152
marketing strategy 85–86

Additional Resources from The Oasis Press®

The Oasis Press,® publisher of the PSI Successful Business Library has been providing straight-forward, easy-to-understand business solutions for over 25 years. Our library has grown to offer ideas along every step of the small business cycle — from startup issues to adding employees to determining how to manage your success and business' growth. On the following pages, we are proud to offer additional ideas that build off of the issues presented in *People-Centered Profit Strategies*.

Use these icons to identify what aspects of business each of our books covers:

| Home-Based Business | Startup | Money Matters | Growth | People Concerns | Marketing | Internet |

Developing International Markets
Shaping Your Global Presence
Gerhard Kautz

Explore sales avenues outside of the United States. Learn to position your products effectively in the international marketplace. *Developing International Markets* stresses the differences between domestic and foreign markets such as labeling requirements and requests for under-the-table payoffs.
Paperback: 19.95
ISBN: 1-55571-433-1

Pages: 308

Improving Staff Productivity
Ben Harrison Carter

This book gives you proven techniques for evaluating business functions. It explains how you can measure company morale and the effectiveness of your company's organizational structure to reduce costs and improve productivity.
Paperback: 16.95
ISBN: 1-55571-456-0
Pages: 113

The Leader's Guide
How to Control Your Business'
Legal Costs & Problems
Randall D. Ponder

Hone your management skills. Transform the roles to become effective leaders and training leaders to better manage — a distinction often overlooked by other "leadership" books.
Paperback: 19.95
ISBN: 1-55571-434-X
Pages: 221

Managing People
A Practical Guide
Byron Lane
This action-oriented guide helps you increase efficiency and productivity by: thinking strategically; motivating your staff; working as a team; evaluating employees; setting goals; delegating; and coping with stress.
Paperback: 21.95
ISBN: 1-55571-380-7   Pages: 217

Not Another Meeting!
A Practical Guide for Facilitating Effective Meetings
Frances A. Micale
With the help of this book, you'll be able to make your meetings more productive by establishing and reinforcing ground rules, facilitating discussions, handling difficult individuals, and guiding groups toward their goals.
Paperback: 17.95
ISBN: 1-55571-480-3   Pages: 154

Renaissance 2000
Liberal Arts Essentials for Tomorrow's Leaders
Luigi Salvaneschi
In an age when most businesses have the potential to be international, communication must break through the barriers of language and customs. Renaissance 2000 addresses eight specific liberal arts principles that will lead to better communication and a deeper understanding of the players in the global marketplace.
Paperback: 19.95
ISBN: 1-55571-434-X   Pages: 221

Truth About Teams
A Facilitator's Survival Guide
J. T. Houston, Ed.D.
Written from a practical perspective, it includes a realistic look at the evolution of teams, their struggles in the workplace, and techniques for maximizing their effectiveness.
Paperback: 18.95
ISBN: 1-55571-482-X   Pages: 152

ORDER DIRECT FROM THE PUBLISHER

The Oasis Press
The Leading Publisher of Small Business Information
— **1-800-228-2275** —
[U.S. AND CANADA ONLY]

HOW TO ORDER

Mail: Send this completed order form and a check, money order or credit card information to:
PSI Research/The Oasis Press®, P.O. Box 3727, Central Point, Oregon 97502-0032

Fax: Available 24 hours a day, 7 days a week at **1-541-476-1479**

Email: info@psi-research.com (Please include a phone number, should we need to contact you.)

Web: Purchase any of our products online at our Website at **http://www.psi-research.com/oasis.htm**

Inquiries and International Orders: Please call **1-541-479-9464**

Indicate the quantity and price of the titles you would like:

4/99

TITLE	ISBN	BINDER	PAPERBACK	QTY.	TOTAL
Advertising Without An Agency	1-55571-429-3		☐ 19.95		
Before You Go Into Business Read This	1-55571-481-1		☐ 17.95		
Bottom Line Basics	1-55571-329-7 (B) ■ 1-55571-330-0 (P)	☐ 39.95	☐ 19.95		
BusinessBasics	1-55571-430-7		☐ 16.95		
The Business Environmental Handbook	1-55571-304-1 (B) ■ 1-55571-163-4 (P)	☐ 39.95	☐ 19.95		
Business Owner's Guide to Accounting and Bookkeeping	1-55571-381-5		☐ 19.95		
businessplan.com	1-55571-455-2		☐ 19.95		
Buyer's Guide to Business Insurance	1-55571-310-6 (B) ■ 1-55571-162-6 (P)	☐ 39.95	☐ 19.95		
California Corporation Formation Package	1-55571-368-8 (B) ■ 1-55571-464-1 (P)	☐ 39.95	☐ 29.95		
Collection Techniques for a Small Business	1-55571-312-2 (B) ■ 1-55571-171-5 (P)	☐ 39.95	☐ 19.95		
College Entrepreneur Handbook	1-55571-503-6		☐ 16.95		
A Company Policy & Personnel Workbook	1-55571-364-5 (B) ■ 1-55571-486-2 (P)	☐ 49.95	☐ 29.95		
Company Relocation Handbook	1-55571-091-3 (B) ■ 1-55571-092-1 (P)	☐ 39.95	☐ 19.95		
CompControl	1-55571-356-4 (B) ■ 1-55571-355-6 (P)	☐ 39.95	☐ 19.95		
Complete Book of Business Forms	1-55571-107-3		☐ 19.95		
Connecting Online	1-55571-403-X		☐ 21.95		
Customer Engineering	1-55571-360-2 (B) ■ 1-55571-359-9 (P)	☐ 39.95	☐ 19.95		
Develop and Market Your Creative Ideas	1-55571-383-1		☐ 15.95		
Developing International Markets	1-55571-433-1		☐ 19.95		
Doing Business in Russia	1-55571-375-0		☐ 19.95		
Draw the Line	1-55571-370-X		☐ 17.95		
The Essential Corporation Handbook	1-55571-342-4		☐ 21.95		
Essential Limited Liability Company Handbook	1-55571-362-9 (B) ■ 1-55571-361-0 (P)	☐ 39.95	☐ 21.95		
Export Now	1-55571-192-8 (B) ■ 1-55571-167-7 (P)	☐ 39.95	☐ 24.95		
Financial Decisionmaking	1-55571-435-8		☐ 19.95		
Financial Management Techniques	1-55571-116-2 (B) ■ 1-55571-124-3 (P)	☐ 39.95	☐ 19.95		
Financing Your Small Business	1-55571-160-X		☐ 19.95		
Franchise Bible	1-55571-366-1 (B) ■ 1-55571-367-X (P)	☐ 39.95	☐ 24.95		
The Franchise Redbook	1-55571-484-6		☐ 34.95		
Friendship Marketing	1-55571-399-8		☐ 18.95		
Funding High-Tech Ventures	1-55571-405-6		☐ 21.95		
Home Business Made Easy	1-55571-428-5		☐ 19.95		
Improving Staff Productivity	1-55571-456-0		☐ 16.95		
Information Breakthrough	1-55571-413-7		☐ 22.95		
Insider's Guide to Small Business Loans	1-55571-488-9		☐ 19.95		
InstaCorp™ Book & Software	1-55571-382-3		☐ 29.95		
Joysticks, Blinking Lights, and Thrills	1-55571-401-3		☐ 18.95		
Keeping Score: An Inside Look at Sports Marketing	1-55571-377-7		☐ 18.95		
Know Your Market	1-55571-341-6 (B) ■ 1-55571-333-5 (P)	☐ 39.95	☐ 19.95		
Leader's Guide: 15 Essential Skills	1-55571-434-X		☐ 19.95		
Legal Expense Defense	1-55571-349-1 (B) ■ 1-55571-348-3 (P)	☐ 39.95	☐ 19.95		
Legal Road Map for Consultants	1-55571-460-9		☐ 18.95		
Location, Location, Location	1-55571-376-9		☐ 19.95		
Mail Order Legal Guide	1-55571-193-6 (B) ■ 1-55571-190-1 (P)	☐ 45.00	☐ 29.95		
Managing People: A Practical Guide	1-55571-380-7		☐ 21.95		
Marketing for the New Millennium	1-55571-432-3		☐ 19.95		
Marketing Mastery	1-55571-358-0 (B) ■ 1-55571-357-2 (P)	☐ 39.95	☐ 19.95		
Money Connection	1-55571-352-1 (B) ■ 1-55571-351-3 (P)	☐ 39.95	☐ 24.95		
Moonlighting: Earning a Second Income at Home	1-55571-406-4		☐ 15.95		
Navigating the Marketplace: Growth Strategies for Small Business	1-55571-458-7		☐ 21.95		
No Money Down Financing for Franchising	1-55571-462-5		☐ 19.95		
Not Another Meeting!	1-55571-480-3		☐ 17.95		
People-Centered Profit Strategies	1-55571-517-6		☐ 18.95		

Sub-total for this side:

TITLE	ISBN	BINDER	PAPERBACK	QTY.	TOTAL
People Investment	1-55571-187-1 (B) ■ 1-55571-161-8 (P)	☐ 39.95	☐ 19.95		
Power Marketing for Small Business	1-55571-303-3 (B) ■ 1-55571-166-9 (P)	☐ 39.95	☐ 19.95		
Proposal Development	1-55571-067-0 (B) ■ 1-55571-431-5 (P)	☐ 39.95	☐ 21.95		
Prospecting for Gold	1-55571-483-8		☐ 14.95		
Public Relations Marketing	1-55571-459-5		☐ 19.95		
Raising Capital	1-55571-306-8 (B) ■ 1-55571-305-X (P)	☐ 39.95	☐ 19.95		
Renaissance 2000	1-55571-412-9		☐ 22.95		
Retail in Detail	1-55571-371-8		☐ 15.95		
The Rule Book of Business Plans for Startups	1-55571-519-2		☐ 18.95		
Secrets of High Ticket Selling	1-55571-436-6		☐ 19.95		
Secrets to Buying and Selling a Business	1-55571-489-7		☐ 24.95		
Secure Your Future	1-55571-335-1		☐ 19.95		
Selling Services	1-55571-461-7		☐ 18.95		
SmartStart Your (State) Business	varies per state		☐ 19.95		
Indicate which state you prefer:					
Small Business Insider's Guide to Bankers	1-55571-400-5		☐ 18.95		
Smile Training Isn't Enough	1-55571-422-6		☐ 19.95		
Start Your Business	1-55571-485-4		☐ 10.95		
Strategic Management for Small and Growing Firms	1-55571-465-X		☐ 24.95		
Successful Network Marketing	1-55571-350-5		☐ 15.95		
Surviving Success	1-55571-446-3		☐ 19.95		
TargetSmart!	1-55571-384-X		☐ 19.95		
Top Tax Saving Ideas for Today's Small Business	1-55571-463-3		☐ 16.95		
Truth About Teams	1-55571-482-X		☐ 18.95		
Twenty-One Sales in a Sale	1-55571-448-X		☐ 19.95		
WebWise	1-55571-501-X (B) ■ 1-55571-479-X (P)	☐ 29.95	☐ 19.95		
What's It Worth?	1-55571-504-4		☐ 22.95		
Which Business?	1-55571-390-4		☐ 18.95		
Write Your Own Business Contracts	1-55571-196-0 (B) ■ 1-55571-170-7 (P)	☐ 39.95	☐ 24.95		

Success Series	ISBN		PAPERBACK	QTY.	TOTAL
50 Ways to Get Promoted	1-55571-506-0		☐ 10.95		
You Can't Go Wrong By Doing It Right	1-55571-490-0		☐ 14.95		

Oasis Software	FORMAT	BINDER		QTY.	TOTAL
Company Policy Text Files	CD-ROM ☐		☐ 49.95		
Company Policy Text Files Book & Disk Package	CD-ROM ☐	☐ 89.95 (B)	☐ 69.95 (P)		
Financial Management Techniques Standalone	Floppy Disks ☐		☐ 99.95		
Financial Management Techniques Book & Disk Package	Floppy Disks ☐	☐ 129.95(B)	☐ 119.95(P)		
Insurance Assistant	Floppy Disks ☐		☐ 29.95		
Insurance Assistant & Buyer's Guide to Business Insurance	Floppy Disks ☐	☐ 59.95 (B)	☐ 39.95 (P)		
Winning Business Plans in Color CD-ROM	CD-ROM ☐		☐ 59.95		

Ordered by: _Please give street address_

NAME _____ TITLE _____

COMPANY _____

STREET ADDRESS _____

CITY _____ STATE _____ ZIP _____

DAYTIME PHONE _____ EMAIL _____

Ship to: _If different than above_

NAME _____ TITLE _____

COMPANY _____

STREET ADDRESS _____

CITY _____ STATE _____ ZIP _____

DAYTIME PHONE _____

Shipping:

YOUR ORDER IS:	ADD:
0-25	5.00
25.01-50	6.00
50.01-100	7.00
100.01-175	9.00
175.01-250	13.00
250.01-500	18.00
500.01+	4% of total

Subtotal from other side	
Subtotal from this side	
Shipping	
TOTAL	

PLEASE CALL FOR RUSH SERVICE OPTIONS.
INTERNATIONAL ORDERS, PLEASE CALL FOR A QUOTE ON CURRENT SHIPPING RATES.

Payment Method:
☐ CHECK ☐ MONEY ORDER
☐ AMERICAN EXPRESS ☐ DISCOVER
☐ MASTERCARD ☐ VISA

CREDIT CARD NUMBER

EXPIRATION (MM/YY) NAME ON CARD (PLEASE PRINT)

SIGNATURE OF CARDHOLDER (REQUIRED)

OASIS PRESS
BOOKS & SOFTWARE

Fax this order form to: (541) 476-1479 or mail it to: P.O. Box 3727, Central Point, Oregon 97502
For more information about our products or to order online, visit http://www.psi-research.com